POPULAR science ALMANAC

FOR KIDS

POWERED BY

Brain POP®

TIME INC. HOME ENTERTAINMENT

PRESIDENT: Rob Gursha
VICE PRESIDENT, NEW PRODUCT DEVELOPMENT: Richard Fraiman
EXECUTIVE DIRECTOR, MARKETING SERVICES: Carol Pittard
DIRECTOR, RETAIL & SPECIAL SALES Tom Mifsud
DIRECTOR OF FINANCE: Tricia Griffin
DIRECTOR, NEW PRODUCT DEVELOPMENT: Peter Harper
ASSISTANT MARKETING DIRECTOR: Ann Marie Doherty
PREPRESS MANAGER: Emily Rabin
BOOK PRODUCTION MANAGER: Jonathan Polsky
ASSOCIATE PRODUCT MANAGER: Kristin Walker

Special thanks: Bozena Bannett, Alexandra Bliss, Bernadette Corbie, Robert Dente, Gina Di Meglio, Anne-Michelle Gallero, Suzanne Janso, Robert Marasco, Natalie McCrea, Margarita Quiogue, Mary Jane Rigoroso, Steven Sandonato, Grace Sullivan

POPULAR SCIENCE

EDITOR-IN-CHIEF: Scott Mowbray
DEPUTY EDITOR: Mark Jannot
DESIGN DIRECTOR: Dirk Barnett
FEATURES EDITOR: Emily Laber-Warren
SCIENCE EDITOR: Dawn Stover

BRAINPOP

CHAIRMAN AND CEO: Avraham Kadar, M.D.
CHIEF OPERATING OFFICER: Yves Saada
CREATIVE DIRECTOR: Mike Watanabe
CONTENT DIRECTOR: Lisa Ebersole
WRITERS: Lisa Ebersole and Jon Feldman
BOOK AGENT: Alfredo Santana

Adults should supervise young readers who undertake the activities and experiments in this book. The publisher and the author assume no responsibility for any damage or injury caused or sustained while performing the activities or experiments in this book.

We welcome your comments and suggestions about Popular Science For Kids Books.
Please write to us at:
Popular Science For Kids Books
Attention: Book Editors
PO Box 11016
Des Moines, IA 50336-1016

If you would like to order any of our books, please call us at 1-800-327-6388 (Monday through Friday, 7:00 a.m.– 8:00 p.m. or Saturday, 7:00 a.m.– 6:00 p.m. Central Time).

A ROUNDTABLE PRESS BOOK

For Roundtable Press, inc.:
DESIGN: Georgia Rucker
DIRECTORS: Julie Merberg and Marsha Melnick
PROJECT EDITOR: John Glenn
PHOTO RESEARCH: Sarah Parvis
SCIENCE FAIR PROJECTS: Michael Orlep

POPULAR Science

For the past 133 years, *Popular Science* magazine has brought discoveries, inventions and cutting-edge research into the homes of its readers. It has always searched for topics and subjects that are interesting, important, and exciting—from space exploration to animal cloning to the building of the world's tallest buildings. So when we set out to make the POPULAR SCIENCE ALMANAC FOR KIDS, we knew what we wanted to do: show just how fun and fascinating science can be.

The purpose of this book is not to replace your science textbooks and science class in school. This is about what's new and exciting in science and technology—with enough basic information to make it all make sense. Experiments and projects throughout these pages are designed to let you bring science into your own kitchen or backyard. And "Did You Know" boxes offer offbeat facts about the topic at hand—cool stuff that you probably won't hear in the classroom. In the "Debate" sections, we've spotlighted some of the most controversial issues—topics you hear mentioned a lot in the news—and given both sides their say.

Science has always been *Popular Science*'s focus and fascination. We hope this book makes you look at the world around you, at yourself, at the technology that you depend on every single day ... in a new and exciting way.

The editors of *Popular Science*

All of the experiments in this book come to you courtesy of BOB the Ex-Lab Rat! BOB also does experiments on BrainPOP. You can try them too—choose any subject on BrainPOP and you'll see one of his experiments!

SCIENCE

MATH

ENGLISH

SOCIAL STUDIES

TECHNOLOGY

HEALTH

Also on BrainPOP.com:
- Comics with Cassie & Rita
- How-to with Gary & gary
- Activity Pages
- Timelines
  . . . and much, much more!

Every topic on BrainPOP features a comic strip with Cassie & Rita! You can also e-mail them with questions about homework, friendship, school, what's up with your body, just about anything . . . They love answering them, so shoot them a message anytime!

BrainPOP is the leading producer of animated educational movies for K-12. Three million kids in thousands of schools watch award-winning BrainPOP movies every day!

http://www.BrainPOP.com

CONTENTS

Chapter 1
HUMAN BEINGS
2

Chapter 2
THE HUMAN BODY
14

Chapter 3
FOOD FOR THOUGHT
40

Chapter 4
ANIMALS

54

Chapter 5
EARTH MATTERS

68

Chapter 6
THE ENVIRONMENT
84

Chapter 7
WEATHER
98

Chapter 8
THE NATURE OF SCIENCE
114

Chapter 9
ENERGY

128

Chapter 10
ELECTRICITY
140

Chapter 11
COMPUTERS AND COMMUNICATION
154

Chapter 12
SOUND AND MUSIC
170

Chapter 13
PICTURES AND MOVING IMAGES
182

Chapter 14
GETTING AROUND
194

Chapter 15
SPACE
208

Chapter 16
BUILDING THE WORLD
228

Index 244

Credits 249

CHAPTER 1

HUMAN BEINGS

It's easy to forget that human beings (*Homo sapiens*) are really just animals after all. It's true—we're part of the primate group that includes chimpanzees and orangutans. Our brains have evolved to be much more complex than those of our fellow mammals, but we all came from the same place. With all of our inventions—cars, skyscrapers, bridges, governments, this book you're reading now—it's amazing to think that we evolved from single-celled organisms! However you slice it, humans are just as much part of the web of life on Earth as anything else.

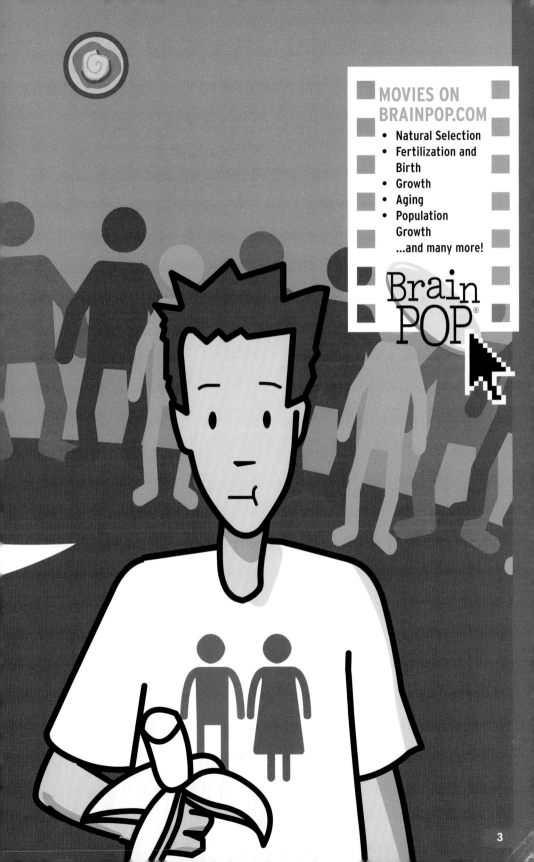

THINK YOU COULD HAVE SURVIVED ON EARTH 4 BILLION YEARS AGO? Think again! Earth wasn't such a comfortable place to live. The weather was extremely violent, volcanoes erupted all the time, and meteors bombarded Earth's surface. Even if you could have put up with the natural world's ferocity, there wasn't even any free oxygen in the air! Humans can't breathe without oxygen.

Earth chilled out eventually, and its surface calmed down enough for steam from the volcanoes to condense into clouds and fall as rain. The rain formed oceans that covered much of Earth's surface. It was in the ocean that scientists believe life began. The ocean water was a safe place for delicate new life. Though they still argue over details, most scientists agree that life began around 3.5 billion years ago.

The Earliest Life

Way back then, life forms weren't based on **DNA**, the way life as we know it is. The earliest living things were simple organisms, far less complex than the virus that gave you a cold last winter. In fact, by today's standards, you would hardly call these substances "life" at all. But they did share one important trait with today's life forms: they had the ability to reproduce. Simple as they were, they eventually evolved into more complex organisms.

DNA stands for deoxyribonucleic acid, the stuff that makes up our chromosomes and carries genetic information from parent to child.

One of the first complex organisms to appear on the scene (that we know about) was **cyanobacteria (blue-green algae)**, which has the ability to live in **anaerobic** (no oxygen) environments. Just like a tree, blue-green algae takes in carbon dioxide and releases oxygen. Once this algae reproduced and spread around the world, it was just a matter of time (a long time) before Earth's atmosphere contained its own free oxygen. Oxygen was the key that eventually allowed more complex animals, like people, to survive on Earth.

FROM CELLS TO PEOPLE All of us can trace our roots back to these ancient, single-celled ancestors. That's why your blood is so salty—now that we don't live in the ocean, we literally carry it around inside of us, in our veins.

TIMELINE OF LIFE ON EARTH

BLUE-GREEN ALGAE ARCHEAN EON		**3.8-2.5** billion years ago
METAZOANS **(MULTICELLULAR ANIMALS)** VENDIAN PERIOD		**650-543** million years ago
TRILOBITES CAMBRIAN PERIOD	 	**543-490** million years ago
LAND PLANTS ORDOVICIAN PERIOD		**490-443** million years ago
AMPHIBIANS DEVONIAN PERIOD		**417-354** million years ago
DINOSAURS TRIASSIC PERIOD		**248-206** million years ago
BIRDS JURASSIC PERIOD		**206-44** million years ago
MAMMALS CRETACEOUS PERIOD		**144-65** million years ago
PRIMATES EOCENE EPOCH	 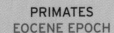	**54.8-33.7** million years ago
HOMINIDS PLIOCENE EPOCH		**5.3-1.8** million years ago
MODERN MAN **(HOMO SAPIENS)** PLEISTOCENE EPOCH (Now we're in the Holocene epoch.)	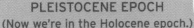	**1.8 million to 11,000** years ago

5

MILLIONS OF YEARS AGO

5.0	4.0	3.5	3.0	2.5

ARDIPITHECUS RAMIDUS (5.8-4.4)

AUSTRALOPITHECUS ANAMENSIS (4.2-3.9)

AUSTRALOPITHECUS AFARENSIS (3.6-2.9)

KENYANTHROPUS PLATYOPS (3.5-3.3)

Evolution of Humans

How did human beings come to be?

Paleontologists, the scientists who study fossils, believe that our earliest **hominid** (human-like) ancestors lived in Africa. The oldest hominid fossil we have found belongs to *Ardipithecus ramidus*. This creature looked more like an ape than a human, with a smaller brain and a hairy body. It lived as early as 5.8 million years ago! As time went on, the early African hominids continued to evolve, developing more and more human traits, like larger brains, more upright skeletons, and less body hair. *Homo habilis* was the first of the human species, and the first of our ancestors to make and use tools. *Homo erectus* came next. He was the first human who definitely used speech.

Did you know...

The earliest **Homo sapiens** remains ever found are about 160,000 years old!

FAMOUS FACES

LUCY In 1973, Dr. Donald Johanson discovered the skeleton of an **Australopithecus afarensis**. He and his team named their 3.2-million-year-old find Lucy. Lucy stood just over 3 feet high, and she was bipedal (that means she walked upright). Scientists consider bipedalism to be one of the most important factors in determining whether a fossil is a human relative.

FLAT-FACED MAN In 2001, it was announced that Maeve Leakey had discovered an even older hominid than Lucy, **Kenyanthropus platyops**, also known as the Flat-Faced Man of Kenya. Flat-Faced Man is clearly not of the same species as Lucy, but he lived at the same time. Since his discovery, debate has raged over where he fits in the puzzle of human history. Is he an ancestor of human beings or not? What's his relationship to Lucy? Scientists are still gathering facts.

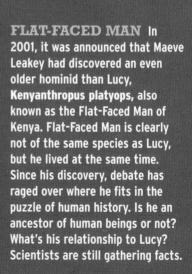

◀ Dr. Donald Johanson with Lucy

HOMINID SPECIES

MILLIONS OF YEARS AGO

2.0	1.5	1.0	0.5	0

HOMO HABILIS
(1.9–1.6)

HOMO ERECTUS
(1.8–0.3)

AUSTRALOPITHECUS ROBUSTUS
(1.8–1.5)

HOMO SAPIENS (ARCHAIC)
(0.5–0.2)

HOMO SAPIENS SAPIENS
(0.12 TO PRESENT)

HOW EARLY HUMANS LIVED The life of the earliest *Homo sapiens* was focused on one thing: survival. Most of their days were probably spent getting food and finding shelter. They were hunter-gatherers, which means that they didn't know how to farm crops or breed animals. They lived off the land and moved around in packs. Unlike other predators, humans didn't have deadly teeth and claws. Fortunately, they had one huge advantage: intelligence. Their large brains allowed our early ancestors to construct weapons and hunt in coordinated groups. Like the animals they hunted, human tribes were sure to live near water. Without water, no animal can survive for very long.

As we continue to collect data from our distant ancestors, we find more and more similarities between them and modern humans. They had an interest in art—some early cave paintings date back 30,000 years. They were also family oriented. Most paleontologists agree that even the earliest hominids, like Lucy, lived in communities that were centered on families. So maybe we haven't come that far after all.

Did you know...

While many bands of humans lived in caves and other natural shelters, scientists have found evidence of simple huts dating back 500,000 years in Japan. European hut remains date as far back as 400,000 years ago!

A collection of tools used by a paleontologist

THE HUMAN LIFE SPAN

Birth

Human beings procreate by sexual reproduction. The females of our species give birth to new life. It takes nine months for a human fetus to fully develop in a mother's womb. The fetus goes through a lot of changes during those nine months of pregnancy.

When a baby is born, he leaves the mother's body and begins breathing air on his own immediately. Your belly button is the leftover part of the umbilical cord that once fed you with nutrients from your mother!

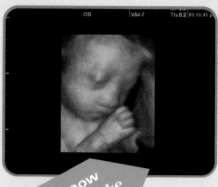

How do we know what a fetus looks like inside the womb?

MOVIES ON
BRAINPOP.COM

Scientists can make images of embryos with sonograms, which use sound waves to take pictures through a pregnant woman's skin. But we can get even more detailed pictures now using actual tiny cameras inside the womb!

FETAL DEVELOPMENT

FIRST THREE MONTHS: The embryo grows from a shapeless lump of cells into a tiny version of a baby, complete with teeth, organs, and even a thumb that it sucks!

BY SIX MONTHS: A fetus can hear and breathe air if it is born prematurely.

BY NINE MONTHS: The fetus develops finer motor skills, like the ability to grasp objects.

Did you know...

Some parents save all or part of their baby's umbilical cord. This can be for sentimental reasons, but it's also because "cord blood" that can be extracted from the umbilical cord shortly after birth is rich in stem cells. Stem cells not only generate all the cell types found in blood, but they may also give rise to other cell types such as heart, brain, and liver cells. They can be used to treat diseases like cancer, blood and immune disorders, and sickle-cell anemia.

Death

The average life span for people living in developed countries is about 75 years (even higher for women). That's up from 1900, when it was just 47 years! What gives—do we lead healthier lives now than back then? Well . . . not really. While we may have healthier diets than our great-grandparents, we also exercise less. Our longer life span probably has more to do with advances in medicine than with better eating.

Before modern medicine, it was common for young kids and older people to die of basic infections and illnesses like the flu and pneumonia. Deaths during childbirth have decreased dramatically: infant mortality has gone down 90 percent since 1900. And maternal mortality has decreased 99 percent! Antibiotics and vaccinations do a lot to keep us healthy and fight off those nasty bacteria that try to make us sick. As science progresses, the average human life span continues to grow.

From 1920 to 1960, average life expectancy in the US shot up from 54 years to 70 years. Many scientists attribute this extraordinary rise in part to the use of penicillin (the first antibiotic), which became commercially available in 1940.
▶▶ FOR MORE ON PENICILLIN, SEE P. 35.

Telomeres

Even though we're living longer on average, death is an inevitable part of the human life cycle. It's one of those things that there's no getting around. As humans grow older, we are more likely to get ill and catch diseases. The question is, why? Genetic researchers think the answer may be in our **telomeres**. Many scientists now believe that once the telomeres of a cell reach a certain length, they signal the cell to stop dividing. That means the cell won't replicate itself anymore. Pretty soon, it will stop working and die. Now imagine that process happening to cells throughout your body. Geneticists are now investigating ways to keep our telomeres long, and keep us alive longer.

Telomeres are the "tail ends" of our DNA strands, and they shorten every time a cell divides.

Did you know...

The average American can expect to live 77.14 years at birth. This may seem like a long time, but in fact the US ranks just 48th for life expectancy around the world.

The countries with the highest life expectancy at birth are:
1. Andorra: 83.49 years
2. Macau: 81.87 years
3. San Marino: 81.43 years
4. Japan: 80.93 years
5. Singapore: 80.42 years

HOW DO MUMMIES HAPPEN?

Normally, when animal or human remains are buried, the exposure to moist air causes bacteria to eat away at the corpse. But without that moisture, bacteria don't get to do their job. The body eventually dries out and a mummy is born. Ancient cultures used special chemicals to embalm their dead and ensure this preservation process.

POPULATION EXPLOSION

A population is the total number of individuals of a particular species in a particular area.

The human population on Earth stands at 6 billion, give or take a few. At our present rate of growth, we're looking at having 8.9 billion people on Earth by 2054! WHOA! The United Nations estimates that the population will stabilize at 9 billion by 2300.

PERSONS/SQUARE KILOMETER

☐ 0-50   ▨ 100-200   ▧ 300-500

☐ 50-100   ▧ 200-300   ■ 500-1000

UNITED STATES

New York

THE MOST POPULOUS CITY IN THE US
New York: 8,084,316
New York is the 17th most populous city in the world!

San Marino

The Vatican

WORLD POPULATION
6,357,633,241

Buenos Aires

THE LEAST POPULOUS COUNTRIES IN THE WORLD
The Vatican: 911
Tuvalu: 11,305
Nauru: 12,570
Palau: 19,717
San Marino: 28,119

WHY IS OUR POPULATION EXPLODING? In developed countries, the population is growing for the same reasons we're living longer lives. Improvements in medicine, sanitation, and nutrition over the last few hundred years have meant that more people started living longer and more babies survived to become adults. These adults had more babies, and so on. In developing countries, people are just having more babies, usually as a means of ensuring that some survive.

Usually, this expanding population is a good thing for a species. But as far as resources go in some areas, humans are really starting to push the limit. The issue is not whether or not there's enough standing room on our planet. Earth has a carrying capacity, a point at which the natural resources can't support any more people. We're using up natural resources like fossil fuels and producing a whole lot of waste. And human activities like clearing forests have a harsh effect on animal populations.

Karachi

CHINA

Delhi
INDIA

Mumbai

Manila

Palau

Nauru

Tuvalu

THE MOST POPULOUS COUNTRIES IN THE WORLD
China: 1,294,629,555
India: 1,065,070,607
United States: 293,027,571

THE MOST POPULOUS CITIES IN THE WORLD
Mumbai (Bombay), India: 12,383,100
Buenos Aires, Argentina: 12,116,400
Karachi, Pakistan: 10,537,200
Manila, Philippines: 10,232,900
Delhi, India: 10,203,700

WHAT'S NEW?

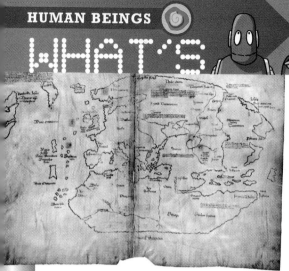

▲ Using carbon dating, scientists have determined that the parchment on which the Vinland Map is drawn dates to 1434. This would appear to make the map—which shows the voyages of Leif Eriksson—the earliest drawing of North America. However, some scholars believe it was drawn much later and is not as old as the parchment.

Carbon-14 Dating

HOW DO WE KNOW HOW OLD FOSSILS ARE? In the late 1940s, a scientist named Willard Libby discovered a way to determine the age of dead plants and animal remains. All living things are made of carbon. A very small amount of this carbon is carbon-14, a radioactive isotope. Once a plant or animal dies, the carbon-14 in its body begins to disintegrate. Since we know exactly how fast carbon-14 decays, we can determine the approximate age of organic matter by looking at how much of its carbon-14 has decayed.

Before carbon dating, scientists could only determine the *relative* age of fossils. For example, they could look at how fossils collect in layers of rock. (The deeper the fossil is buried, the older it is.) But carbon dating is an *absolute* technique. Since carbon-14 decays completely after 50,000 years, other radioactive materials with slower decay rates are used to date really old remains.

WHAT'S NEXT?

Cryonic Research

WHAT IF YOU COULD FREEZE YOUR BODY AND DEFROST IT IN THE FUTURE? Let's say you have an incurable disease. Is it possible for you to have yourself frozen, with the hope that scientists in the future can cure you? Yes! The question is, will you survive the thawing process? As far as most scientists know, freezing the human body results in massive damage. Ice crystals forming in cells can cause them to burst, and cracks can form in your body, just like in an ice cube!

Still, there are a bunch of different companies that offer cryonic freezing services right now. It'll cost you, though: anywhere from $30,000 to over $100,000! According to the scientists at these companies, special chemicals injected after death will prevent freezing damage. And, they argue, any damage caused by the freezing will be reparable by future medicine. One thing's for sure: it'll be a long time, if ever, before this technology is perfected.

SCIENCE FAIR PROJECT #1

A fossil is the remains of anything that used to be alive. By studying fossils, scientists can learn a lot about the history of life on Earth. Many fossils form in ways that are too hard for you to try to reproduce on your own. However, some fossils form by leaving an impression in soft mud that later gets changed into rock. This process is easy enough that you can do it yourself.

YOU WILL NEED:

◎ Plaster of paris

◎ Small plastic tubs (margarine tubs are good)

◎ Large mixing bowl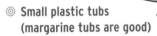

◎ Wooden spoon

◎ Objects that you would like to fossilize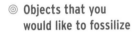

◎ Nonstick cooking spray

1. Mix 1 cup of plaster with 1/2 cup of water in the bowl and mix well.

2. Spray the inside of each tub with cooking spray. Pour the plaster mixture into the tubs. Each tub should be about 1/3 filled with plaster mixture.

3. Cover the items to be fossilized with cooking spray. Press each item into the plaster mixture and remove it right away.

4. Leave the tubs in a place where they will not be disturbed. Let the plaster harden overnight.

5. You have your first fossils! Fossils formed in this way are called molds. Leave the molds in the plastic tubs for now.

6. Make a new plaster mixture like you did in step 1.

7. Cover the surface of each of your molds with cooking spray.

8. Add the wet plaster mixture to each of your molds.

9. Leave the tubs in a place where they will not be disturbed. Let the plaster harden overnight.

10. Gently remove the top section of dried plaster from each tub and turn it over.

11. You made another fossil! Fossils formed in this way are called casts.

12. Remove the molds from the plastic tubs.

◎ Compare the molds, casts, and original objects. How are they the same? How are they different? What information about the object are your fossils missing?

◎ What types of objects do you think make molds and what types make casts?

CHAPTER 2

THE HUMAN BODY

Your body's design is even more impressive than the newest computers and gadgets out there. The human body grows, feeds itself, senses the world around it, and handles all the ups and downs of life. It's an efficient machine brought about by millions of years of evolution. Our bodies have a basic pattern; we're all built with more or less the same parts inside and out. But we don't all look the same! That would be kind of freaky. One thing's for sure: your body works hard to keep you going. You can help it out by eating right, getting good sleep, and exercising regularly.

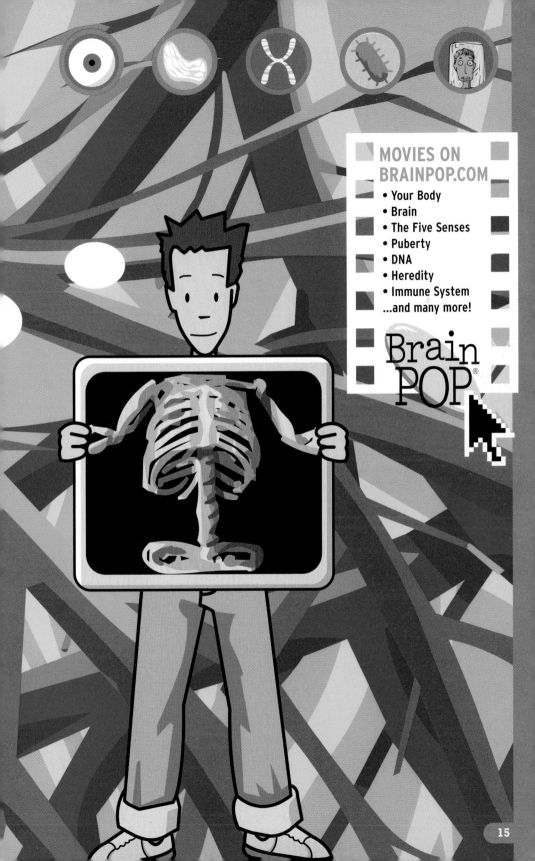

BODY SYSTEMS

There are 12 body systems that each carry out an important and very complicated task. These body systems depend on each other.

Where would your brain be without blood?

Where would your muscles be without oxygen?

How could you feel anything without nerves?

The list goes on. No one body system can function without help from the others.

1

The **Nervous System** is the control center for your entire body. It's made up of your brain, your spinal cord, and a huge network of nerves. Nerve cells in the spinal cord carry chemical messages back and forth from the brain to the rest of the body, kind of like telephone wires. The brain uses information it receives from nerves to coordinate all of your actions and reactions. ▸▸ FOR MORE ON THE BRAIN, SEE PP. 24-26.

There are three parts of your nervous system that work together:

The **somatic nervous system** controls voluntary actions like talking or petting your cat.

The **peripheral nervous system** includes nerves that branch off from the brain and spinal cord and carry nerve impulses to the muscles and glands.

The **autonomic nervous system** handles all the things that seem to happen on their own, like your heart beating.

Did you know...
Your brain has about 100 BILLION nerve cells.

Did you know...
When you touch something, neurons are stimulated. Each neuron generates a tiny electrical impulse. The impulse travels the full length of the neuron, then jumps on to the next neuron. The chain reaction keeps going until the information reaches your brain. And it all happens in a split second!

The **Endocrine System** includes all of the glands that control body growth and reproduction. These glands make more than 50 types of hormones, each with its own special job.

The **pituitary gland** is like the king of the endocrine system—it sends out its own chemical messages and rules the actions of most of the other major endocrine glands. It tells your cells when to divide and when to stop dividing. Cell division is how we grow!

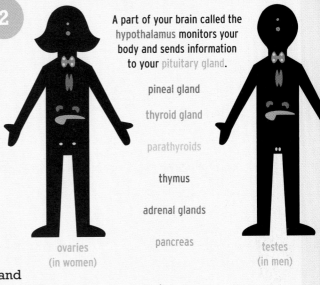

A part of your brain called the hypothalamus monitors your body and sends information to your pituitary gland.

pineal gland

thyroid gland

parathyroids

thymus

adrenal glands

pancreas

ovaries
(in women)

testes
(in men)

The **Immune System** is your friend. It battles **pathogens**, all those germs and bacteria that try to make you sick. The immune system has some general defenses: **skin** prevents pathogens from entering your body, **mucus** traps pathogens you breathe in, and **stomach acids** kill bacteria in the food you eat.

The most important part of your immune system is its army of **white blood cells**; they patrol your body, looking for trouble. There are two types of white blood cells at work: **T cells** survey the body to pick out invading pathogens, and **B cells** investigate the invading pathogens and build proteins, called antibodies, to fight them.

When enough antibodies form, the pathogen is beaten and you feel better. Lots of times, those antibodies stay in your blood just waiting to fight off that same illness when it shows up again. Your immune system sends lots of germs running for their lives on a daily basis!

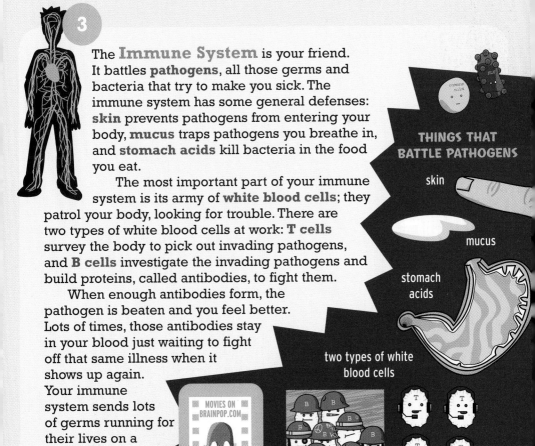

THINGS THAT BATTLE PATHOGENS

skin

mucus

stomach acids

two types of white blood cells

MOVIES ON
BRAINPOP.COM

17

4

The **Digestive System** breaks down the food you eat into protein, carbohydrates, and fats, so that your body can use those nutrients as fuel. Anything that doesn't get absorbed is solid waste that your body gets rid of when you have a bowel movement.

Digestion begins in your **mouth**: your teeth chew food into small bits, while enzymes in your saliva make the food easier to swallow.

Food moves down the esophagus into the **stomach**, where it spends 2 or 3 hours mixing with all sorts of acids and digestive juices.

By the time food is ready to pass through to the **small intestine**, it's the consistency of a thick milk shake. It takes about 3 hours for the small intestine to break food apart and soak up all of the nutrients your body needs.

From the small intestine, digested food moves to the **large intestine**. The large intestine absorbs water from what's left of your food and processes nondigestable material for defecation.

5

The **Reproductive System** lets humans make babies. The **penis** and **testicles** are the male reproductive organs. The testicles are two rounded glands that hang under the penis inside a pouch called the **scrotum**. Tiny male **sperm cells** are produced in the testicles. Sperm can't survive if they are too warm. That's why the testicles are outside the body—so they can stay slightly cooler than the body's average 98.2°F (36.8°C).

Sperm move through the sperm duct to mix with fluids from the **seminal vesicles** and **prostate gland**. This mixture of sperm and fluids is called semen. In an adult male, millions of sperm cells are made every day.

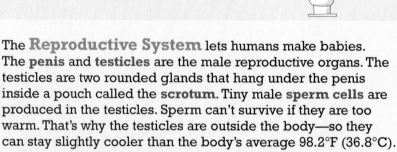

prostate

penis

testicles

seminal
vesicles

scrotum

sperm cells

Unlike male genitals, the female reproductive organs are found inside the body. The reproductive glands in women are called ovaries. During **puberty** the **ovaries** start to release one egg cell, or ovum, each month. ▶▶FOR MORE ON PUBERTY, SEE PP. 30-31.

It travels down the **fallopian tube** to the **uterus**. If sperm fertilizes the egg cell, it plants itself in the uterine wall and an embryo begins to grow. If not, it passes on through the **vagina** and the woman has her menstrual period. This cycle repeats itself every 28 days or so. Women's bodies don't make new egg cells; instead, they're born with a lifetime supply.

ovaries

uterus

fallopian tubes

vagina

As cells in your body do their jobs, they create waste. This is stuff your body doesn't need—chemicals that could actually harm you if they stay too long. The **Urinary System** gets rid of chemical waste from cells by flushing it out of your body.

Your two kidneys have millions of tiny filters called nephrons that remove waste from the blood and carry it to the **bladder**. When the bladder is about half full, you feel the urge to pee. A mixture of water and chemical waste, called **urine**, leaves your body through a tube called the **urethra**.

6

Blood moves through your body and into the **kidneys**, where useful substances like sugars are extracted and returned to the body.

Waste filtered out by the kidneys is carried to your **bladder** through a tube called the **ureter**.

The **Respiratory System** allows your body to take in **oxygen** and get rid of **carbon dioxide**.

When you breathe in, air enters your body through your nose or mouth.
Air travels down the trachea to your lungs where it fills tiny sacs called alveoli.

7

▶ Alveoli get oxygen from the air and pass it on to your blood.

▲ Bronchi branch into bronchioles.

▶ Blood distributes oxygen to your body so that cells can use it. When blood carries oxygen to cells, it picks up carbon dioxide, a waste gas produced by those cells. Carbon dioxide travels back to the lungs and leaves your body when you exhale.

19

8

The **Circulatory System** moves blood through your body, getting valuable nutrients to all the parts that need them and carrying away cell waste. When your **heart** beats, it pumps blood to a network of **arteries** and **veins**. Blood is carried away from the heart by arteries (the biggest one is called the **aorta**). These arteries branch into **capillaries** that connect up with veins. Capillaries are where blood cells exchange oxygen for carbon dioxide. Veins carry blood back to the heart. The heart pumps blood into the lungs so that carbon dioxide can be expelled and the blood can pick up fresh oxygen. This cycle repeats every time your heart beats!

Blood enters the heart (from the body) through the vena cava.

aorta

The pulmonary arteries send blood to the lungs.

Blood returns to the heart (from the lungs) through pulmonary veins.

Did you know...

The adult body is 50-65 percent water and contains about 6-10 pints of blood depending upon height and weight!

Did you know...

Not everyone's blood is the same. Do you know what your blood type is? In the early 20th century, an Austrian scientist named Karl Landsteiner broke blood down into four types—and he won the Nobel Prize for doing it! There are two different molecules on the surface of red blood cells. One is called "A," and the other is called "B."

IF A RED BLOOD CELL HAS...	THAT BLOOD TYPE IS...
Only "A" molecules on it	Type A
Only "B" molecules on it	Type B
A mixture of both molecules	Type AB
Neither "A" nor "B" molecules	Type O

GIVING BLOOD, AND GETTING IT

In most states, you have to be 16 years old to donate blood, but anyone can receive blood when they need it. But not just any blood will do. If two different blood types mix, the blood cells can clump in the blood vessels and cause major problems. Matching blood types is tricky business. Here's the deal:

IF YOU ARE...	YOU CAN DONATE TO SOMEONE WITH	YOU CAN RECEIVE FROM SOMEONE WITH
Type A	Type A or type AB	Type A or O
Type B	Type B or type AB	Type B or O
Type AB	Type AB	Any type of blood*
Type O	Any type of blood*	Type O

*A person with type AB blood is known as a universal receiver, and type O blood is known as the universal donor.

9 The **Lymphatic System** works with the circulatory system to absorb fat from the small intestines. "Lymph" is a milky body fluid that contains a type of white blood cells, called "lymphocytes," along with proteins and fats. Lymph is continuously passing through the walls of the capillaries. It transports nutrients to cells and collects waste products. Along the lymphatic network in certain areas of the body (neck, armpit, groin, abdomen, chest) are small reservoirs called lymph nodes, which collect bacteria and act as a barrier against the entrance of these substances into the bloodstream. When you're sick, the lymph nodes may become filled with bacteria to the point that you can actually feel them. Swollen lymph nodes are often a sign of infection.

10 The **Skeletal System** is made up of **bones**, **ligaments**, and **tendons**. The bones that make up your skeleton are pretty useful—they protect soft parts like your brain and vital organs from getting hurt. The skeleton also acts as a framework for your body—it holds the body up and works with the muscular system to make your body move! Ligaments hold bones together, while tendons attach muscles to the bones.

Did you know...
You have 206 bones inside of you—the tiniest ones are in your ears.

11 The **Muscular System** is made up of tissues that work with the skeletal system to make the body move. Anytime you move, you know there's a muscle at work. The muscles you can control are called skeletal or **voluntary** muscles and you have over 600 of them. The muscles that you don't control are called **involuntary** muscles. Involuntary muscles like the heart and stomach muscles are controlled by your nervous system.

12 The **Integumentary System** includes **skin**, **hair**, and **nails**. Skin is the largest organ in your body. It keeps your internal organs safe from germs and prevents them from drying out or getting too hot. Hair and nails are made mainly of the protein **keratin**. Hair helps to regulate your body's temperature and protects sensitive body parts. Nails let you pick up tiny objects, pull things apart with precision, and scratch those itches!

Did you know...
Hair grows 6 inches (15.2 cm) per year on average. And nails grow 1-2 inches (2.5-5 cm) per year on average.

Did you know...
Scientists have discovered that baby teeth are chock full of stem cells—those amazing cells that can form almost every kind of cell in your body. So far, researchers have used baby teeth stem cells to form nerve, bone, and tooth cells. ▶▶FOR MORE ON STEM CELLS SEE P. 8.

BODILY FUNCTIONS

GROSSOLOGY
Burping, farting, the goop in your nose . . . Eewww! Now, now, no need to be squeamish. These bodily substances and functions each have a specific purpose.

BRAAAP!

Burping and Farting

It's all a matter of gas. When you eat, you also swallow air, and air is made up of gas molecules. Sometimes gas in your stomach comes back up the esophagus and before you know it . . . BUURRRP! But often the gas moves on, passing through your digestive system as food moves through the body. The process of breaking down food in the large intestine makes more gas (the smelly kind). Between the gas you swallowed and the gas from digestion, that's a lot of gas in your body—and it can't stay in you. The gases that make it past your stomach leave your body as farts.

Dandruff

Those pesky oil glands are at it again. Your skin is always shedding cells—all day long, every day of the year. (Dust is actually made up largely of dead skin cells!) Sometimes, the glands on your scalp produce too much oil and cause the shedding skin to stick together in flaky clumps. That's dandruff.

FRRRNT

Snot and Boogers

They're made of mucus—a thick slimy substance that lives in your nose. Mucus traps dust and dirt that you breathe in, so that it doesn't get through to your lungs. Mucus also protects the delicate skin inside your nose. When mucus clumps up around dirt and debris, you have a booger.

Scabs and Pus

Scabs are natural bandages. When you get a cut, blood rushes to the scene of the wound. Platelets in your blood cause it to clot and harden at the surface of the skin so that the cells below can repair themselves. When the repair work is done, the scab will fall off. Sometimes, yellowish goo called pus seeps out of a cut. Pus is just dead cells, bacteria, and some leftover white blood cells that your body is pushing out.

Zits

Annoying as they are, zits are actually just clogged pores (those nearly invisible holes in your skin). Usually, the oil glands inside pores produce just the right amount of sebum (oil) to lubricate your skin and everything is fine and dandy. But sometimes, like during puberty, they produce too much oil and the pore itself becomes clogged with the excess oil and dead skin cells. When the pore becomes inflamed, you see a red bump pushing all that gunk to the surface. Sometimes it even has a white tip or whitehead. When the gunk oxidizes and hardens at the surface, you see a dark spot or blackhead.

FRAAARGH

Vomit

Bleh. Vomiting is your body's automatic response to harmful bacteria, too much food, nerves, or motion sickness. Here's how it happens: the muscles in your stomach contract and press down on your abdomen, forcing partially digested food back up through the esophagus, into your mouth, and out (hopefully into the toilet)!

Earwax

It does for your ears what mucus does for your nose—protects the delicate insides of your sense organs and catches dust and debris that you don't want inside your body. Earwax also has the very important job of channeling sound waves to your eardrum.

Eye Gunk

Tears clean your eyes and get gunk and debris off their surface. Usually, your eyelids wipe them away when you blink. But at night, your eyes don't open and close fully, so that mixture of tears and debris collects at the corner of your eye and hardens into the crusty stuff you wipe away in the morning.

Poop

Poop is the waste that's left over after your body has used up everything it needs from the food you ate.

THE BRAIN

What's going on inside your head? Lots. Your brain is the most complex part of your body. It's made up of billions of nerve cells that control all of your actions, including the ones you don't have to think about, like your heartbeat. Your brain is also what lets you think, remember, and dream. All that work takes a lot of energy.

The brain is divided into several parts with different functions:

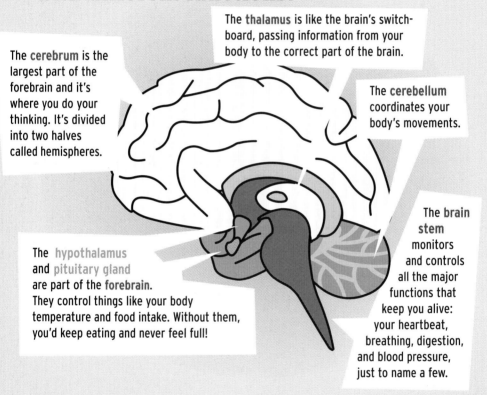

The **thalamus** is like the brain's switchboard, passing information from your body to the correct part of the brain.

The **cerebrum** is the largest part of the forebrain and it's where you do your thinking. It's divided into two halves called hemispheres.

The **cerebellum** coordinates your body's movements.

The hypothalamus and pituitary gland are part of the **forebrain**. They control things like your body temperature and food intake. Without them, you'd keep eating and never feel full!

The **brain stem** monitors and controls all the major functions that keep you alive: your heartbeat, breathing, digestion, and blood pressure, just to name a few.

Did you know...

It's not time, but distractions that affect your memory. In 1924, two psychologists, John Jenkins and Karl Dallenbach, did an experiment to test memory. Students learned lists of nonsense syllables either late at night or first thing in the morning. If the students learned the material just before bed, they slept between the study session and the test. If they learned the material in the morning, they were awake in the time before the test. The researchers tested the students' memories of the syllables after 1, 2, 4, or 8 hours. And guess what? The students forgot more while they were awake than while they were asleep! What seemed to cause the forgetting was not the passage of time, but interference from all the stuff you see and do in a day.

Memory

It's so annoying to forget things! And why is it that you remember something that happened when you were 4 years old, but you can't remember what you had for breakfast last week? There are three types of memory at work inside your head:

SENSORY MEMORY Sensory memories are just that—memories that come from the senses.

A sensory memory exists for each sensory channel: When you recognize a sound, like a friend's voice, that's a sensory memory!

SHORT-TERM MEMORY These are the memories that are easy to forget. Short-term memory is for temporary recall of information. When you're reading a paragraph, you have to remember what happened in the one before that. If you're paying attention, your short-term memory will keep that info stored for you, but not for long . . . Short-term memories fade quickly, unless they're passed on to your long-term memory!

LONG-TERM MEMORY These memories aren't going anywhere. The memories stored in your long-term memory are strong enough that you can recall them at almost any time. The name of your first cat, how to ride a bike, how to play a musical instrument . . . As long as you think of them from time to time, these guys are there to stay! Memories that you don't recall will fade and eventually be . . . forgotten.

SLEEPING AND DREAMING YAWN . . . ZZZzzzzzz . . . After a full day of working and playing, your body needs to take a break. That's when it's time to sleep. During sleep, your breathing slows down and your muscles relax. Your body temperature drops and your blood pressure decreases. It's rest time for your body, but your brain is another story! No one is entirely sure what our brains are up to when we sleep, but we know that our nerve cells are hard at work even while our consciousness is shut down.

Whatever's going on in there is important. If you miss one night of sleep, you'll probably feel cranky and a little uncoordinated. Miss a couple of nights in a row and you'll actually start seeing things.

Sleep happens in cycles that repeat throughout the night.

CYCLE	LASTS FOR	WHAT HAPPENS?
NREM, or non-rapid eye movement sleep, is the first part of the cycle	1 ½ to 2 hours	During NREM sleep, the brain and eyes are pretty inactive but your body might move around. If you've ever experienced sleepwalking, that happens during NREM sleep.
REM, or rapid eye movement sleep, is the second part of the cycle	10-60 minutes; repeats a few times	The brain is busy and your eyes and eyelids move around (that's where we get the rapid eye movement thing). Dreams and nightmares happen during REM sleep.

DREAMS

Some people think dreaming cleans up your memory, sorting through the events and emotions of the day. Others think that dreams are symbolic, concealing a greater meaning. Whatever you choose to believe, dreaming brings together elements from your unconscious mind—images, thoughts, feelings, experiences, and people—and forms them into a story.

Sigmund Freud

FAMOUS FACES

Psychoanalysts **Sigmund Freud** and **Carl Jung** wrote the books on dreaming, literally. Their theories about dreaming may differ, but Freud's **The Interpretation of Dreams** and Jung's **Man and His Symbols** are the major dream books of our time! Freud believed that dreams were expressions of the unconscious mind, your mind's way of revealing hidden desires and fears. Jung believed that dreams allow your unconscious mind to help your conscious mind work through problems and gain understanding.

THE FIVE SENSES

VISION

HEARING

SMELL

TOUCH

TASTE

THEY'RE HOW YOU EXPERIENCE THE WORLD!

1 Vision

Your eyes let you see the world. They're like a camera that captures images and works with your brain to make sense of what you see.

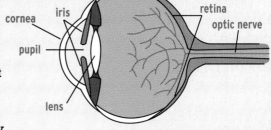

cornea · iris · pupil · lens · retina · optic nerve

SEE WHAT YOU SEE When you "see" something, you are actually seeing beams of light bouncing off of that object. Light bounces off objects and is reflected into your eyes. Light rays pass through the **cornea** to the **iris,** which contracts or expands to let light through the **pupil** to the **lens**. Together with the cornea, the lens focuses light onto your **retina**. On the retina, there are millions of light-sensitive cells called **rods** and **cones**. Rods identify shapes and work well in low light. Cones identify color and work best in bright light. Rods and cones send signals with the information they gather to the brain through the optic nerve. The brain makes sense of these signals and tells you what you are looking at.

I CAN'T SEE!
Eyes can develop all types of problems. Some people are blind, which means that they can't see at all. Lots of people wear glasses or contact lenses to correct their vision. And did you know that eyes get damaged by the sun's ultraviolet rays? Especially light-colored eyes. You can help your eyes by wearing sunglasses on bright days!

WHAT'S NEW? LASER EYE SURGERY

Want to say good-bye to your glasses? Laser eye surgery is becoming more and more popular as a way for people to correct their vision permanently. To see clearly, the cornea and the lens have to bend light rays so they focus on the retina. If the light rays don't focus on the retina, the image you see is blurry. Glasses and contacts help your eyes by focusing light onto the retina so that you can see things clearly.

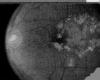

Laser eye surgery

During laser eye surgery, a doctor uses a laser to reshape the cornea so that light is focused properly. Laser eye surgery is an outpatient surgical procedure that takes 10–15 minutes for each eye. But before you run off to the doctor, be warned— laser eye surgery is not recommended for kids under the age of 18, mostly because your vision is still changing. And, while it can help a person see better, keep in mind that some patients have developed problems as a result of laser eye surgery.

2 Hearing

Ears serve two very important purposes: they process sound and keep you balanced.

LISTEN CAREFULLY When an object makes a noise, it sends sound waves through the air. These vibrations are channeled into your **ear canal** where they strike your eardrum. The eardrum vibrates and sets off a chain reaction, vibrating the three smallest bones in your body: the **hammer**, then the **anvil**, and finally the **stirrup**. The stirrup passes the vibrations into a coiled tube in the inner ear called the **cochlea**. When the fluid in the cochlea vibrates, tiny hairs called **cilia** move and sway. The vibrating cilia send electrical messages to the brain via the **auditory nerve**. The auditory nerve carries messages from 25,000 receptors in your ear to your brain. Your brain makes sense of the messages and tells you what sounds you are hearing!

Diagram labels: hammer, auditory nerve, cochlea, ear canal, eardrum, anvil, semicircular canals, eustachian tube, stirrup

NOISE

Sound pressure is measured in decibels (dB). Most people can hear sounds down to about 0 dB, the level of rustling leaves. Exposure to sounds of 85 dB or more (especially over a period of time) can damage the cilia, leading to hearing loss.

Sound	Decibels
Whisper	20
Normal talking	50–60
Car traffic	70
Alarm clock	80
Lawn mower	95
Rock concert	100
Jackhammer	115
Jet engine	130
Gunshot	140

DON'T FALL OVER Near the top of the cochlea are three loops called the **semicircular canals**. The canals are also full of liquid. When you move your head, the liquid moves. It pushes against nerve endings, which send messages to your brain. From these messages, your brain can tell whether or how your body is moving. When you feel dizzy, it's because the liquid is swirling around inside your ears. This makes the hairs of the sensory cells bend in all different directions, so the cells' signals confuse your brain.

WAIT, WHAT DID YOU SAY? Some people have trouble hearing, and some can't hear at all. Hearing aids can help people who are partially deaf, but people who are entirely deaf have to rely on their other senses to help process all of the information from the world around them.

Ears are delicate, so take care of them. Wear earplugs if you're exposed to loud sounds like construction.

3 Smell

Smell is a powerful thing. Tiny odor particles are all over the place, just waiting to be sniffed by your nose!

olfactory bulb

olfactory nerve

olfactory membrane cilia

SNNIFFF As you breathe in through your nose, air enters your nostrils. Hairs in the nostrils filter all kinds of things trying to enter your nose, even bugs! Past your nostrils, air moves through a thick layer of **mucus** to the **olfactory bulb**. There the smells are recognized because each smell molecule matches up with a particular nerve cell. The cells send signals along your **olfactory nerve** to the brain. The brain makes sense of sweet-smelling cookies and the moldy sandwich in your backpack from two weeks ago.

4 Touch

cold   heat

Touch doesn't come from one body part— it's experienced all over. Touch originates in the **dermis**, the bottom layer of your skin. The dermis is filled with tiny nerve endings that send information about what you touch to the spinal cord. Heat, cold, pressure, and pain are all felt by nerve endings in the skin. The spinal cord receives information and sends messages to the brain, where the feelings are registered.

pressure   pain

When nerve endings are cut off from the spinal cord, you no longer have the ability to feel. That's why damage to the spinal cord can result in paralysis-the inability to feel and move certain body parts.

Papillae are the bumps you see on your tongue.

5 Taste

YUCK OR YUM? Your tongue is covered with thousands of tiny **papillae** that contain **taste buds**. When you eat something, saliva helps break down your food. This causes the receptor cells located in your taste buds to send messages through sensory nerves to your brain. Your nose helps out by sensing odors and sending its own signals to the brain. The brain processes this information from your nose and mouth and decides whether or not you like the flavor!

Close-up of a papilla with salivary glands below and tastebuds lining the sides

You lose taste buds as you grow older, so taste your favorite foods while you can.

Did you know...

There are four types of taste buds—sensitive to sweet, salty, sour, or bitter chemicals.

PUBERTY

WHAT'S GOING ON WITH MY BODY?!?

Puberty is the name for all the things that happen to your body as it makes the transition from childhood to adulthood. It's caused by **hormonal** changes. Pubertal changes don't happen overnight—they take years to run their course. But when you're through with puberty, you'll be an adult! Physically anyway.

> **Hormones** are those chemical substances released by glands like the pituitary gland, a tiny but important pea-size organ located near your brain.

Girls

Girls start puberty first, around the age of 10 or 11. The pituitary gland releases hormones that tell the ovaries to start producing the hormones estrogen and progesterone and to start releasing eggs each month. These hormones cause changes to happen in a girl's body.

Breasts start to develop.

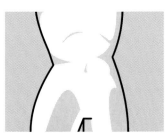

Hips gain some extra padding.

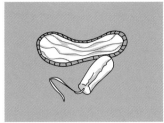

Pubic and underarm hair starts to grow.

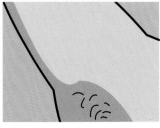

Menstruation begins.

Boys

Boys begin puberty later, around the age of 12 or 13. Hormones from the pituitary gland tell the testes to let out more of the hormone testosterone and to start making sperm. The increased level of testosterone causes changes in boys.

Boys begin their growth spurt later than girls, but they grow for a longer time. That's why guys generally end up taller than girls.

Just like in girls, pubic and underarm hair starts to grow. Facial and body hair starts growing too.

The genital organs start to enlarge.

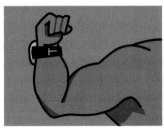

Muscles become more developed.

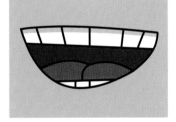

The larynx enlarges, making a guy's voice a lot deeper.

Hormones and Emotions

Along with all those physical changes that hormones cause, there are some emotional changes too. Guys and girls may start thinking about each other ... differently, and that can cause some awkwardness.

MOVIES ON
BRAINPOP.COM

HELLO

DNA AND HEREDITY

Why do you look the way you do?

Because of your parents, and their parents, and their parents' parents . . . We inherit our looks, height, size, and chemical makeup from our parents.

That passing of traits from parents to offspring is known as heredity. The genes from your parents combine to form your genes. No two people have the same genetic makeup, except for identical twins.

DNA stands for deoxyribonucleic acid.

A very important molecule called **DNA** acts like a blueprint for your body.

Every cell in your body has DNA in it, and each strand of DNA contains all of the information about your body's plan. It's a chemical record of your inherited characteristics like hair color, eye color, height, bone structure, and so on. So even if you don't know how tall you're going to be when you're 18, your DNA has a pretty good idea! What we look like is determined by the genes we inherit, but factors like environment and nutrition can play a role too. For example, humans in general are much taller than their ancestors because their diet is different and their environment has changed.

A strand of DNA has a double helix structure that encodes information.

Siblings can look a lot alike, or very different. It's all up to the gene mix!

Did you know...

Babies are usually born with blue eyes, regardless of the eye colors of their parents. Why? Well, newborns do not have the dark brown pigment melanin in the irises of their eyes. As babies get older, their bodies start to produce melanin and their eye color may change.

Brown Eyes, Blue Eyes

How is your eye color determined? It's **genetics**, of course. If your mother has brown eyes and your father has blue eyes, the chances are your eyes will be brown. This is because the gene for brown eyes is **dominant** and the gene for blue eyes is **recessive**. In most cases, the gene for brown eyes will block out the gene for blue eyes, but not always. If one of your father's parents had blue eyes, your father is still carrying that gene, even if his eyes ended up brown. Your father can still pass that trait on to you! And it's possible that your eyes might be a totally different color than both of your parents. If that's the case, take a look at your grandparents' eyes. If you wind up with a recessive blue-eye gene from each of your brown-eyed parents, your eyes will be blue!

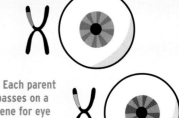

▶ Each parent passes on a gene for eye color.

▲ A visual family tree can show where your eye color came from.

Did you know...

Do your earlobes dangle down or do they attach directly to your head? Check 'em out. This is an example of a **genetic** trait. Try looking at your family members to see if their lobes are attached or detached.

WHAT'S NEW?

Pre-implantation Genetic Diagnosis (PGD)

Some couples have trouble having babies. Human reproduction can be tricky, and it's often the very start of a pregnancy that causes the most problems. IVF (in vitro fertilization) is nothing new—with IVF, eggs are removed from a woman's ovaries and fertilized in a laboratory with male sperm cells. About three days later, once the embryo begins to grow, it is implanted into the mother's womb and the pregnancy proceeds normally.

The new part is PGD. Nowadays parents-to-be can not only learn the sex of their child, but also whether their child will be able to supply tissue-matched bone marrow to a dying sibling and whether she may be predisposed to develop breast cancer or Huntington's disease. In the case of PGD, all of this information could be gathered by examining cells before the embryo gets implanted into the mother's womb. A couple might decide to reject an embryo based on its genetic makeup.

BACTERIA, DISEASES, AND EPIDEMICS

Viruses

AHHHH-CHOO! Yep, that cold you got last winter was a virus. A virus is a little pack of chemicals that attacks the cells inside your body. Viruses work by taking over healthy cells. With a virus inside of them, those cells start making copies of the virus instead of reproducing normally. If your immune system can't fight them off in time, you get sick.

Gesundheit! When your buddy sneezes, it's best to say "bless you" from afar. A sneeze from a person with a runny nose forces out drops of moisture containing millions of tiny virus cells. If you're close enough to breathe these in, you might get sick.

Bacteria

Bacteria are the most common living things on Earth. Most bacteria are good guys; they actually help your body digest food and break down waste. Then there are the bad, disease-causing bacteria that can make you really sick.

Having a bacterial infection is different from having a virus. Bacteria don't need the help of your cells to reproduce. They can pretty much do that on their own, given a warm, moist place to hang out. And they reproduce quickly—about once every 20 minutes! Because of this, bacteria have caused some major problems over time, especially before we had antibiotics to fight them. You've probably heard of **cholera**, **tuberculosis**, and **smallpox**—these **epidemics** were all caused by persistent bacteria that multiplied quickly.

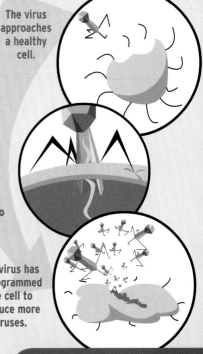

The virus approaches a healthy cell.

The virus injects its genetic material into the cell.

The virus has reprogrammed the cell to produce more viruses.

Did you know...

HIV (human immuno-deficiency virus) specifically attacks the body's immune system, making it difficult for the body to fight off infections like the common cold. HIV destroys those helper T-cells of the immune system. When a person's T-cell count reaches a very low number, he is said to have **AIDS**.

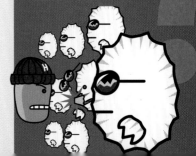

▶ HIV is the bad guy who attacks the helper T cells that normally fight off illnesses for your immune system.

Antibiotics

In the fight against bacteria, antibiotics have made an enormous difference. They kill the harmful bacteria that get into our cells, without

▲ Alexander Fleming accidentally grew a bacteria-killing mold on a culture plate in his lab. After further experiments proved its bacteria-fighting properties, he named the substance penicillin.

damaging our bodies. The discovery of penicillin in 1928 by **Alexander Fleming** changed our world. Prior to that, people would die from what are now minor, common infections. **Penicillin** is an antibiotic that's made from mold and fungi. It's effective, but many people are allergic to it. Newer antibiotics are chemically formed to break bacteria down and prevent them from multiplying. These newer antibiotics are more targeted to specific strains of bacteria.

FAMOUS FACE

Back in the late 1700s, **Edward Jenner** noticed that milkmaids who had contracted cowpox (and successfully fought it off) seemed immune to the disease smallpox as well. Jenner intentionally infected a young boy with cowpox, allowed him to recover, and then infected him with smallpox to show that his body had built the necessary antibodies to resist the infection. (Jenner was convinced that antibodies for cowpox would be effective against smallpox germs.) It was a risky experiment and certainly unethical by today's standards, but Jenner's gamble paid off—he developed the smallpox vaccine. Today, smallpox vaccinations are rarely even given because it is so uncommon to see cases anymore.

Vaccines

They protect you from deadly diseases, but what's inside that shot? Vaccines themselves contain either bits of the very bacteria or virus they protect against or deactivated forms of the pathogens. Disease-causing organisms have at least two distinct effects on the body. First, they make us feel sick. Second, they cause our immune systems to respond. The immune system builds proteins called antibodies to fight off the invader cells, and we eventually get better. So vaccines contain organisms that will cause the second response to happen, but not the first.

FLU SHOTS

Each year, scientists develop a new influenza (flu) vaccine. There are different strains of the flu virus and each one has a different genetic makeup. In any given year, one strain becomes more prominent than the others. The vaccine is developed to immunize people against one particular flu strain. Here's the catch—if the wrong strain of flu virus comes your way, you can still get the flu, even if you get a flu shot. In the winter of 2003/2004, a particularly deadly strain caused the deaths of more than 100 children. Babies and the elderly—people with weak immune systems—are at the greatest risk.

TIMELINE OF **EPIDEMICS**

Before there were vaccines, unsanitary living conditions and mixing of populations (exposing one another to new germs) led to devastating epidemics.

1300s
BUBONIC PLAGUE
BUBONIC PLAGUE (A.K.A. THE BLACK DEATH) IS FIRST REPORTED IN ASIA BUT MOVES INTO EUROPE WITH DEVASTATING RESULTS: 1/3-1/2 OF EUROPE'S POPULATION IS KILLED DURING EPIDEMICS IN THE 13TH AND 17TH CENTURIES. THIS INFECTIOUS BACTERIUM ORIGINATED IN RATS AND WAS SPREAD TO HUMANS BY FLEAS.

1518
SMALLPOX
SMALLPOX (SO NAMED BECAUSE VICTIMS ARE COVERED WITH POCKMARKS) FIRST BREAKS OUT AND CONTINUES TO DECIMATE NATIVE POPULATIONS FOR CENTURIES. IT IS SPREAD THROUGH THE AIR (COUGHING) OR CLOSE CONTACT.

1732-33
INFLUENZA
THE WORLD IS HARD HIT BY THIS DEADLY BOUT WITH THE FLU. THE FLU COMES BACK AGAIN AND AGAIN, WITH A SEVERE AND DEADLY OUTBREAK OF THE "SPANISH FLU" KILLING 20-30 MILLION PEOPLE WORLDWIDE IN 1818-19.

1800s
MEASLES
NORTH AMERICA IS THE TARGET OF THIS MEASLES OUTBREAK.

1826-37
CHOLERA
CHOLERA SPREADS FROM ASIA TO EUROPE AND INTO NORTH AMERICA, CAUSING MAJOR DESTRUCTION IN CITIES. THE BACTERIA, WHICH ARE FOUND IN CONTAMINATED FOOD AND WATER, CAUSE SEVERE DIARRHEA LEADING TO DEHYDRATION.

1898
YELLOW FEVER
MORE THAN 5,000 AMERICAN SOLDIERS DIE OF THE DISEASE (SPREAD BY MOSQUITOES) DURING THE SPANISH-AMERICAN WAR. SYMPTOMS INCLUDE HIGH FEVER AND JAUNDICE.

1940s-50s
POLIO
AT ITS HIGH POINT IN 1952, THERE ARE OVER 58,000 CASES OF POLIO IN THE US ALONE. THE MOST SEVERE CASES LEAD TO PARALYSIS OR DEATH.

1981-PRESENT
HIV/AIDS FIRST APPEARS IN 1981. THERE IS STILL NO CURE OR VACCINE, AND IT REMAINS A THREAT, PARTICULARLY IN PARTS OF AFRICA.

DEBATE: Traditional vs. Alternative Medicine

Some people believe that if you're sick, you should go to a "real" doctor. But for a large portion of the world's population, traditional "Western" medicine seems weird. In Eastern countries like China, people regularly see herbalists or acupuncturists who treat their conditions with needles, herbs, and ointments. In India, ayurveda is a widespread holistic approach that treats the mind and body. Some examples of widely used "alternative" therapies include:

CHIROPRACTIC: The spine and neck are manipulated to realign the vertebrae and release the muscles and tensed nerves.

ACUPUNCTURE: Needles and herbs are used to unblock the body's "vital energy" within its pathways, known as "meridians" and "channels."

OSTEOPATHY: Soft-tissue stretching and gentle release techniques are used to re-position the bones and release tensed muscles.

HOMEOPATHY: Patients are treated with small amounts of a substance that in a larger dose would cause symptoms similar to those being treated.

REFLEXOLOGY: Pressure on the sole of the foot stimulates the nervous system to balance and restore energy to various organs in the body.

Because many alternative healing methods are not regulated, some people are nervous about trying them. Others will only check them out if prescription drugs, surgery, or more mainstream approaches don't work for them. But there are also plenty of people who will opt for an herb, like garlic, before they'll take an antibiotic.

While it's good to be open to trying new things, it's also important to be very careful about your health. The safest bet is to check out any natural or alternative remedies with your family doctor or practitioner first.

WHAT'S NEW?

Body Monitoring

Why wait for a visit to the doctor to find out if something's up with your body? Shirts and armbands that tell you how your body is doing will allow you to keep tabs on your daily health. Heart-rate monitors are old news compared with this new wave of body-monitoring gadgets:

Smart Shirts, like Georgia Tech's Wearable Motherboard™, have sensors that measure breathing, heart rate, temperature, and other vital signs. Optical fibers can even detect bullet wounds. It's lightweight, so it's easy for anyone to wear—from infants (who could be monitored for sudden infant death syndrome) to soldiers in combat.

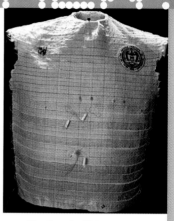

▲ The Smart-Shirt prototype Wearable Motherboard™ developed by Georgia Tech

Armbands also contain sensors that constantly collect data like heart rate, movement, heat flow, and skin temperature from your body. Handily enough, the armbands are outfitted with wireless technology, so they can transmit your body's data to a personal computer.

WHAT'S NEXT?

Brain Slushy

What if you could freeze your brain? It's not as gross as it sounds, and it's actually a potential lifesaver. If someone's heart suddenly stops beating, they're in trouble. A person can often be saved by resuscitation, but the problem is that while the heart can survive up to 20 minutes without beating, brain damage starts to happen after 4–6 minutes. It's a fact that cell damage slows down at colder temperatures. With that in mind, the National Institutes of Health are funding the study of a "brain slushy" as an emergency paramedic tool that would be administered in certain situations where a person's heart has stopped beating, but there is the possibility of saving his life if brain damage can be avoided. The slushy works by cooling brain cells, and therefore slowing cell damage. The hope is that a patient could reach the hospital with a fighting chance! Human trials of the brain slushy are slated to begin in 2007.

SCIENCE FAIR PROJECT #2

When your brain gets signals that don't agree with each other, you may feel uncomfortable and have a hard time doing things that require thinking. In this experiment, you will show test subjects colors and words that do not match in order to find out whether they can recognize words or colors faster.

YOU WILL NEED:

- ◎ 40 index cards
- ◎ Felt-tipped markers (basic colors—red, orange, yellow, green, blue, purple, brown, and black)
- ◎ Stopwatch
- ◎ 10 volunteers (they should all be about the same age)

1. On one side of each of 20 index cards, write the name of a color using a magic marker of a DIFFERENT color (for example, use a red marker to write the word BLUE; yellow to write GREEN, etc.). On the back of each card, write the word you used in black marker. (If you wrote BLUE on the front with a red marker, write BLUE on the back in black.) Put this group of cards aside and label it group 1.

2. On the last 20 index cards, write the same names in the same colors as you did in group 1. However, on the back, write the marker color you used on the front. (If you wrote BLUE on the front with a red marker, write RED on the back in black.) Put this group of cards aside and label it group 2.

3. Before you start showing your volunteers the cards in group 1, ask them to read the word on the front of each card. Start timing with your stopwatch when you show the first card. When the volunteer correctly reads the word, show her the next card. Stop the stopwatch when your volunteer has correctly read all 20 cards. Record the time that appears on your stopwatch.

4. Repeat step 3 with the cards in group 2, but ask your volunteer to name the color that she sees (NOT the word that is written on the front of the card).

◎ Did your volunteers name (and therefore recognize and process) the words or the colors faster? Making a bar graph of your results may help you to present and understand them more clearly.

◎ The ages of your volunteers may affect whether they recognize words or colors faster. Try this experiment with groups of volunteers of different ages (including adults, people your own age, and young children who have recently learned to read).

CHAPTER 3

FOOD FOR THOUGHT

Food is the fuel our bodies use to do everything they do. Like cars need gasoline, humans need food. What's inside the food you eat? And why are some foods better for you than others? What is the future of food and our food supply? Read on to find out!

NUTRITION

Human beings are **heterotrophic**. That means we rely on outside sources for food (as opposed to **autotrophic** plants that can create food from the help of sunlight). The fact is, everything we do requires fuel. Our body's fuel is a balance of carbohydrates, protein, fats, vitamins, and minerals.

The Food Guide Pyramid

The US Department of Agriculture (USDA) and the Department of Health and Human Services (HHS) have created a helpful little chart called the **Food Guide Pyramid** to help us navigate the complex world of nutritional needs.

Most **protein** comes from animal products, so vegetarians have to be very careful to get enough of the protein, calcium, iron, and zinc found in meat and dairy.

FATS, OILS, AND SWEETS
USE SPARINGLY
Your body doesn't need much extra fat, even though they taste good! Most of us don't need to be too careful about consuming enough of these.

Too much **fat** in your diet can lead to all sorts of health problems later in life.

MEAT, POULTRY, FISH, DRY BEANS, EGGS, AND NUTS GROUP
2-3 SERVINGS
Protein is important because it helps our bodies rebuild tissue.

MILK, YOGURT, AND CHEESE GROUP
2-3 SERVINGS

VEGETABLE GROUP
3-5 SERVINGS
Fruits and veggies provide vitamins, minerals, and fiber. They keep your hair shiny, your skin healthy, and your digestive system on track, among other things.

FRUIT GROUP
2-4 SERVINGS

BREAD, CEREAL, RICE, AND PASTA GROUP
(CARBOHYDRATES) 6-11 SERVINGS
Our energy comes from carbs. They are broken down by our bodies into a simple sugar called **glucose**, and that glucose is what our cells use for energy.

Most **glucose** that isn't used by the body right away is stored for later as **fat**.

DRINK MILK?

Yes, ideally. Milk is one of those funny things that's REALLY good for you, but also hard for some people to stomach. Thank goodness there are some alternatives:

LACTOSE-FREE MILK is real milk, with the lactose removed. Most milk allergies come from lactose intolerance. Two cups of lactose-free milk delivers almost all of your daily calcium intake requirement. And the calcium in milk is the kind most easily absorbed by the body.

SOY MILK is made from soybeans. It contains a lot of good things like protein, vitamin A, magnesium, potassium, and folate. Plus, soy is good for you.

RICE MILK is made from rice. Like soy milk, there's a lot of good stuff in it, but it's low in protein and is missing some essential vitamins and the blast of calcium that real milk delivers. Calcium-fortified rice milk can help out in that department.

VITAL NUTRIENTS

Your body needs VITAMINS and MINERALS to function properly. Here's a sample of what you need, where you can get them, and what they do for you!

WHAT YOU NEED	WHAT IT DOES	WHERE IT COMES FROM
VITAMIN A	Prevents eye problems, helps the immune system, contributes to growth and development of cells, keeps skin healthy	Milk, eggs, liver, orange or green vegetables, and orange fruits
VITAMIN C	Forms collagen, a tissue that helps to hold cells together; keeps bones, teeth, gums, and blood vessels healthy; helps the body absorb iron and calcium; helps heal cuts and scrapes	Fruits and veggies like oranges, grapefruits, kiwi, red berries, tomatoes, broccoli, and spinach
VITAMIN D	Strengthens bones by helping the body absorb bone-building calcium	Made by your body when you get sunlight on your skin! Also found in egg yolks, fish oils, and fortified foods like milk
VITAMIN E	Helps protect cells from damage and contributes to the health of red blood cells	Vegetable oils, nuts, leafy green vegetables, avocados, wheat germ, and whole grains
B VITAMINS: B12, B6, THIAMIN, RIBOFLAVIN, FOLATE	Help build DNA, make red blood cells, and break down proteins; important for heart health and nerve-cell function	Fish, red meat, poultry, milk, cheese, eggs, leafy green vegetables, asparagus, and oranges and other citrus fruits
CALCIUM	Builds strong bones and teeth	Milk, dairy products, and broccoli and dark green, leafy vegetables like kale; soy foods and foods fortified with calcium, including some kinds of orange juice and soy milk
MAGNESIUM	Helps muscles and nerves to function, steadies the heart rhythm, keeps bones strong, helps the body to create energy and make proteins	Whole grains, nuts and seeds, leafy green vegetables, potatoes, beans, avocados, broccoli, bananas, kiwi, shrimp, and chocolate!
PHOSPHORUS	Helps to form healthy bones and teeth, helps the body to make energy, helps cells function normally	Dairy foods, meat, and fish
POTASSIUM	Helps with muscle and nervous-system function, helps maintain the balance of water in the body	Broccoli, potato skin, leafy green vegetables, citrus fruits, bananas, dried fruits, peas, and lima beans
ZINC	Helps with normal growth, sexual development, strong immunity, and healing cuts and scrapes	Red meat, poultry, seafood, nuts, dried beans, soy foods, dairy products, whole grains, and fortified breakfast cereals

Calories

Just what are calories anyway? Everyone talks about them. Some people count them. But what do they do for us? Calories are a measure of the amount of energy that the body can get from a given food. So the more calories you get, the more energetic and better off you'll be, right? Wrong! There is such a thing as consuming too many calories—which can wind up stored as an unhealthy amount of fat in your body.

▲ A typical slice of cheese pizza can have as many as 300 calories. Add sausage or pepperoni, and it can have as many as 500-600 calories.

There are other important things to be gained from food: Protein not only gives us energy, but helps us rebuild tissues. Vital nutrients (vitamins and minerals) keep our systems running. Fats can help us process certain vitamins . . . Daily calorie needs vary from person to person, depending on your age, size, gender, and level of activity.

So, what's for lunch?

Decisions, decisions. Get the maximum nutrients out of your meal and you'll feel better and more energized for the rest of the day. See how these two very different lunches stack up:

	SUBWAY ROASTED CHICKEN BREAST SALAD	MCDONALD'S SMALL FRENCH FRIES
Calories	140	209
Fat	3 g	10 g
Cholesterol	45 mg	0
Saturated Fat	1 g	2 g
Carbs	12 g	26 g
Protein	16 g	3 g
Iron	6% RDV	3% RDV
Vitamin A	15% RDV	*
Vitamin C	50% RDV	14% RDV
Calcium	4% RDV	1% RDV

RDV is Recommended Daily Value

The fries have more calories and more fat. They also have more saturated fat and fewer micronutrients. Not only that, but the carbs in the fries are simple carbohydrates. That means that they are broken down into glucose quickly and their energy is released quickly. If you're sprinting a mile right away, you might be able to use the energy up—you'll feel a quick high from the fries, but it won't last. Excess glucose gets stored as fat if you don't use it up. The chicken breast gives the salad its healthy protein. And complex carbohydrates—like those found in the salad's leafy greens—break down and release energy more slowly, for the long haul.

Fortified and Enriched Foods

MOVIES ON BRAINPOP.COM

You get some help along the road to good nutrition—certain foods are **fortified**. This means that vitamins and/or minerals are added in order to increase their nutritional content. The government and food companies work together to fortify certain foods in order to ensure that people are getting the right amounts of some vital nutrients.

Then there are foods that have lost some of their nutritional value in the process of being refined for packaging and sale. These foods are **enriched** with the vitamins and minerals they have lost along the way. Bread and pasta, for example, are enriched with **B vitamins** and **iron**.

TV IS BAD FOR YOUR HEALTH

A recent study showed that kids who watch a lot of TV are more likely to be overweight than those who do not. Guess why? Commercials! The junk food that's presented in commercials (by your favorite cartoon characters) is so appealing that you just want to go out and get it! Kids who watch a lot of TV (and those persuasive commercials) are also likely to be getting less exercise.

Mrs. Cheever's CHEESE POPCORN

Weight Problems

It's true that people come in all shapes and sizes. Some of us are naturally thin, some of us are muscular, others are heavyset. Having a little baby fat or even being on the round side is perfectly okay. If everyone looked the same, the world would be pretty boring.

However, when your weight gets to be too high, it can cause stress and strain on your body. Overweight people are at a higher risk for health problems like heart disease and diabetes. Being overweight is sometimes due to heredity, but it's a problem that you can control with attention to diet and exercise.

Obesity has become a big problem in the last 20 years, especially among kids. On account of a combination of poor diet and lack of exercise, the majority of Americans are overweight.

"NATURAL" FOODS

These days, there's lots of confusion and concern about what's in the food we're putting into our bodies.

The Meaning of Organic

You've probably heard the term organic or seen it in your supermarket aisles. But what does it mean? Here's the deal—organic farmers emphasize the use of renewable resources to conserve soil and water and to protect the environment. Organic produce is grown without the use of synthetic pesticides and fertilizers. Milk, meat, poultry, and eggs are considered organic if the animals they come from are not treated with hormones (as is common with dairy cows) or antibiotics (as a means of warding off disease).

In the grocery store, organic food is labeled "organic," as compared with produce that is "conventionally grown." Because there is growing concern about the environment and the effect of pesticides and fertilizers on the humans who eat conventionally grown fruits and vegetables (which do contain traces of pesticides), many health-minded people are going organic.

In addition, for the government to certify food as organic, it can't be bioengineered (see below) or irradiated (a process that kills microorganisms).

Genetically Altered Foods

Super-succulent strawberries. Purple carrots with twice the recommended value of beta-carotene per carrot. Pest-resistent corn. Seedless watermelons . . . Sound futuristic? It's not. The technology currently exists to produce all of the above and more through a process called bioengineering.

In a way, humans have been messing around with plant genetics for quite a long time—almost as long as plants have been cultivated. In the beginning this meant cross-pollinating certain plants, grafting plants together, or saving only the best seeds from the most desirable plants.

Genetic engineering is a science that takes traditional plant-breeding methods to a new level—scientists are able to take a set of genes from one plant (or animal), and insert it into another (this is called splicing). The results are combinations that don't happen in nature. We call them transgenic or genetically modified plants.

▲ Scientists draw circles on mangos so they can monitor the fruits' color changes during an experiment.

Now we can create vegetables that are fortified right on the vine; change the shape, color, and flavor of produce; and grow soybeans that are resistant to weed killer.

Scientists are even starting to explore

▶ Scientists created 'Black Emerald' seedless grapes because no other grape of its type was available in mid-May.

produce with medicinal value: one interesting example is golden rice, which has been engineered using a daffodil gene to have high levels of beta-carotene, a substance that the body converts to vitamin A. In theory, this rice will be used in regions where vitamin A deficiency is widespread, though it hasn't yet been proven effective. Another goal of genetic modification is to extend the shelf life of food.

▶ Scientists engineered 'Endless Summer' tomatoes to stay on the vine longer to enhance flavor.

Pharm Crops Plants contain protein, and protein is required to produce certain types of drugs and vaccines. Until recently, these protein drugs were most often made by inserting a protein-producing human gene into cultured hamster cells, which are grown and monitored in very expensive, complicated machinery in a lengthy process. In the last few years, scientists have found a cheaper, faster way to grow **pharmaceutical protein**: they isolate the gene for the protein they want to reproduce, inject it into developing plants—most commonly corn—and later extract the protein they need from the harvested corn. Though pharmed drugs aren't available just yet, drugs for cystic fibrosis, vaccines for cholera and measles, and other therapies are undergoing testing.

While this is great news for pharmaceutical companies, scientists and environmentalists are concerned about the contamination of our food supply. It's difficult to control interbreeding, especially in a crop like corn. Pharm crops—which are not intended to be eaten—have never been tested to see if they're safe for human consumption.

Did you know...

Currently, 10 to 30 percent of our food is lost because it spoils before reaching the consumer. This is a huge problem, especially in developing countries.

DEBATE: To Bioengineer or Not to Bioengineer

Bioengineering is a hot topic for debate these days. On the one hand, it could lead to bigger crop yields and "new and improved" fruits and vegetables. Though technology is more sophisticated now—in terms of isolating and extracting genes from one species and implanting them in another—you could look at bioengineering as a high-tech version of cross-pollination, which happens naturally with certain types of plants.

So what's the problem? Well, we don't know much about the dangers of genetically altered food. There's no telling what the long-term effects will be just yet. And because it is difficult to control cross-pollination (genetically modified crops interbreeding with conventional crops), there is also the risk that some native (nonmodified) species could become extinct. We have no idea how this would impact not only the people who eat the crops, but the wildlife that feeds on them and the environment as a whole.

47

FOOD SICK!

As much as food keeps us going, there's always a chance that it will make you sick. We're not talking about the stomachache you get from eating too much in one sitting. Food poisoning comes from eating something that is contaminated with harmful bacteria or viruses.

This happens most often when food spoils or when it is not properly cooked.

BOTULISM is caused by bacteria found primarily in home-canned vegetables. Infants under 12 months can also get botulism from eating honey.

E. COLI infection comes from eating undercooked infected meat, drinking unpasteurized milk or juice, or swimming in or drinking sewage-contaminated water.

LISTERIA BACTERIA is found in soil and water. Humans can get it from raw meat products, raw vegetables, or unpasteurized milk and cheese.

SALMONELLA comes from food contaminated with animal or human feces, especially unpasteurized milk and raw or undercooked meat, poultry, and eggs.

Did you know...

Reptiles, including turtles, often carry salmonella. So be sure to wash your hands after handling one

Did you know...

They're not seen that often, but tapeworms are parasites that can enter your body through raw or undercooked fish or meat. A tapeworm takes up residence in your intestine, eating the food you eat, getting bigger and bigger, and making you really sick!

The best way to steer clear of food poisoning? Wash, wash, wash: your hands, your food, your countertops. Don't eat raw cookie dough (because it contains raw eggs)! It's also important that food be cooked well, especially poultry.

Preservatives

In the battle to keep food fresh, preservatives have made a huge difference. Not too long ago, food only lasted on the shelf for a few days before it spoiled. People came up with all sorts of ways to make food last—freezing it outdoors in the winter, using vinegar to pickle vegetables and fruits, salting

VINEGAR

canned eggs

or drying meats . . . More recently, food has been canned, vacuum-packed, and even irradiated to make it last!

Since the first practical refrigerator came along in 1873, it's been a whole lot easier to keep food fresh. Even so, leave a piece of meat in the fridge for more than a few days and your dinner is spoiled.

Scientists have found that chemical compounds can help to prevent food from rotting or oxidizing. Today, many processed foods contain natural and artificial preservatives. Ascorbic acid (vitamin C), an antioxidant, keeps food from changing color and taste when exposed to air. Sodium benzoate prevents the growth of microorganisms in pickles and other acidic foods. Sulfites prevent discoloration in dried foods and are used in wine-making to inhibit bacterial growth. And emulsifiers, such as lecithin, keep oil and water from separating in ice cream, chocolate, and margarine.

TRICK OR TREAT?

HAGGIS (a tasty treat from Scotland) Take one sheep's stomach and stuff it with oatmeal, fat, lamb's liver, and onion. Sew it up and drop it in boiling water for 5 hours and what do you get? Yummy yummy haggis! Five million Scotsmen can't be wrong—they've been eating it for hundreds of years!

SWEETBREADS (not necessarily for the sweet tooth) It ain't cake, that's for sure. Sweetbreads are the edible glands of an animal, including the pancreas, where the body creates insulin, and the thymus, which makes T cells. Believe it or not, fancy restaurants actually serve this stuff up for lots of money.

1,000-YEAR-OLD EGGS (a Chinese delicacy) They're not really 1,000 years old, but they're still pretty gross. This recipe starts with a duck egg, which you coat in a mixture of lime, salt, ash, and tea leaves. Bury the eggs in a pot full of garden soil and store in a cool, dry place. Wait . . . and wait—100 days in all. Then dig your eggs out of the dirt, rinse, peel, and enjoy!

HEAD CHEESE (wherever gross foods are served) If you think anything that's called head cheese has to be disgusting . . . you're right! Head cheese is made from all those little parts of cows and pigs that are too small to sell on their own: cheeks, skull muscles, tongues, feet, and hearts. Take all that good stuff and suspend it in some gelatin, and you've got yourself a head cheese. Some people can't bear to throw anything away!

WITCHETTY GRUBS (Australian for nasty) Aborigines are wild about witchetty grubs, the larvae of the ghost moth. They're fat, white, and squirmy, and usually eaten alive! Despite being totally disgusting, these insects provide the aborigines with an easy source of fat and protein. Try it, you might like it!

BALUT (a shocking snack from the Philippines) The eggs you buy in the supermarket haven't been fertilized, but the eggs used for balut have—and they've been allowed to develop! Boil them in salt water at just the right time, and you've got a mouthful of yolky goodness garnished with a morsel of chicken! Hooray!

FUN FOOD FACTS

OiL AND WATER

You've heard it over and over again: oil and water don't mix. The chemical bonds that keep atoms of oxygen and hydrogen together are not similar enough to the bonds that keep the hydrogen and carbon atoms of oil together to allow them to combine. Atoms have polarity, just like magnets. If the strength of the charge between any two given atoms is similar, then they will readily combine. If it's not, they will keep to themselves. Pour oil and water into the same glass and watch what happens!

WHY CHEWING GUM iS CHEWY

People have been chewing on things for centuries—bark, resin, even paraffin wax. But modern chewing gum wasn't born until the late 1800s, when Thomas Adams started experimenting with chicle. Adams wasn't the first to enjoy chicle, which is made from the latex sap of the Central American sapodilla tree—people in Mexico had already been chewing it for centuries!

WHY SODA iS FiZZY

Soda gets its zip from a gas called carbon dioxide (CO_2). Without CO_2, soda would be, well . . . flat. Soda is sealed in containers under pressure with CO_2. The CO_2 gas doesn't want to stay in the liquid (it isn't truly dissolved), and it wants to go back to regular atmospheric pressure. So, when you open a bottle and let air in, the fizzing that happens is a result of CO_2 gas escaping as the interior of the bottle goes from high pressure to a lower pressure.

WHY GARLiC iS HEALTHY

It may not make your breath smell good, but chomping on garlic has health benefits. It reduces cholesterol and triglycerides in the blood. Garlic is also a natural antibiotic with antiviral and antifungal properties. There's garlic in pill form, but to get the full benefits you've got to eat the real thing.

CHiCKEN SOUP FOR THE COLD

Like your grandma said, chicken soup is good for the body. It contains several ingredients that affect the body's immune system. Lab tests found that chicken soup helps to stop the movement of neutrophils, white blood cells that kill germs and cause inflammation. Neutrophils can cause mucus build-up, which may be at the heart of coughs and stuffy sinuses and noses.

SPACE FOOD

Food carried into space has to be freeze-dried (all the water is sucked out!) and vacuum-sealed to prevent spoilage. Space food is sealed in packages that have a shelf-life of two years or more, and it doesn't need refrigeration.

BROCCOLI CAN FIGHT CANCER

Broccoli contains sulforaphane—a substance known to block carcinogens. Feeding sulforaphane-rich broccoli sprouts to lab rats exposed to a carcinogen was shown to reduce the size and number of the rats' tumors.

SEAWEED IS IN YOUR FOOD!

You've probably eaten seaweed without knowing it. An ingredient called carrageenan is present in many of the foods you eat: salad dressings, hamburger patties, even ice cream. Carrageenan is a gum derived from red seaweed and used as a filler for some sandwich meats and to improve the texture of things like ice cream and desserts.

FAST-FOOD NATION

Fast-food consumption has increased fivefold among American children since 1970. Eaters of fast food consume more carbohydrates, fats, sugars, and about 187 more calories per meal overall. That could add up to about 6 pounds (2.7 kg) per year.

WHY POPCORN POPS

Corn kernels pop when they are heated to 400°F (204°C). At this temperature, the water inside each kernel changes to steam. Popcorn's hard cover keeps the steam from escaping, so pressure builds up inside the kernel until it bursts and we have a popped piece of corn!

Instant Ice Cream

Leave two chemists in a lab for too long and they come up with some wacky projects. Ice cream in 30 seconds? Sounds like a fun afternoon.

The secret to the rapid freeze is found in liquid nitrogen. Liquid nitrogen is COLD—we're talking minus 320°F (minus 196°C). It's so cold, in fact, that it can produce a half gallon of ice-cream in 30 seconds!

Here's how it happened in the lab:

- A regular old ice cream recipe was used, and the concoction was mixed in a well-ventilated lab.
- Once the basic recipe had come together, liquid nitrogen syrup was stirred into the mix.
- As it was stirred, the liquid nitrogen rapidly froze the cream mixture, and tada, ice cream!

WARNING! Liquid nitrogen is NOT something you can or should get your hands on. Leave this one to the chemists.

WHAT'S NEXT?

Protecting Food from Bioterrorism

In the wake of September 11th, the United States and other countries have a new concern when it comes to food and water supplies: terrorism. Like our bridges, tunnels, and power plants, food and water need increased measures of protection.

Step 1 in protecting our food is being aware of potential threats. Farms, food-packaging plants, and distributors and others are putting in place a more stringent screening process for employees. They're also revamping security systems to catch potential threats.

Step 2 is detecting contamination once it has occurred. Special labs in development will help detect disease and bacterial toxins. Veterinary and agricultural labs are also being trained and placed on alert so that they can respond as quickly as possible in the event of an emergency. There has even been a National Surveillance Coordinator appointed to help farms and food producers respond quickly to suspected terrorist activities. Still, the government admits that there is a lot of work to be done to ensure the safety of our food supply. What new technologies and procedures will be developed to protect us in the next 10 years? In the next 20 years?

SCIENCE FAIR PROJECT #3

Food companies often fortify their food with vitamins and minerals. One of the minerals your body needs is iron. Many companies fortify their cereal by spraying it with tiny pieces of iron metal. In this experiment, you will compare the amount of iron in different cereals by removing the iron with a magnet.

YOU WILL NEED:

- ◎ 40 index cards
- ◎ Different brands of cereal (look for brands that list "iron" or "reduced iron" in the ingredients. Brands with high amounts—over 80%—of the recommended daily amount of iron will work best)
- ◎ Measuring cup
- ◎ Blender
- ◎ Glass or ceramic bowl
- ◎ Bar magnets (the stronger the better, but they all must be the same), painted white (you will need one for each brand of cereal)
- ◎ Resealable plastic bags
- ◎ Magnifying glass

1. Measure 1 cup of your first brand of cereal. Pour the cereal into the blender and cover the cereal with water. Blend the cereal and water into a soupy mixture.

2. Pour the cereal mixture into the bowl. Stir the mixture slowly and carefully with the magnet for 15-20 minutes.

3. Gently dip the magnet into a bowl of water to clean off any excess cereal. Be careful not to wash away any tiny bits of iron that are stuck to the magnet.

4. Leave the magnet in an undisturbed place to dry. Place the dry magnet with the iron pieces into a plastic bag. Label the bag with the brand name of the cereal.

5. Repeat steps 1-4 with the other brands of cereal. Use a new magnet with each brand so you can compare the amounts of iron from each one. (If you have access to a laboratory balance, you can weigh the magnets both before and after gathering the iron to see how much iron you picked up, but a regular scale will not be sensitive enough.)

- ◎ Which brand appears to have left the most iron on the magnet?
- ◎ Does the nutritional information on the boxes agree with your observations?

CHAPTER 4

ANIMALS

Lizards, bugs, birds, bears, humans, and tiny creatures you never see . . . We all belong to the animal kingdom! Animals, by definition, are multicelled organisms that eat food to survive. Animals tend to move around, although some, like coral for example, don't move much at all. There are about 1 million known animal species on earth, and there are way more out there, just waiting to be discovered. About 10,000 new species of animals, most of them insects, are discovered every year! The bad news is, we don't know how many undiscovered animals go extinct every year. Threats to animal habitats, like pollution and deforestation, are still major problems in our world. It's important to find as many new species as we can, before they disappear!

MOVIES ON
BRAINPOP.COM
• Six Kingdoms
• Vertebrates
• Invertebrates
• Food Chains
• Dinosaurs
• Birds
• Insects
...and many more!

Brain
POP®

WILD THINGS

How do we keep track of every living thing on Earth?
Scientists like to organize stuff into categories. Every living creature
fits into a certain group or kingdom.

LIVING THINGS ARE DIVIDED INTO SIX KINGDOMS:

 1. EUBACTERIA are single-celled creatures with no nuclei (that's
the plural of "nucleus"!). They live in mild conditions all over the planet.
Some eubacteria live in our intestines and help us break down food.
Others can make us really sick if they get inside our bodies.

 2. Like eubacteria, ARCHAEBACTERIA are single-celled
organisms. But they can live in harsh climates, like lava-spewing
trenches deep beneath the ocean's surface!

 3. PROTISTS are single-celled too, but they have nuclei. The most
famous protist is probably the amoeba: a shapeless cell that lives in
water and reproduces by dividing in two.

 4. You know those mushrooms in your salad? That's right, they're
FUNGI. They may look like plants, but they're not. Fungi can't make
their own food, like plants can. Instead, fungi suck up nutrients that
have been made by other organisms.

 5. PLANTS are organisms that can feed themselves. They contain
the chemical chlorophyll, which reacts with sunlight to create a simple
sugar. This process is called photosynthesis. Chlorophyll is also what
gives plants their green color.

 6. The ANIMAL kingdom contains multicelled organisms that
eat food to survive. Mammals, birds, reptiles, and insects all belong
to the animal kingdom.

The six kingdoms of life are
just the beginning. Each of
these kingdoms has **six
different subdivisions**!

**FROM BIGGEST TO
SMALLEST, THEY ARE**  **Phylum** **Class**

So how do biologists decide what goes where? Well, they look at all sorts of traits in order to classify something—there's appearance, cell structure, DNA, and behavioral traits. The classification gets a lot more specific as you move down the line—members of the same species have much more in common than members of the same phylum.

CLASSIFY ME!

Subject: Humpback Whale

Kingdom: Animalia
All animals belong here!

Phylum: Chordata
Now we're just talking about animals with backbones.

Class: Mammalia
Female mammals have mammary glands that produce milk to feed their young.

Order: Cetacea
Whales, dolphins, and porpoises belong to this order.

Family: Balaenopteridae
A family is a collection of species that share general traits. Instead of teeth, 270–400 short, broad baleen plates line the upper jaw of the six whale species in this family. The whales feed by sifting crustaceans and fish through the plates.

Genus: Megaptera
Generally, very similar species form a genus. The humpback whale, however, is the only species in the genus *Megaptera*.

Taxonomy is the study of scientific classification.

Species: Megaptera novaeangliae
This species is for humpbacks only!

 Order   **Family**   Genus Species

PETS

▲ Ferrets make cute pets but they tend to poop everywhere!

So You Say You Want a Pet . . .

Not to sound like your parents, but taking care of an animal is a big responsibility. Think about it—a creature is going to depend on you for its life! Even something as simple as a hermit crab needs attention. If you do think you're ready for an animal of your own, first think about what pet is right for you. Do you want something that won't take a lot of your time? Maybe a goldfish is what you need. Looking for something that'll sleep in your bed? A cat is a good bet. Just think carefully about what you want and how much time you're willing to spend on it.

▼ You can walk a pig!

▲ Dogs need to go to the dentist too!

Did you know...

Not everyone looks at certain animals the way we do in the US.

- In INDIA, cows are considered sacred! They are allowed to walk around free, and eating beef is forbidden to the followers of several religions.

- In KOREA and a few other countries in Asia, some people eat dogs. (If you think that's gross, think of how people from India must view our eating cows!)

- In GIBRALTAR, there are baboons running around all over the place. Sometimes they even steal tourists' cameras!

▲ The recent discovery of a cat skeleton buried alongside what could have been its owner's skeleton in a late Stone Age grave on Cyprus is evidence that cats may have been pets for as many as 9,500 years.

EXPERIMENT

with Bob the Ex-Lab Rat

MAKE YOUR OWN BUTTERFLY GARDEN

Like most other animals, butterflies spend the bulk of their waking hours on one thing: finding food. So what do butterflies eat? Sweet, fresh nectar. You know, from flowers. Want to attract butterflies to your yard? You'll have to become something of a gardener.

Follow these instructions, and come summer, your garden could be thick with Lepidoptera (that's butterflies).

YOU WILL NEED:
- A yard that gets at least 6 hours of sunlight in summer. If you live in an apartment, you can use your fire escape or windowsill, as long as there's plenty of sun.
- Seeds for one or more of these plants: marigold, lilac, zinnia, milkweed, verbena, black-eyed Susan, meadow sage, lavender, marjoram, primrose, mint, ivy, honeysuckle, daisy, thistle, parsley, passionflower.

STEP 1 Choose an assortment of seeds to plant in your garden.

STEP 2 Follow the instructions on the back of your seeds regarding when to plant them and how to care for the seedlings. Try to plant your flowers in big bunches, not just one here and one there. You may have to plant your flowers months in advance of summer, so be patient!

STEP 3 Starting in butterfly season (late spring), place some shallow bowls of water near your garden. That sun makes butterflies thirsty too.

STEP 4 Enjoy watching these amazing animals!

WORKING LIKE A DOG

Dogs aren't only good for looking cute and playing fetch—they also help us in a lot of different ways. Dogs have been evolving as human companions for thousands, maybe even tens of thousands of years. Early humans may have used dogs in much the same way we do now: to guard their homes (or caves) against intruders. They probably also used them on hunts, just like hunters today. Here are just a couple of the more advanced jobs for dogs:

GUIDE DOGS Guide dogs literally act as their blind owners' eyes, helping them avoid obstacles and get around more easily. They're even smart enough to disobey a command if it would put their owner in danger! This is called "selective disobedience." Only the smartest, most loyal dogs are chosen to go to guide-dog training schools. Once there, it takes about two years and thousands of dollars to train each one.

POLICE DOGS Man's best friend is making an important contribution to law enforcement. At airports, drug- and bomb-sniffing dogs make sure that nothing dangerous gets on a plane. Police dogs called K-9 units are also helping out on the streets. They can chase down suspects that human officers might never catch. Even more important, they help cut down on the use of guns. A suspect is more likely to give up peacefully when staring down the bared fangs of a German shepherd!

▲ Dogs helping out their masters.

ENDANGERED SPECIES

When an animal species is listed as "endangered," that means that its population in a certain area, or in some cases, its population worldwide, has lessened dramatically.

ENDANGERED SPECIES GET PROTECTED STATUS, BECAUSE THEY ARE CLOSE TO EXTINCTION, AND THAT'S WHAT WE WANT TO AVOID AT ALL COSTS!

A species is classified as "threatened" when its numbers are falling quickly, or have almost reached endangered levels. Animals can become endangered for all sorts of reasons—overhunting, habitat loss, pollution, environmental changes. When it comes to conservation, it's up to humans to help out the animals. Often it's our practices that cause the problems in the first place—in 1967, the bald eagle was listed as endangered, mainly because of the pesticide DDT. We used DDT to kill bugs that harmed our crops, but DDT also made the eagles' eggshells too thin, causing reproduction problems. Since DDT was banned, the bald eagle—though still threatened—has made a huge comeback!

Here's a look at some animals from around the world that are currently listed as endangered.

GRIZZLY BEAR (North America) Grizzlies can be found in Wyoming, Montana, Idaho, and Washington. There are in the neighborhood of 700 grizzlies left in the continental US. In Alaska, the grizzly, or brown bear population, is estimated at more than 30,000. And then there are about 22,000 grizzly bears living in Canada.

MANATEE (Florida) The West Indian or Florida manatee is found mostly along the Florida coast. Manatees are counted from airplanes, so distance and water conditions make it tough to get an exact number. In the most recent survey, 1,856 manatees were spotted in Florida waters.

CALIFORNIA RED-LEGGED FROG (California) Only about 350 adults currently live in three or four areas of its California habitat.

GREEN SEA TURTLE (coasts of Africa, India, South East Asia, and Australia) Green turtle population numbers are hard to nail down because they migrate. Surveyors base their counts on nesting females that stay in one place to lay eggs, but the numbers are still fuzzy—current estimates put the number of breeding female green turtles worldwide at 203,000.

GIANT PANDA (China) There are only about 1,000 giant pandas left roaming in the wild. There are 120 pandas in captivity in China, with another 20 spread out in zoos around the world.

BENGAL TIGER (India, Nepal, Bhutan, Bangladesh) In the early 1900s there were about 40,000 Bengal tigers in India alone. Today, there are only 3,000-4,000 Bengal tigers in the wild, as well as roughly 1,300 in nature reserves.

A MURDER OF CROWS

That's what you call a group of crows! The names for groups of the same animal can sound kind of funny—check them out:

Ants: colony	Lions: pride
Bears: sleuth	Oxen: yoke
Cattle: drove	Parrots: company
Elk: gang	Ponies: string
Goats: trip	Swans: bevy
Hens: brood	Toads: knot

EXTINCT ANIMALS

TIMELINE OF EXTINCTION

Many scientists think that because of humanity's widespread destruction of natural habitats around the world, the rate of animal extinctions is at an unprecedented level. In the last 100 years a lot of animals have been wiped off the planet forever. Here are just a few:

PYRENEAN IBEX
JANUARY 2000

PIG-FOOTED BANDICOOT
1950s
•
"TASMANIAN TIGER" (THYLACINE)
SEPTEMBER 1936

PASSENGER PIGEON
SEPTEMBER 1914

Crazy but True

Our planet has seen its fair share of weird animals come and go. Check out these bizarre creatures that once walked the earth!

▶ **WOOLLY MAMMOTHS** Woolly mammoths were big, furry elephants with curved tusks! They were around for a couple of million years, with the last ones dying out around 10,000 years ago. A number of well-preserved mammoths have been found recently in the Siberian ice. Who knows, one may have enough intact DNA for scientists to clone it!

▼ **SMILODON FATALIS (SABER-TOOTHED "TIGER" OR CAT)** There have been several saber-toothed cats throughout history, but **Smilodon** was the biggest. It weighed in at well over 400 pounds (181 kg) and had curved, 7-inch (18 cm) canine teeth! To accommodate those big choppers, experts think **Smilodon** could open its mouth at an angle of at least 90 degrees (some think as much as 120 degrees). Just to give you an idea of how wide that is, lions can open their mouths only 65 degrees! **Smilodon** first appeared as early as 35–40 million years ago and lived until just 11,000 years ago.

▶ **INCISIVOSAURUS** What's up, doc? This very strange-looking theropod (that's a type of two-legged dinosaur) lived around 128 million years ago. Scientists think this 3-foot (1 m) long dinosaur used its goofy front teeth to eat plants, making it different from all the other theropods, which ate meat and eggs.

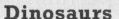

Dinosaurs

You won't run into them on Earth today, but the dinosaurs ruled our planet for over 120 million years.

They've been called the most successful land animals ever.

WHERE THEY CAME FROM

The first dinosaurs evolved from early reptiles around 230 million years ago. Scientists have been able to find out a lot about dinosaurs just by studying their fossilized bones and eggs. Their footprints and droppings too! These clues give scientists a really basic idea of how dinosaurs looked and behaved, but there are still many mysteries.

Did you know...

Many scientists believe that modern-day birds are the descendants of the dinosaurs!

Did you know...

The word dinosaur means "terrible lizard."

WHAT THEY WERE LIKE

Dinosaurs came in all shapes and sizes. Some walked on two legs, some on four. Some were fast, and others were . . . not so fast. You could find dinosaurs with thick, bumpy skin or plates or frills or horns. The biggest dinosaurs grew to be around 50 feet (15 m) tall and over 100 feet (30 m) long. And the littlest dinosaurs were the size of chickens.

The FASTEST dinosaur was the **Ornithomimus**. It looked a lot like an ostrich and it could run 40–50 mph (64–80 km/h)!

The DUMBEST dinosaur was the **Stegosaurus**. It weighed 3 tons (2,700 kg), but its brain was only the size of a walnut!

The LARGEST dinosaur was the **Seismosaurus**. It was 120 feet (37 m) from head to tail and 18 feet (5 m) tall!

The SMALLEST dinosaur was the **Compsognathus**. It weighed just 6.5 pounds (3 kg)!

HERBIVORES, like the **Plateosaurus**, were dinosaurs that ate plants. They had dull, flat teeth, perfect for mashing leaves and greenery.

CARNIVORES, like the **Tyrannosaurus rex**, ate meat. They had sharp, pointed teeth for pulling apart flesh, and horns and plates on their bodies for defense. These guys got in lots of fights.

▲ Paleontologist Paul Sereno poses with a copy of the 90-million-year-old carnivorous dinosaur he unearthed in Morocco in 1995.

WHERE'D THEY GO?

Around 65 million years ago, the dinosaurs suddenly died out. No one is totally sure why, but a lot of scientists think it had something to do with an asteroid colliding with Earth. Such a massive impact would have kicked up enough dust to block out the Sun for a long time. And without sun, the dinosaurs couldn't survive.

FUN ANIMAL FACTS

Sea Creatures

With tens of thousands of animals living in the oceans, there's a lot going on beneath those waves. Here's a sampling of the incredible variety of life that most of us never see!

ANIMAL	HABITAT	COOL FACTS
HAMMERHEAD SHARK	Tropical and subtropical waters, along the coasts	Hammerheads can get up to 20 feet (6 m) long, weighing over 1,000 pounds (450 kg). These sharks are such fierce hunters, they sometimes even eat each other!
MANTA RAY	All over the world, preferring water near shore	Some mantas grow to be 30 feet (9 m) wide! They may look scary, but these animals are completely harmless to people. 
SEA HORSE	Warm and temperate water	Sea horses are a unique species of animal—their eggs are carried by the male, not the female, until hatching.
DOLPHIN	All over the world, in fresh and salt water	Like whales, dolphins are mammals. They live in the sea and give birth to live young, which nurse on milk! Sailors have long considered dolphins to be good luck. 
BEARDED ANGLERFISH	Most oceans, at depths of up to 3,300 feet (1,000 m)	Female bearded anglerfish have glowing lures dangling from their snouts. They use these to lure other fish in . . . and eat them! 
GIANT SQUID	Most oceans, in very deep water	It may sound like something out of a science fiction movie, but in 1965, sailors aboard a Soviet whaler witnessed a fight between a giant squid and a sperm whale. Both animals died. Giant squids can be 65 feet (20 m) long .

Land Creatures

There are some amazing animals that do extraordinary things in order to eat, reproduce, get around, and stay alive in their natural habitats. Here are just a few examples of these curious creatures.

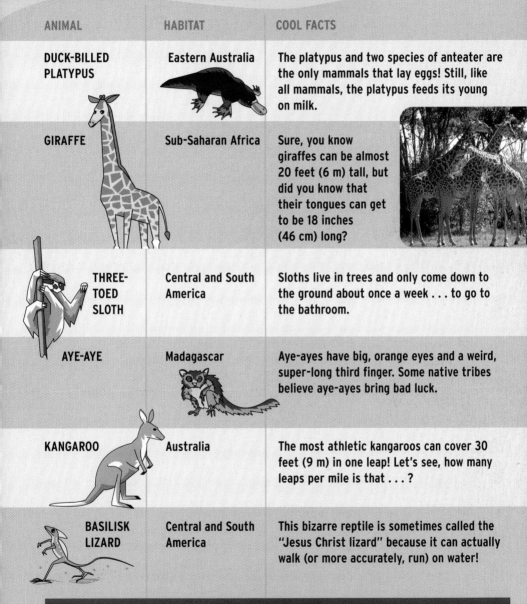

ANIMAL	HABITAT	COOL FACTS
DUCK-BILLED PLATYPUS	Eastern Australia	The platypus and two species of anteater are the only mammals that lay eggs! Still, like all mammals, the platypus feeds its young on milk.
GIRAFFE	Sub-Saharan Africa	Sure, you know giraffes can be almost 20 feet (6 m) tall, but did you know that their tongues can get to be 18 inches (46 cm) long?
THREE-TOED SLOTH	Central and South America	Sloths live in trees and only come down to the ground about once a week . . . to go to the bathroom.
AYE-AYE	Madagascar	Aye-ayes have big, orange eyes and a weird, super-long third finger. Some native tribes believe aye-ayes bring bad luck.
KANGAROO	Australia	The most athletic kangaroos can cover 30 feet (9 m) in one leap! Let's see, how many leaps per mile is that . . . ?
BASILISK LIZARD	Central and South America	This bizarre reptile is sometimes called the "Jesus Christ lizard" because it can actually walk (or more accurately, run) on water!

FAMOUS FACES

Mary the Self-Cloning Python. That's right, a Burmese python in Amsterdam's Artis Zoo has been producing eggs on her own without the help of a male snake. About 40 percent of Mary's eggs have tiny embryonic replicas inside. It's no secret that some female snakes can reproduce without a male sperm cell, but Mary's self-cloning abilities are a new thing. And, just like Mary, all the embryos are female!

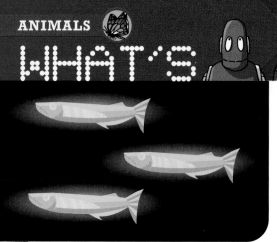

Glow-in-the-Dark Fish

Want to really light up your aquarium? In Taiwan, you can already buy a genetically modified glow-in-the-dark fish as a pet. Using a gene from a jellyfish, a researcher at National Taiwan University accidentally made the animal's entire body glow. Knowing a good idea when they saw one, a Taiwan company started selling the **Night Pearl Fish** as pets. Here in the United States, you can get a genetically engineered zebra fish called a **GloFish** (except in California, where they're banned). Idea—how about a glow-in-the-dark dog that won't get hit by cars?

The Missyplicity Project

The Missyplicity Project set out to clone a dog named Missy, but sadly, Missy died in 2002 before she could be cloned. Scientists did, however, manage to clone a cat. In 2001, Rainbow the cat was joined by a cloned version of herself called Cc (short for "carbon copy"). Although they look similar, Rainbow and Cc are not identical and their personalities are very different. So, it doesn't look like cloning will bring your favorite cat back and so far, no dog has been successfully cloned.

DEBATE: Animal Cloning

Animal cloning—growing a new animal from a single cell of another (parent) animal—might sound really weird and scary. Though cloning experiments are primarily for the sake of research, in theory, cloning could prevent the extinction of endangered species. And in theory, cloning animals could lead to cloning humans—a serious ethical concern.

In addition to the fact that it's like something out of a horror movie, another issue with cloned animals is that they don't live very long. The science is still inexact and unpredictable.

If helping endangered animals is the goal, protecting animal habitats and eliminating poaching are safer, more effective, less controversial methods.

SCIENCE FAIR PROJECT #4

How Does the Shape of a Bird's Beak Help It Gather Food?

The shape of a bird's beak affects the types of food it can gather. Think about different birds you are familiar with. Are all their beaks shaped the same? This experiment will help you understand how different shapes of beaks can help a bird gather different types of food.

YOU WILL NEED:

◎ Tweezers

◎ Chopsticks

◎ 2 spoons

◎ A pair of tongs

◎ 40 marbles

◎ Uncooked rice or seeds

◎ 40 pieces of yarn (each about the length of a finger)

◎ 40 toothpicks

◎ Timer or stopwatch

◎ Large bowl or cup

◎ Clean 20-ounce soda bottle

1. The tweezers, chopsticks, spoons, and tongs represent different shapes of beaks. (The tweezers are comparable to smaller, pointed beaks, such as sandpipers' or chickadees'. The chopsticks represent long-billed birds like pelicans or herons. The spoons work similarly to many ducks' bills. The tongs grasp like gulls' beaks. The marbles, rice, yarn, and toothpicks are shaped like different types of bird food—berries, seeds, and worms, for example.

2. Spread one food type on a flat surface, like a large table or countertop. Set your timer for 1 minute. Pick up as many food pieces as you can using one of the beak shapes. Place the food pieces in the bowl or cup. At the end of 1 minute, count the number of items in the bowl. Record the type of food, type of beak, and number of food pieces collected.

3. Repeat step 2 with the other beak shapes. Then change the food type and repeat with each beak shape.

4. Sometimes a bird's food is in a hard-to-reach place. Repeat steps 2 and 3, but place the food pieces in the soda bottle instead of on a flat surface. When you record your results, be sure to note that you tried to gather the food pieces from the bottle.

5. Make a chart of your results.

◎ What beak shapes were best at gathering the different types of food? Was one shape successful at collecting more than one food type? What do you think would happen to a bird if only one type of food were available?

◎ Try this experiment with other food shapes and beak shapes. Find pictures of birds with different beak shapes and try to find things to represent these shapes in your experiment.

◎ Research the beak shapes of different birds and the foods those birds eat. Does this information agree with your results?

CHAPTER 5

EARTH MATTERS

We've learned a lot about Earth in the past 50 years. Scientists used to speculate about what was inside our planet—some even thought it might be hollow! Now we know better. Earth is divided into different layers: the thin rock **crust**, the **mantle**, the molten, iron-rich **outer core**, and the solid **inner core**. Even though we live on top of the crust, these other layers of Earth have a huge effect on the features we see on the surface.

PLATE TECTONICS

If you look at the shapes of Earth's continents, Africa and South America look like pieces of a puzzle that could snap together. Believe it or not, they used to be right next to each other. Hundreds of millions of years ago, Earth looked very different. According to a scientific theory called **plate tectonics**, all of the continents used to be part of a huge land mass called **Pangaea**.

Plate tectonics explains that Earth's crust isn't just one solid piece, like an eggshell. Instead, it's broken up into different pieces, called plates.

▲ Earth's crust is broken up into large plates, and smaller ones.

This is what Earth probably looked like 200 million years ago. All of the continents were locked together in a big land mass called **Pangaea (pan-GEE-uh)**.

And here's Earth about 100 million years ago. Pangaea started to break up about 80 million years earlier.

This is Earth about 50 million years ago. It looks similar to the way it looks today.

Scientists disagree about the exact number of plates—there are around seven large plates, and a bunch of smaller ones. These plates move around like rafts—very, very slowly! Their movement is called **continental drift** because the continents sit on top of these plates. Plate movement is what caused Pangaea to break apart and eventually form the continents we see today.

How Plate Tectonics Works

The plates are moving, slipping under one another, sliding past one another... There are three main types of plate margins where movement happens:

▲ At a **CONSTRUCTIVE MARGIN,** two plates are moving apart, creating a gap or crack that has to be filled. **Magma** from Earth's mantle comes to the rescue, bubbling up in the empty space and making new crust material. When this happens to an oceanic plate, an underwater mountain range called a **mid-ocean ridge** is created. When it happens to a continental plate, a **rift valley** is created as the land between plates drops down.

Magma is hot, molten rock.

▲ At a **DESTRUCTIVE MARGIN,** a dense oceanic plate slides beneath a lighter continental plate, and the friction created causes the oceanic plate to melt into magma. The friction from the plate movement also builds up a lot of energy that is released in earthquakes along the plate margin, and in volcanoes where magma is forced up through the continental plate. This sliding beneath, or **subduction** of plates can cause the continental plate to buckle, pushing its crust up into a folded mountain range.

▲ At a **CONSERVATIVE MARGIN,** two plates slide horizontally past each other, rubbing together as they go. The friction creates a lot of energy with no place to go. That energy is eventually released in an earthquake.

Effects of Plate Tectonics

Mount Everest, the highest peak in the world, grows a few millimeters per year. Like a lot of different mountain ranges around the world, the Himalayas were formed by two plates smashing together and pushing up land. And they're still rising! In addition to giving rise to mountains, the shifting of plates is responsible for earthquakes and volcanoes. ▶▶ SEE PP. 81-83 FOR MORE ON EARTHQUAKES AND VOLCANOES.

Did you know...

The **Ring of Fire** contains 75 percent of the world's volcanoes. The "ring" is actually an arc-shaped area where Earth's Pacific Plate rubs against and slides beneath the plates around it. This active area sees plenty of earthquakes too!

HOW SCIENTISTS SOLVED THE PUZZLE

Scientists found a lot of different evidence to support the plate tectonics theory.

- As far back as the 17th century, when mapmaking became more precise, Sir Francis Bacon noticed the jigsaw-puzzle look of Africa and South America.
- Paleontologists have found fossils for the same types of dinosaurs on totally different continents. This supports the idea that the continents were once stuck together to form Pangaea.
- Deep-sea submarines have traveled to the ocean floors and recorded video of magma forming new land along the ridges. You can't get better evidence than that!

ROCKS AND MINERALS

Earth's crust is made of rock. The sand on the beach, the mountains, the soil in our yards—all of it is technically rock. And every kind of rock is made up of different **minerals**. They're the building blocks of rock.

The size of the crystals in igneous rocks depends upon how long it took the rock to form.

CLAY **SANDSTONE**

COAL **CALCITE**

SEDIMENTARY rocks form when layers of sediment build up over time and get compressed into rock. Sediment is mainly just particles of dirt and dust—the broken bits of other rock. But it can also be made of the remains of living things. Limestone is a sedimentary rock formed mainly from the shells and skeletons of sea creatures.

TOPAZ **GRANITE**

PUMICE **OBSIDIAN**

IGNEOUS rocks are formed by cooled magma (molten rock). Obsidian, or volcanic glass, forms in lava flows on Earth's surface.

TALC **CORUNDUM**

MARBLE **DIAMOND**

METAMORPHIC rock forms when igneous or sedimentary rock is placed under enormous heat and/or pressure. Marble is a metamorphic rock that forms when limestone is subjected to a lot of heat.

MOVIES ON BRAINPOP.COM

The Rock Cycle

Not all rocks are created equal. The rock cycle shows how the different types of rock on Earth form. Geologists classify rocks based on how they form:

Magma that reaches the surface to cool is extrusive (volcanic) igneous rock.

Sediment collects in layers underwater and on the surface.

Magma that cools underground is intrusive (plutonic) igneous rock.

Pressure cements the sediment together to form sedimentary rock.

When rock makes it down to Earth's mantle, incredible heat melts it into magma.

Igneous and sedimentary rock, subjected to enormous heat and pressure, become metamorphic rock.

WHAT'S NEXT?

Man-Made Diamonds

Diamonds form deep below the Earth's surface, when carbon is heated to 2,200°F (1,093°C), under pressure equal to 50,000 atmospheres! Scientists have been able to make synthetic (man-made) diamonds for years. These industrial diamonds are useful for lots of different things, like making very hard drill bits. But none of them were ever perfect enough to fool a jeweler.

Now, a team of Russian inventors working with scientists at the University of Florida may have cracked it. Their machine actually "grows" diamonds by subjecting carbon plus a seed (a chip of real diamond) to the same heat and pressure as in Earth's mantle. And it can be done cheaply. To date, the largest diamond they've made is 1.6 carats, but the machine should be able to produce a 6-carat rock. It takes about 50 hours to make a 1-carat stone.

Did you know...

Plutonic igneous rocks form underground, starting off as magma. The overlying layers of dirt and rock insulate the cooling magma, so the crystals form slowly. That gives them a chance to get really big. Because the big gemstones form underground, people have to dig mines to find them.

Volcanic igneous rocks form on the surface, completely exposed to the elements. They cool off quickly, so their crystals don't have a chance to get very big.

SCIENCE FAIR PROJECT #5

How Does the Speed of Crystallization Affect the Size of Crystals?

Geologists can tell how long an igneous rock took to form by looking at the size of the mineral crystals in the rock. In this experiment, you will make crystals of salt by dissolving the salt in water and letting the water evaporate. Find out how forming crystals at different speeds results in different sizes.

YOU WILL NEED:

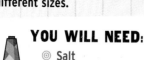

◎ Salt

◎ Tap water

◎ Saucepan

◎ 2 large glasses

◎ Pyrex or porcelain bowl

◎ String

◎ 2 paper clips

◎ 2 pens or pencils

◎ Magnifying glass

HAVE AN ADULT HELP YOU WITH STEPS 1 THROUGH 5!!

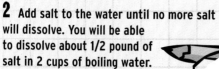

1. Pour about 2 cups of water into the saucepan and bring to a slow boil.

2. Add salt to the water until no more salt will dissolve. You will be able to dissolve about 1/2 pound of salt in 2 cups of boiling water.

3. Pour about 2/3 of your salt water mixture into the Pyrex or porcelain bowl. Be careful—pouring hot water into ordinary glass can crack the glass!!

4. Keep boiling the salt water in your saucepan until all the water has evaporated. Collect the salt crystals and label them.

5. After the salt water in the bowl has cooled a bit, pour it into the 2 glasses (half into each glass). Cut 2 pieces of string a bit longer than the glasses are tall. Tie a paper clip onto the end of each string. Tie the other end around a pencil. Rest the pencils on the top of each glass so the string hangs into the salt water with the paper clip weighing it down. The rough surface of the string will help your crystals form.

6. Leave one glass at room temperature in a place where it will not be disturbed. Leave the other glass in an undisturbed place in your refrigerator. Both glasses should be left uncovered so the water can evaporate.

7. The water may take several days or even a week or two to evaporate. Once the water has evaporated, observe the crystals in each glass.

◎ How do crystals that form slowly look different than crystals that form quickly?

◎ You can make crystals from other household substances besides salt. Try sugar, baking soda, alum, or borax.

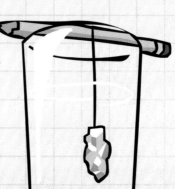

Fossils

A fossil forms when any part of a creature is preserved in rock. The imprints of living things on hardened soil, like dinosaur footprints and leaf impressions, are also considered fossils.

There are lots of different ways for fossils to form:

PETRIFICATION is how most bone fossils form. The process starts when an organism's remains are covered in sediment and mineral-rich water seeps into the remains. Slowly, over millions of years, the minerals in the water replace the bone minerals. Eventually, the entire skeleton is replaced with a stone replica. That's right—those dinosaur bones you see in the museum aren't really bone. They're rock replacements of bone!

UNALTERED PRESERVATION is when an organism's entire body is encased in something that preserves it. The most common unaltered preservations are insects trapped in amber (hardened tree sap). But there are also organisms that get preserved when they are trapped in tar pits or hardened in ice.

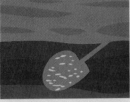

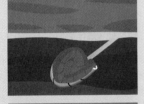

Sometimes an organism's entire body will decay, except for the carbon in it. When that happens, it's called **carbonization**. Coal is carbonized plant matter. When an entire forest gets carbonized, you've got a coal mine!

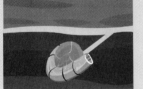

Like petrification, **replacement** occurs when an organism's hard parts are replaced with rock. But in replacement, the organism's parts dissolve first, resulting in a mold or a cast. A mold is a hole in a rock formed by the dissolved body of an organism. If there is time for minerals to fill that hole in the organism's shape, it forms a cast.

Did you know...

Woolly mammoths walked the earth 26,000 years ago, and we know this because mammoth fossil remains have been uncovered in bogs, lakes, tar pits, and ice. Fully preserved mammoth specimens have been chipped out of the permafrost in Siberia and Alaska. "Baby Dima," a woolly mammoth baby, was discovered by gold miners in Siberia in 1977!

OCEANS

MOVIES ON
BRAINPOP.COM

Oceans cover more than 70 percent of Earth's surface.

The Ocean Floor

Despite the fact that water covers such a large part of our planet, the oceans are still an unexplored territory. We do know that most of the ocean's floor is just a flat plain. But there are huge mountain ranges and unbelievably deep trenches below the waves too.

Features of the Ocean Floor

CONTINENTAL SHELVES refer to the edges of a continent where the water is shallow.

CONTINENTAL SLOPES are the area where continental shelves gradually decline to abyssal plains.

A **SEAMOUNT** is an underwater mountain formed by a very tall volcano—with a peak that's at least 3,300 feet (1,000 m) above the ocean floor.

RIDGES are under-water mountains.

ABYSSAL PLAINS are the flatlands that form the bulk of the ocean floor.

TRENCHES are deep valleys in the floor.

FAMOUS FACES

Born in France way back in 1910, **Jacques Cousteau** was responsible for much of the public's interest in the oceans today. He produced two Academy Award-winning underwater documentaries: THE SILENT WORLD (1956) and WORLD WITHOUT SUN (1964). In the 1960s and 1970s, he starred in a television series called **The Undersea World of Jacques Cousteau**. From his boat, **Calypso** he brought sharks, sunken treasure, and coral reefs to a whole new audience.

UNDERWATER ROBOTS

Since their invention, robots have been used to go places where people can't. Scientists today use unmanned subs, or **Remotely Operated Vehicles (ROVs)** for oil exploration, rescue missions, archaeological finds, and scientific experiments. These robots—which are connected to a ship via a tether cable called the "umbilical"—can withstand the tremendous pressure created by thousands of feet of ocean water.

KAIKO

In 1995, Japan's $50 million robot submarine **Kaiko**, was the first ROV to reach the bottom of the **Mariana Trench**. It even sent back some cool video images!

The Mariana Trench in the Pacific Ocean, just east of the Philippines, is the deepest ocean trench in the world. It's over 35,000 feet (10,500 m) deep. That's nearly six times as deep as the Grand Canyon!

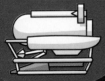

HROV

Developed by the Woods Hole Oceanographic Institute, the battery-powered Hybrid ROV (HROV) was designed to explore the ocean's most remote regions—as deep as 36,000 feet (11,000 m) below the surface.

SUPER SCORPIO

The **Super Scorpio** is used for US Navy rescue missions and to survey the sites of naval accidents.

Alvin, a human-operated submersible, explored the sunken **Titanic**.

77

MOUNTAINS

Mountains make Earth's surface a whole lot more interesting. Mountains are one of the three basic types of landforms on Earth, along with plains and plateaus. They're formed when plate movement causes pressure to build up inside the earth. Mountains cover about a fifth of Earth's surface, and they're found on all continents. There are even mountains under the surface of the ocean!

The **ANDES** mountain range in South America is the longest continuous mountain chain on Earth, spanning 4,500 miles (7,240 km).

The **ROCKIES** are the major mountain system in North America. They extend north-south from Canada to New Mexico. Most of North America's skiing happens in the Rocky Mountains!

The **ALPS** are the second highest mountain range in the world. They're located in Europe, extending over 600 miles (about 1,000 km) through southern France, northern Italy, Switzerland, Liechtenstein, Germany, Austria, and Slovenia. The Alps are made up of several hundred peaks and glaciers. Mont Blanc is the tallest one, measuring 15,771 feet (4,807 m).

The **HIMALAYAS** are the great mountains of Asia. They're home to the highest peaks in the world, and they extend 1,500 miles (2,414 km) through northeastern Pakistan, northern India, southern Tibet, Nepal, Sikkim, and Bhutan.

MAJOR MOUNTAIN RANGES ON EARTH

Making a Mountain . . .

There are four basic types of mountains, categorized by how they were formed:

FOLDED MOUNTAINS form when forces inside Earth push horizontal rock layers together. When the rock layers collide, they buckle and their edges form long, parallel folds.

Sharp peaks and ridges are characteristic of **UPWARPED MOUNTAINS.** They form when forces inside Earth push up parts of the crust. Environmental factors like rain and wind wear soil and vegetation away over time, causing rock to become exposed and weathered.

FAULT BLOCK MOUNTAINS are made of huge, tilted blocks of rock that are separated by faults. A fault is a large crack in the rock where movement happens. One block is tilted and pushed up while the other is pushed down. These mountains have jagged peaks.

VOLCANIC MOUNTAINS form when molten magma is forced through cracks in Earth's crust. The magma cools in layers that form a cone shape over time, and we have a volcanic mountain.

Did you know...

🏔 The 14 highest mountains in the world are all found in the Himalayas.

🏔 The tallest mountain on Earth, measured from its base (16,178 feet (4,931 m) below the sea surface) is Mauna Loa in Hawaii. It rises to 13,678 feet (4,169 m) above sea level.

🏔 Measuring from sea level, Mount Everest is the world's tallest mountain at 29,035 feet (8,848 m).

🏔 The highest mountain in North America is Mount McKinley in Alaska, measuring 20,320 feet (6,194 m).

FAMOUS FACES

In 1953, **Sir Edmund Hillary** became the first person to reach the top of Mount Everest. That may not seem like a big deal these days, when someone seems to do it every year, but before Hillary, people weren't even sure if it was possible. The air at that altitude contains so little oxygen that most climbers have to lug their own, in tanks! After finishing the climb, Hillary was knighted by Queen Elizabeth II. He went on to lead expeditions to the South Pole, but was always remembered for Everest. And to think he used to be just an unknown beekeeper from New Zealand! (By the way, Hillary wasn't alone in his conquest of Everest—a Nepalese Sherpa, Tenzing Norgay, made the climb too.)

WHEELS DOWN

NATURAL DISASTERS

▲ Mount Etna, Europe's largest volcano, is located in Sicily, Italy. When it erupted in October 2002, ashfall was reported over 350 miles (560 km) away in Libya.

Shifts in tectonic plates are responsible for many natural disasters on Earth.

Volcanoes

When one tectonic plate is ground down beneath another, it melts, producing magma. This molten rock is under enormous pressure from all of the rock lying above it. Sometimes the pressure becomes so great that overlying rock ruptures. This rupture can be a violent explosion or a gentle flow. Most volcanic eruptions occur at plate boundaries, but some, like those on the Hawaiian islands, form over **hot spots.** These are isolated areas of volcanic activity above unusually hot parts of the Earth's mantle.

STEAM

MAGMA CHAMBER

◀ **ANDESITIC VOLCANOES** are steep-sided, cone-shaped mountains. This cone forms from millions of years' worth of magma exploding out of the ground, hardening in layer upon layer. If the explosion is great enough, the entire side of the mountain can collapse, sending up huge volumes of dust, rock, and white-hot ash over the surrounding area. This is called a nuée ardente.

▼ **PYROCLASTIC FLOWS** are avalanches of hot gas, bits of rock, and bits of super-cooled magma.

MAGMA CHAMBER

◀ **BASALTIC VOLCANOES** tend to form over "hot spots" or places where material from the mantle rises through the surface to form a new plate. The material—runny, dark lava called basalt—flows a long time before hardening, forming low, broad volcanoes. Also called "shield" volcanoes, they mostly form underwater. Although these volcanoes tend to be gentler than the andesitic type, in places like Volcanoes National Park in Hawaii, the eruptions can be quite violent, shooting up jets of lava called fire fountains.

Subducting plate fuels volcanic activity

EXPERIMENT
with Bob the Ex-Lab Rat

MAKE YOUR OWN VOLCANO

Ever wish you had an erupting volcano in your backyard? Well, this is your chance to make that wish come true. Follow these instructions to make your own erupting volcano!

WARNING: DO THIS OUTSIDE—IT'S REALLY MESSY! AND MAKE SURE YOU HAVE A GROWN-UP AROUND TO HELP YOU.

YOU WILL NEED:
- A sheet of cardboard
- Tape
- A cardboard toilet-paper tube
- Enough clay to make your volcano
- Baking soda
- Clear vinegar
- Red food coloring

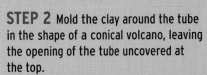

STEP 1 Use some tape to make the toilet-paper tube stick upright on the sheet of cardboard.

STEP 2 Mold the clay around the tube in the shape of a conical volcano, leaving the opening of the tube uncovered at the top.

STEP 3 Wait until the clay is dry.

STEP 4 Fill the toilet paper tube with baking soda.

STEP 5 Mix the vinegar and red food coloring together.

STEP 6 Add the vinegar to the baking soda in the tube and step back! Watch that volcano erupt!

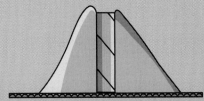

Did you know...

Entire ecosystems thrive around the lava vents deep under the sea. Tiny microbes feed off of the hydrogen sulfide emitted by the vents. They in turn are fed on by larger sea creatures. There are hundreds of species whose lives depend on the ocean's hydrothermal vents!

Earthquakes

Tectonic plate movement is responsible for earthquakes as well as volcanoes. See, Earth's plates are constantly growing at one end, getting consumed at the other, shifting alongside other plates, and pushing headlong into others. All of this causes a tremendous amount of pressure build-up. Rocks are rigid. Since they don't break easily, they resist this pressure for a long, long time. But after a while, something's got to give. Rapid movement of massive blocks of rock releases the tension . . . at least for the time being.

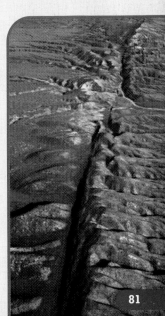

▶ The San Andreas Fault in California falls at the boundary of two tectonic plates. The slipping of these plates is often the cause of earthquakes in the region.

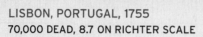

TIMELINE OF THE MOST DEVASTATING EARTHQUAKES

LISBON, PORTUGAL, 1755
70,000 DEAD, 8.7 ON RICHTER SCALE

GANSU, CHINA, 1920
200,000 DEAD, 8.6 ON RICHTER SCALE

SHANSI, CHINA, 1556
830,000 DEAD, 8 ON RICHTER SCALE

KWANTO, JAPAN, 1923
143,000 DEAD, 7.9 ON RICHTER SCALE

PERU, 1970
66,000 DEAD, 7.9 ON RICHTER SCALE

IRAN, 1990
50,000 DEAD, 7.7 ON RICHTER SCALE

USSR, 1948
110,000 DEAD, 7.3 ON RICHTER SCALE

MESSINA, ITALY, 1908
70,000-100,000 DEAD, 7.2 ON RICHTER SCALE

Did you know...

Often the majority of deaths, damage, and destruction from earthquakes are really a result of the fires, tsunamis, and landslides triggered by the quakes.

ANATOMY OF AN EARTHQUAKE

The **EPICENTER** is the area on the surface directly above the focus.

AFTERSHOCKS are little earth-quakes following the initial one. They can go on for days.

The **FOCUS** of an earthquake is its underground point of origin. It's where the most rock movement occurs.

A **FAULT** is the break in the rock where the movement that caused the earthquake occurred.

HOW EARTHQUAKES ARE MEASURED

An earthquake's size is measured on the Richter scale. Each point on the Richter scale is 10 times more powerful than the point below. A 6 on the Richter scale is a pretty nasty earth-quake, but some have gotten as high as 8.9, almost 1,000 times more powerful!

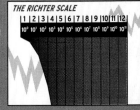

THE RICHTER SCALE

Scientists measure an earthquake's size using a seismograph. It uses a heavy weight that won't budge at all to measure the relative movements of the room during an earthquake. These movements are recorded by a pen attached to a rotating drum of paper.

▶▶ FOR INFORMATION ON DISASTER-PROOFING BUILDINGS, SEE P. 238.

Tsunamis

Tsunamis, a.k.a. tidal waves, are giant sea waves caused by underwater earthquakes. Tsunamis can be as tall as 50 feet (15 m), and travel at speeds of up to 600 mph (965 km/h)! If such a wave hits a populated area, the damage can be devastating. In 1964, a tsunami hit Alaska, killing 125 people and causing $311 million dollars in damage.

▶ Tsunami damage in Kodiak, Alaska

CHAPTER 6

THE ENVIRONMENT

Our environment is made up of the air, land, water, plants, and animals that surround us. We're talking about the natural world here. People have a funny relationship with the environment: we depend on our natural resources a great deal, and at the same time, human technology and growth can harm the environment. It's up to us to take care of Earth and maintain nature's balance.

LAND BIOMES

WHAT'S IT LIKE WHERE YOU LIVE?

Grassy? Sandy? Icy? It might be hot, cold, dry, moist, or any combination of those things.

Every **biome** has its own special characteristics. Factors like temperature, rainfall, and altitude all decide what types of plant and animal life a biome can support. Biomes refer to large regions that house similar ecosystems. There are countless species of plants and animals living on Earth, and they've all evolved to become specially adapted to their environments.

A **biome** is home to systems of plants, animals, and land. The living things interact with their environment in what's called an ecosystem.

What's your biome?

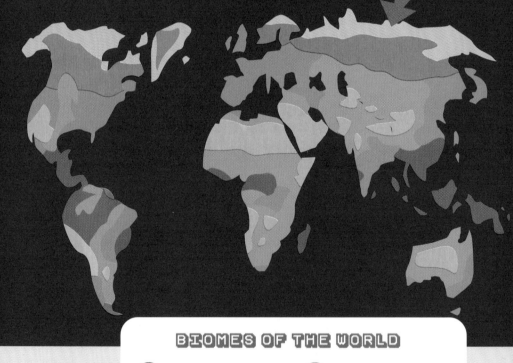

BIOMES OF THE WORLD

- Tropical rainforests
- Grasslands
- Temperate forests
- Taiga
- Deserts
- Tundra
- Permafrost

MOVIES ON BRAINPOP.COM

1 Tropical Rainforests

WHERE THEY ARE: Tropical rainforests are found in areas along the equator. They're in Asia, Africa, South America, Central America, and on many islands.

WHAT THEY'RE LIKE: Hot! And humid. They get more than 59 inches (150 cm) of rainfall each year. Rainforests grow in three levels—the canopy is at the top, followed by the understory, and then the forest floor.

WHAT LIVES THERE:
Scientists think that more than half the animal and plant species in the world live in rainforests. In fact, scientists believe that rainforests contain all sorts of undiscovered species.

Nearly half of the world's tropical rainforests are in Brazil.

The hyacinth macaw, native to Brazil, survives on seeds, palm fruits, and nuts.

Anteaters, monkeys, toucans, and jaguars are some of the animals that live in rainforests. They make their homes among bamboo, medicinal plants, banana trees, and rubber trees, just to name a few.

2 Temperate Forests

WHERE THEY ARE: Temperate forests are found in areas of mid-latitude (between 30 and 60 degrees north and south of the equator) in North America, South America, Asia, Africa, Europe, and Australia.

WHAT THEY'RE LIKE: They have moderate rain and four seasons. Trees and other plants grow easily in the fertile forest soil.

WHAT LIVES THERE: Deciduous trees like oaks and maples—they lose their leaves in the winter and grow new ones in the spring. Evergreens, trees that keep their foliage year-round, grow there too. Animals such as foxes, deer, and a variety of birds can be found in temperate forests.

◀ Rocky Mountain National Park, Colorado, United States

▼ Dromedary camels, native to the deserts of western Asia and North Africa, can drink up to 25 gallons of water at a time. One drink and they're set for weeks!

3 Deserts

WHERE THEY ARE: There are deserts on every continent except Europe. Most deserts are found in the "horse latitudes," between 15 and 30 degrees north and south of the equator.

WHAT THEY'RE LIKE: Deserts are also called arid regions, and they're the driest places on Earth. Deserts can be hot, like the Sahara in Africa, or cold, like Antarctica. Hot and dry or cold and dry, all deserts get less than 10 inches (25 cm) of rainfall each year.

WHAT LIVES THERE: It takes special types of plants and animals to survive in the desert. Most animals sleep belowground or in patches of shade during the day and come out at night when it's cooler. Plants and animals that live in the desert have to be able to store water. Cacti soak up rainwater when it comes and hold it in their cells.

▲ The saguaro cactus, found only in the Sonoran Desert of Arizona and Mexico, grows 4-8 inches (10-20 cm) a year—it can take as long as 150 years to reach full height.

▼ The jackrabbit's long ears help it to survive under the intense desert sun by radiating excess heat.

4 Grasslands

WHERE THEY ARE: Grasslands are all over the world. Drier grasslands, called savannas, are found in areas like central Africa, and they usually have scattered trees. Cooler grasslands, called prairies, which are treeless, are found in the central United States and Canada.

WHAT THEY'RE LIKE: Savannas have a rainy season followed by a dry season. Prairies have milder seasons, and the soil is rich enough to grow crops. Steppes, another type of grassland, are dry with hot summers and cool winters.

WHAT LIVES THERE: Savannas are home to animals like zebra, giraffes, and elephants. Bison, cattle, and sheep graze on prairies, and smaller animals like the prairie dog make their homes there.

▶ Bison, or buffalo, are North America's largest native land mammals.

◀ Torres del Paine National Park, Chile

5 Taiga

WHERE IT IS: Taiga is found mostly in North America and northern Europe and Asia.

WHAT IT'S LIKE: This biome has cool summers and cold winters, with small amounts of rainfall.

WHAT LIVES THERE: The ground is covered with a thick layer of needles and dead twigs, held together by fungus. Evergreen trees grow in the rocky soil. Animals with heavy fur coats, like moose, caribou, elk, and bears, live in these conditions.

▲ Some caribou migrate over 3,000 miles each year, farther than any other land mammal.

6 Tundra

WHERE IT IS: Tundra covers a fifth of Earth's land surface. Arctic tundra is mostly found in a belt across northern North America, Europe, and Asia. Alpine tundra is found at the tops of mountains.

WHAT IT'S LIKE: It's really cold all the time in the tundra and very windy during the winter. There's little precipitation, less than 10 inches (25 cm) per year.

WHAT LIVES THERE: Grasses, moss, lichen, and low shrubs grow in the tundra. Large hoofed mammals and small rodents show up during the tundra's two months of summer.

Permafrost, a layer of permanently frozen soil, can be as thick as 1,500 feet (450 m).

▶ Denali National Park, Alaska, United States

GLOBAL WARMING AND THE GREENHOUSE EFFECT

EARTH IS HEATING UP

The Sun's radiation comes in through the glass and heats up the air inside.

SUN'S RADIATION

In the last 100 years, the surface temperature of our planet has risen about half a degree Celsius, and some scientists believe it's going to get even warmer in the years to come. One reason for global warming is the increase in "greenhouse gases" like carbon dioxide in our atmosphere. Just as glass traps heat in a greenhouse, these gases trap heat on Earth and cause a natural warming called the **"greenhouse effect."**

The glass traps the warm air, raising the indoor temperature—which is good news for the plants.

SO WHAT'S THE BIG DEAL IF IT GETS A LITTLE WARMER?

Warm winters can be nice, but increased temperatures can cause problems for the environment. They can lead to more extreme weather, which could harm some habitats and species. Coral reefs die because of warmer water temperatures, so fish have to go elsewhere for food. Earth's polar ice caps hold a lot of water. A tiny difference in temperature can melt this ice, causing sea levels to rise, which could flood coastlines, affecting the habitats of plants and animals and people.

The Sun's radiation travels through our atmosphere, heating up Earth's surface.

Excess greenhouse gases in our atmosphere trap that heat.

Recently, scientists have determined that global warming is causing the Arctic ice to thaw earlier each spring, forcing polar bears in the western Hudson Bay region, off the coast of Canada, to cut short their seal-hunting season. Researchers fear that the Hudson Bay bears could be wiped out if the climate continues to heat up.

THE GOOD NEWS IS:

We can stop the accumulation of greenhouse gases in the air.

✔ Things that HELP	✖ Things that HURT
✔ Planting trees (which take in carbon dioxide and produce oxygen)	✖ Using a lot of gas and electricity (fossil fuel-driven power plants produce carbon dioxide)
✔ Recycling and consuming less	 ✖ Wasting paper
 ✔ Walking or riding your bike to keep the air cleaner	 ✖ Burning fossil fuels (driving), which generates carbon dioxide

It's easy when thinking about global warming to forget that Earth—over the billions of years of its existence—has experienced a number of extended periods of severe climate change. In fact, scientists think that Earth has weathered five ice ages.

MOVIES ON BRAINPOP.COM

 TIMELINE OF **ICE AGES**

An ice age is any time in Earth's history when there are glaciers at one or both poles. That's right—we're in an ice age right now! But we happen to be alive during an **interglacial** period. That means that the glaciers from the poles aren't very extensive. During a glacial period, the glaciers expand out from the poles for hundreds, even thousands, of miles. That's when the temperature really starts to drop!

last 5 million years	300 million years ago	450 million years ago	700 million years ago	2,200 million years ago
LATE CENOZOIC	PENNSYLVANIAN AND PERMIAN	ORDOVICIAN	LATE PROTEROZOIC	EARLY PROTEROZOIC

POLLUTION

Pollution is the contamination of air, water, or land by harmful substances. Air pollution creates a number of environmental problems ranging from global climate change to illness in humans.

When harmful gases are released into the air (from cars or factories, for example), they fall back to Earth in the form of acid rain.

MOVIES ON BRAINPOP.COM

Acid rain can damage plants and animal habitats.

Paint, oven cleaner, furniture polish, motor oil, and other toxic substances called hazardous waste can seep into the water supply and contaminate it if they're not disposed of properly.

Contamination of the water supply is most dangerous when it happens on a large scale, over time—for example, if a manufacturing plant disposes of huge quantities of poisonous chemicals, people are affected both because the water we drink may become contaminated and because the fish we eat are consuming poisons that are then passed on to us.

Recently, pollution has led to increased levels of mercury in ocean fish such as tuna, which could pose a health risk, particularly to pregnant women. And contaminated fish meal has led to increased levels of cancer-causing polychlorinated biphenyls (PCBs) in farmed salmon.

Oil spills are bad news for the water and the creatures that live there. When oil is accidentally spilled into the water by a tanker, barge, or burst pipeline, it spreads across the water's surface, forming a thin layer called an oil slick. Sticky oil takes away the insulating ability of fur on sea otters, so they can't stay warm. It also destroys the water-repelling abilities of the feathers on birds, making it hard for birds to stay warm. Birds and animals also swallow oil when they clean themselves, which can poison them. Oil spills are difficult and expensive to clean up, especially if they spread over a large area.

>> THE UNITED STATES USES ABOUT 840 MILLION GALLONS OF OIL EACH DAY.
>> THE WORLD USES ALMOST 3 BILLION GALLONS EACH DAY.

THE OZONE LAYER

Our atmosphere is made of up different layers. The ozone layer is part of the stratosphere, which extends between 6 and 30 miles (10 and 50 km) above Earth's surface. Ozone is a gas made up of molecules with three oxygen atoms (as opposed to the oxygen we breathe, which has two oxygen atoms per molecule). This layer of gas is so important because it protects us from the sun's powerful **ultraviolet (UV) radiation**.

In the United States, the Environmental Protection Agency (EPA) oversees a number of programs designed to help protect the ozone layer. The good news is that ozone is produced naturally, so the idea is that if we stop making ozone-depleting substances like **chlorofluorocarbons (CFCs)**, the ozone layer could be restored to normal conditions in as little as 50 years.

UV radiation can cause skin cancer and eye problems, and weaken your immune system. It's also harmful to plants and animals, upsetting the balance of the food chain.

CFCs are substances that were once used in refrigerators, spray cans, and other household stuff. CFCs take a few years to get up to the stratosphere, but once there, radiation from the sun triggers a series of reactions that cause ozone to break down.

For more information on protecting the environment, go to www.epa.gov

Did you know...

You may have heard ozone discussed on your local weather forecast. Here's why: too much ozone at ground level can irritate your eyes, reduce your lung capacity, and make it hard to breathe. The ozone alert scale goes from green (good) to purple (very unhealthy).

GOOD

BAD

DEBATE: Is the Ozone Hole Really a Problem?

For sure! And we've got to be careful or it will get worse.

I've heard it's a lot of hype. It's there as part of nature, but it's not growing.

It's a fact that there is a hole (or holes) in the ozone layer. Although the hole varies in size throughout the seasons, scientists in the 1980s noticed a drastic thinning of the ozone over Antarctica—in fact, nearly 70 percent of the ozone layer normally found there had been destroyed. And we know that man-made chemicals like **CFCs** destroy ozone. Humans are responsible for releasing CFCs into the atmosphere, increasing the size of the hole.

Now some scientists think that the ozone hole is getting smaller as the ozone gas is replenishing itself. Is that happening naturally, or is it because people have made a big effort to stop releasing CFCs and other chlorine compounds into the atmosphere? What do you think?

GARBAGE

WHAT HAPPENS TO ALL THAT STUFF WE THROW AWAY?

Most of it ends up in **landfills,** a.k.a. dumps. Basically, the garbage is poured into a shallow hole where it builds up and just . . . sits there. It's not very nice to live near landfills—they often smell, they're usually not very pretty, and they can be dangerous if toxic substances are not properly disposed of.

Some garbage is burned in **incinerators**. Once it's burned, it's gone. So lots of communities try to burn their garbage. The problem with burning is that it releases ash and smoke into the air that might contain harmful chemicals.

WHAT'S IN A LANDFILL?*

Metal 9%

Plastic 7%

Random garbage 9%

Food 9%

Glass 8%

Paper products 40%

*Figures have been rounded up.

Yard waste 20%

RECYCLING

A growing percentage of garbage can be recycled. Recycling is one off the three "Rs" for helping the environment: **Reduce, Reuse, Recycle**. Plastic, glass, aluminum cans, steel, and paper are recycled in most communities throughout the US. You can tell when a product is recyclable by the arrows symbol on it. And you can help the planet by recycling waste in your home and at school!

HOW LONG DOES IT TAKE TO DECOMPOSE?

COMPOSTING

*Dissolve-rate estimates for things like Styrofoam cups and plastic bottles are just that—estimates! The only way we'll ever know for sure how long it takes is to wait hundreds, maybe thousands of years and observe what happens. And without sufficient moisture, some things simply don't decompose. Many dry landfills have 50-year-old newspapers that are still readable.

| Styrofoam cup 400–500 years* | Tin can 100 years | Orange peel 6 months | Newspaper 2–5 months |

Dead leaves shouldn't get thrown away. You can make them into compost. It's good for your whole garden—and fun too!

YOU WILL NEED:
- Brown stuff like dry leaves, sawdust, and dry pine needles
- Green stuff like grass clippings, weeds, and old vegetables
- Soil
- Water

STEP 1 A compost bin should be an area or container that is made of something like chicken wire. Set one up in the corner of your yard.

STEP 2 Layer the compost so that there's a layer of brown stuff followed by a layer of green stuff and so on until the bin is full. Spray each layer with water so that the compost is nice and moist. Mix in a little soil here and there to get some microorganisms in the mix.

STEP 3 Leave the compost alone for a few weeks. The microorganisms will gradually break down all the green and brown stuff until they become dark brown, rich, earthy humus that plants love. You can use the compost as mulch or mix it with planting soil. I prefer to roll around in it first, but that's just me.

+

+

+

WATER

=

C
O
M
P
O
S
T

WHAT'S NEW?

Corn Plastics

What if we could make containers out of biodegradable materials?

No one knows for sure how long a plastic water bottle takes to decay— some scientists say it could take thousands of years. But a new type of plastic that's made of corn takes only 47 days to dissolve! It's called polylactide (or PLA), and it's already starting to appear on some store shelves. PLA require 20–50 percent less fossil fuel to manufacture than regular plastic, and it doesn't give off toxic fumes when it's burned.

Sound too good to be true? On the down side, the new plastic can't hold hot foods (it melts) and is much more expensive than traditional plastic. Also, you can't just toss this stuff on the ground like an apple! Corn plastics don't dissolve under normal environmental conditions. They need to be treated in special processing plants, where they are heated to 284°F (140°C). At that temperature, they biodegrade in 47 days.

WHAT'S NEXT?

Glacial Melting

It's official—mountain glaciers and ice caps in certain parts of the world are melting fast. In fact, they may disappear altogether by the year 2020. This is bad news because 70 percent of Earth's fresh water is frozen into glaciers. People in Bolivia, Ecuador, and Peru depend on glaciers as the main source of their fresh water. Most scientists say that the glacial meltdown is happening because of global warming—as Earth gradually heats up, ice in certain parts of the world melts. What to do? By reducing the chemicals in the atmosphere that contribute to the gradual heating of our planet, we can slow the glacial meltdown and keep the glaciers intact.

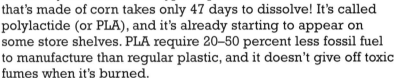

▲ Warm water causes chunks of ice to "calve" or fall off the face of Johns Hopkins Glacier in Alaska. The glacier is so unstable that ships stay at least two miles away to avoid the calving icebergs.

Check out NASA's data on the ozone layer at toms.gsfc.nasa.gov/ozone/ozone.html

SCIENCE FAIR PROJECT #6

Many pollutants can harm aquatic plants and animals. Acid rain is caused by pollutants from factories and cars. Fertilizers from farms and lawns can pollute lakes and ponds. Salt used to clear snow from roads in the winter can find its way into waterways. Find out how these and other pollutants can change aquatic environments by creating your own mini-aquariums!

YOU WILL NEED:

◎ Four clear 2-liter soda bottles (rinsed with hot water) with labels removed

◎ Gravel

◎ Vinegar

◎ Table salt

◎ Plant fertilizer

◎ Eight sprigs of elodea and 40 duckweed plants (from any store that sells aquarium supplies). Note: you can use other aquarium plants instead of elodea and duckweed. And you can choose other contaminants as well.

1. Cut the tops off the four soda bottles to make an opening in each one large enough to put your hand in.

2. Mark a fill line with permanent marker on the outside of each bottle about 1 inch (3-4 cm) from the top, making sure it hits the same place on all four bottles.

3. Add 1 cup gravel and then 5 cups tap water to each bottle.

4. Add two sprigs of elodea and 10 duckweed plants to each bottle.

5. Mix the following solutions separately to act as pollutants:

> ACID RAIN: 1 teaspoon vinegar in 1 pint tap water (vinegar will have a similar effect to acid rain)
> FERTILIZER: 1 teaspoon fertilizer in 1 pint tap water
> ROAD SALT: 1 teaspoon table salt in 1 pint tap water

Use the same ratio for any other contaminants you may want to test.

6. Fill the first bottle to the fill line with tap water. This is your **control bottle**. Fill the second bottle to the fill line with the "acid rain." Fill the third bottle with the fertilizer mixture, the fourth with the road salt mixture, and so on, should you choose to test other contaminants. Be sure to label each bottle clearly so you know what you added to it!

CONTROL ACID RAIN FERTILIZER ROAD SALT

7. Leave the bottles together in a sunny spot. Each day, observe the bottles and record what you see happening. Keep observing for at least two weeks.

8. Over time, some water will evaporate. Keep each bottle filled to the fill line by adding the same liquid you used in step 6.

Compare what happens to the plants in the polluted bottles with the one that contained only tap water. How did the pollutants affect your aquatic environments?

CHAPTER 7

WEATHER

Weather is simply the state of our atmosphere at any particular time. It's caused by the interaction of air, water, and heat from the Sun. That's all there is to it. Well, maybe not all . . . There's extreme weather, changes in weather, winds, air pressure, and predicting the weather too!

MOVIES ON
BRAINPOP.COM

- Water Cycle
- Humidity
- Temperature
- Wind
- Clouds
- Thunderstorms
- Tornadoes
- Hurricanes
...and many more!

Brain
POP®

THE WATER CYCLE AND HUMIDITY

The water cycle is an important component of our weather. The Sun heats up Earth's surface, causing water to evaporate into the air. The air holds on to those water particles sort of like a sponge.

The amount of water vapor in the air is called **humidity**. Humidity varies from day to day. When the **relative humidity** reaches 100 percent, the air is at its maximum moisture capacity (also known as the **dew point**). At this point, water vapor in the air condenses back into water and forms clouds, fog, rain, or snow.

Relative humidity is the amount of water that's in the air, compared with the maximum amount that the air can hold at that temperature.

Dry air, which contains just a few water molecules, has low relative humidity.

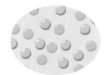

Humid air, which contains lots of water molecules, has high relative humidity.

Clouds

It's no secret that when the sky fills with dense, dark clouds, rain is on the way. But farmers and meteorologists can predict the weather with other kinds of clouds too. Here's a quick guide to clouds and what it means when you see them.

STRATUS Gray and sheet-like, these are the lowest clouds, forming between the ground and 2,000 feet (600 m). Fog and mist are stratus clouds that form on or just above the ground.

NIMBOSTRATUS These are thick stratus clouds that produce precipitation (nimbus means "rain" in Latin), but without thunder or lightning. They can cover the whole sky, blotting out the Sun or Moon.

CUMULUS Plain old cumulus clouds have flat gray bases and puffy white tops, but strong winds can blow them into swirls and streamers. They usually form during the day and disappear at sunset.

CUMULONIMBUS Also called anvil clouds or thunderheads (because they almost always produce rain with thunder and lightning), these are most common in warm, humid regions and often form in the afternoon.

STRATOCUMULUS A blend of layered and puffy clouds forming between 500 and 6,500 feet (150 and 2,000 m). Common in coastal climates, these clouds create cool, damp weather as long as they're around.

ALTOCUMULUS High, layered clouds that can look like fish scales, waves, lenses, castle towers, and tufts of wool. In cold weather, they can signal coming cyclones or rain; in the summer, they often appear at the end of a storm.

CIRRUS High, wispy clouds forming above 18,000 feet (5,500 m). They are sometimes called mare's tails. Cirrus clouds are so thin that the Sun and Moon can shine through them, creating optical effects like halos and sun dogs.

Air Temperature

The tiny building blocks of the universe—subatomic particles, atoms, molecules—are in constant motion. This molecular movement creates heat energy. Temperature is a measure of heat or how fast those molecules are moving.

The more you heat something, the faster the molecules move. The temperature where you live depends on how directly the Sun hits that part of Earth and for how long. Temperatures are always warmest near the equator since the Sun hits that part of Earth directly. Temperatures are coldest at the poles where the Sun's rays hit at an angle. Temperature is measured in most parts of the world using the **Celsius scale**. The **Fahrenheit scale** is used in the United States. Both scales are based on the behavior of water—pure water freezes at 0°C (32°F) and boils at 100°C (212°F).

To convert Celsius to Fahrenheit, it's (9/5 x °C) + 32 = °F
Temperature is measured using a **mercury thermometer**. When the temperature rises, the mercury expands and rises in the thermometer. When the temperature falls, the mercury contracts and falls in the thermometer. Temperature should always be measured in the shade.

▼ The McMurdo Dry Valleys, Antarctica—one of the coldest and driest places on earth.

Did you know...

The coldest temperature ever recorded on Earth: minus 129°F (-89°C), at Vostok Station in Antarctica on July 21, 1983. The hottest temperature ever recorded on Earth: 136°F (58°C), in El Azizia, Libya, on September 13, 1922.

Air Pressure

You may not think of air as having weight, but it does, and its weight is a critical factor in measuring and predicting weather. When meteorologists talk about air pressure, they mean the weight of the atmosphere pressing down on Earth. At sea level, the pressure is greatest. As you go higher, the pressure decreases because there's less air above you.

BAROMETERS are the instruments we use to measure air pressure, in units called millibars (mb). Some barometers use a simple mercury tube, like a thermometer, to measure air pressure. Air pressing down on a dish of mercury causes the level inside the tube to rise.

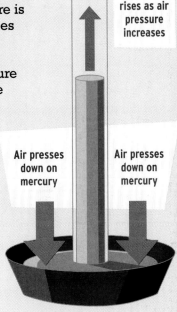

Mercury rises as air pressure increases

Air presses down on mercury

Air presses down on mercury

POP!

EAR POPPING

Ever notice your ears popping when you drive over a mountain or go up in a plane? That's your middle ear reacting to changes in air pressure. When the air pressure inside your ear is different from the air pressure outside, it equalizes with a popping noise!

Ears aren't the only things that go "pop!" When you drive up a really tall mountain, you may notice signs on the road advising you to let some air out of your tires. The difference between the high pressure inside your tires and the low pressure on top of a mountain can be more than they can handle. If you don't deflate them, they could pop!

Did you know...

When the weatherperson on TV says that there's a high-pressure system moving in, it usually means nice weather. Low-pressure systems generally bring clouds and precipitation. That's because the warm air in a low-pressure system sometimes carries water vapor inside it. And when that warm, humid air rises, it can form rain clouds!

Wind

Air pressure isn't the same everywhere on Earth.

At any one time, Earth is covered with millions of little high- and low-pressure areas. That's why there's almost always at least a little bit of a breeze outside. The atmosphere is constantly equalizing between these different pressure areas.

Air sinks within an area of **high pressure**, eventually flowing along into an area of low pressure.

Here, the air rises within the area of **low pressure**, sometimes leading to clouds and precipitation if the rising air contains enough water vapor.

Did you know...

The strongest wind ever recorded was on Mount Washington in New Hampshire, way back in 1934. On April 12, scientists clocked the wind going 231 mph (372 km/h)!

WINDS AROUND THE WORLD

Chicago, Illinois, is known as "the windy city." But it's not the only place known for its winds. People in different places have names for the prevailing winds in their areas.

CHINOOK
a warm, dry wind from the Rockies

MELTEMI
a strong, cool breeze in the eastern Mediterranean

PAPAGAYOS
cool, gale-force northeasterlies from the Gulf of Mexico that bring fine, clear weather

PREVAILING WINDS

Even though there are little winds blowing every which way all over the world, it's not all random. There is an overall pattern. The general direction in which winds move in a certain part of the world is called the prevailing wind. So, for example, the prevailing wind in the northern part of the US moves from west to east. Sure, there are little winds that blow in the opposite direction, but in general, it goes from California to New York.

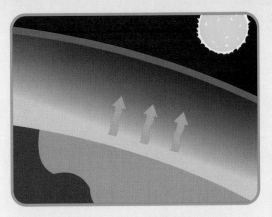

▲ Earth's prevailing winds are powered by the sun-warmed air from the equator. Here, the warm air rises and spreads north and south, moving the warm equatorial air toward the poles in a complex series of patterns. At the same time, cold polar air sinks and then moves toward the equator in another complex series of wind patterns.

◀ Meanwhile, the spin of the earth makes the wind move in a sideways pattern too. This sideways motion resulting from Earth's rotation is called the **Coriolis force**. So you could say that the Sun is the source of Earth's wind. If the Sun were blocked out completely, the air on Earth would slow to a stop.

Did you know...

Ever heard that cool rumor about how the CORIOLIS FORCE (also known as the CORIOLIS EFFECT) makes toilet water swirl in different directions north and south of the equator? Well, unfortunately, it's just that—a rumor. The Coriolis force only has a noticeable, um, effect over time and on large masses of air. So unless your toilet bowl is the size of a small ocean, the way it flushes is determined purely by its plumbing.

SIROCCO
a hot, dry, dusty wind from the Sahara in North Africa

FREMANTLE DOCTOR
a cool sea breeze on the west coast of Australia; the world's most consistent wind—it blows almost every day between 12 and 3 p.m.

SANTA ANA
warm, dry wind in southern California

PRECIPITATION

Precipitation is any form of water that falls from clouds. You know, rain, snow, and hail. The temperatures inside and outside the cloud determine which type of precipitation falls to Earth.

 RAIN   **SNOW**   **HAIL**

RAIN You may hate to wake up and see that it's raining, but think of this: all life on Earth depends on rain. Without it, there'd be no lakes or rivers and no way for plants to grow.

Except in tropical areas, most rain starts off as snow inside clouds. See, clouds form high up in the air, where it's really cold. Water vapor inside clouds forms ice crystals. These collect into snowflakes, and when they get too heavy, they fall from the cloud. If it's warm enough outside the cloud (above 32°F, or 0°C), the snow melts and turns to rain.

In tropical areas, the clouds are warm, so rain starts off inside them as tiny liquid water droplets. The droplets collect, and when they get too big and heavy, they fall from the cloud as rain.

Did you know...

The state of Hawaii boasts both the highest and the lowest average annual rainfall in the United States: a whopping 460 inches (1,170 cm) per year on Mount Waialeale on the island of Kauai, and just 9 inches (23 cm) per year in the town of Puako on the island of Hawaii.

MOVIES ON
BRAINPOP.COM

SNOW Snowflakes start off as individual ice crystals in clouds, created when water vapor freezes around grains of dust. As ice crystals fall from clouds, they bump into each other and combine, forming snowflakes.

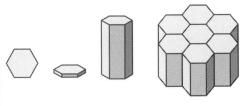

You may have heard that no two snowflakes are alike. This is generally true, and all snowflakes adhere to a six-sided pattern. In fact, every molecule of ice forms a hexagon, a six-sided polygon.

Did you know...

Until very recently, it was commonly thought that all snowflakes were distinct. However, in 1988, while doing research in a plane at 20,000 feet (6,000 m), atmospheric scientist Nancy Knight and her colleagues grabbed two identical snowflakes from the air.

Did you know...

The most snow ever dropped in a single snowstorm in the United States: 189 inches (480 cm) in Mount Shasta Ski Bowl, California, over February 13-19, 1959.

The most snow ever dropped in 24 hours in the United States: 76 inches (193 cm) in Silver Lake, Colorado, over April 14-15, 1921.

HAIL Hailstones are little balls of ice that form inside cumulonimbus clouds (thunderclouds that can grow several miles up). They begin as ice crystals or pellets of snow. Buffeted by strong updrafts, the pellets rise and fall within the clouds, building layer upon layer of ice as drops of rain freeze to their surfaces.

Some hailstones can get to be the size of marbles or golf balls. These can cause massive damage to crops, houses, cars, and other property. The largest hailstone on record fell on Coffeyville, Kansas, in 1970. It weighed 1.67 pounds (0.76 kg)!

EXTREME WEATHER

Winds and precipitation can be incredibly powerful—even threatening lives and property—and making the TV news around the world.

Tornadoes

The most powerful tornadoes create the fastest winds on Earth, over 300 mph (483 km/h)! Actually, scientists don't know for certain how fast the wind inside of a tornado gets, because the instruments they use to measure it get destroyed!

Tornadoes form when warm air rises from the ground as a column of violently rotating air. In the US, favorable conditions for the formation of tornadoes occur when cool, dry air from the Rockies moves east on top of warm, moist air from the Gulf of Mexico. That's why so many tornadoes happen in Texas, Oklahoma, and Kansas. That part of the country is sometimes called Tornado Alley!

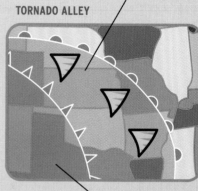

warm air moving north from the Gulf of Mexico

TORNADO ALLEY

cold air moving east from the Rockies

EXPERIMENT with Bob the Ex–Lab Rat

TORNADO IN A BOTTLE

Let's make our own mini-tornado.

YOU WILL NEED:

- Two large plastic soda bottles (with screw tops)
- Glue (not water-soluble)
- One sharp, pointy object (screwdriver; scissors)
- Water
- Food coloring (optional)

STEP 1 Empty all the liquid from the soda bottles and remove their labels. Glue the flat sides of the two screw tops together and let dry.

STEP 2 When the glue is dry, ask your parents to pierce a small hole through both tops using the sharp, pointy object.

STEP 3 Fill one of the soda bottles about two-thirds full of water. Put 1-3 drops of food coloring in the water. I like green. (This step is optional.)

STEP 4 Screw the double top onto the bottle with the water in it. Then screw the empty bottle onto the other side of the top.

STEP 5 Turn the whole thing upside down, giving the water a little swirl to get it going. Watch the water form a spiral in the middle, just like a tornado!

◀ A tornado's signature funnel-shaped cloud approaches the ground near Ardmore, Oklahoma, in 1985.

▼ A house collapses into a sinkhole on Hatteras Island, North Carolina, after weathering Hurricane Isabel in 2003. Isabel killed at least 35 people and caused damage and power outages across 10 states, from North Carolina to New York.

Hurricanes

A hurricane's top wind speed is frequently slower than that of a tornado, but these storms typically cause much more damage with their sustained winds and wide paths of destruction. A hurricane's effects can be felt as far away as 240 miles (386 km) from its center (the "eye" of the storm)! That means in any one place, a hurricane can cover a circular area of close to 500 miles (805 km)! In 1992, Hurricane Andrew left 250,000 Americans homeless in the southeast.

A hurricane is a storm that develops in the tropics with winds of at least 74 mph (119 km/h). Some really strong hurricanes have winds of over 185 mph (298 km/h)! When one of these storms has winds of less than 74 mph, it's called a tropical storm.

◀ A satellite photograph of Hurricane Mitch taken on October 26, 1998.

Did you know...

You can stand in the center of a hurricane and not feel a thing. A hurricane's center is called its eye, and it is perfectly calm in there!

▲ Many businesses and homes, like this one in Florida, were devastated by Hurricane Andrew in 1992. Andrew was one of the most destructive hurricanes ever recorded in America, killing 54 people and forcing the evacuation of more than a million.

HURRICANE NAMES

Ever wonder why meteorologists name hurricanes? Since there can be more than one hurricane in the ocean at a time, they use names to keep them all straight. The first hurricane of the season gets a name starting with "A," the second with "B," and so on. Meteorologists rotate the same six lists of names every hurricane season. When a hurricane causes a lot of damage, the name is retired forever.

SOME RETIRED HURRICANE NAMES:

Agnes in 1972 (Florida and northeastern US)

Gloria in 1985 (North Carolina and northeastern US)

Hazel in 1954 (the Antilles, North Carolina, and South Carolina)

Luis in 1995 (the Lesser Antilles)

Mitch in 1998 (Central America)

Roxanne in 1995 (Mexico)

Thunder and Lightning

Thunderstorms tend to happen on hot, humid days. Inside a storm cloud, tiny droplets of water and ice bump together. This knocks electrons loose from the ice, forming a static charge. It's just like the spark that occurs when you touch a metal doorknob after walking on a carpet, except on a huge scale. After the charge builds up for a while, it gets released through lightning. ◀◀ FOR MORE ON STATIC ELECTRICITY, SEE PP. 142-45.

Lightning heats the air to 54,000°F (30,000°C). That's five times hotter than the surface of the Sun! This causes the air to expand faster than the speed of sound, which is what makes thunder.

▶ Multiple cloud-to-cloud and cloud-to-ground lightning strokes spark up the sky during a nighttime thunderstorm.

Did you know...

Lightning doesn't just travel downward. It can go from the ground up to a cloud or from one cloud across to another too. Some lightning even goes up and down at the same time!

There are many kinds of lightning. How many of these have you seen?

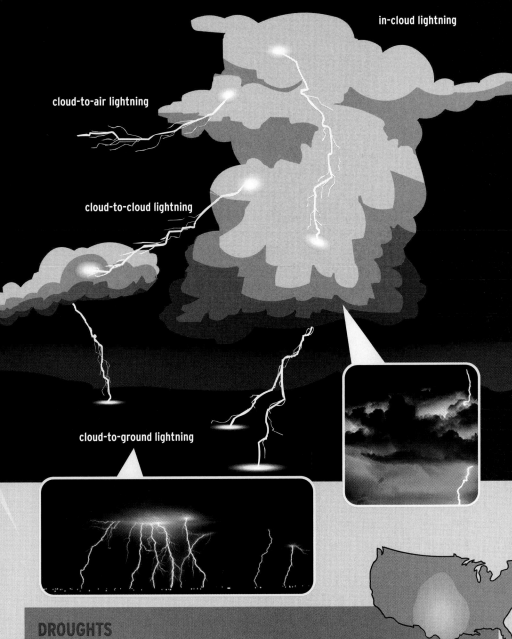

in-cloud lightning

cloud-to-air lightning

cloud-to-cloud lightning

cloud-to-ground lightning

DROUGHTS

Droughts are long periods without rainfall. A lot of droughts are caused by "blocking highs." These are dry high-pressure systems that repel low-pressure systems and their accompanying precipitation.

The Dust Bowl drought of the Great Plains in the 1930s was partly the result of a very long blocking high from the Rockies. ◀◀ FOR AN EXPLANATION OF HIGH- AND LOW-PRESSURE SYSTEMS, SEE P. 104.

WHAT'S NEW?

Predicting Weather

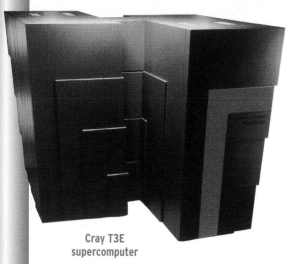

Cray T3E supercomputer

Trying to forecast weather is incredibly complicated. Think about all of the factors that combine to make your local weather: temperature, wind, humidity, sunlight, and the water levels of seas, rivers, and lakes, to name just a few. To do it accurately, you have to collect data from all around the world, because weather in one place is affected by weather patterns nearby. Some scientists believe that totally accurate weather prediction is impossible, because there are too many random elements involved. Right now, we can only "see ahead" a few days.

But at weather-modeling centers like the Hadley Centre for Climate Prediction and Research in England, new techniques are being used to predict weather patterns. Weather modelers use Cray T3E supercomputers to compile data from satellites, weather balloons and stations, ships, and buoys. The supercomputers take this information and create a model of how it thinks all of it will affect our weather. Who knows? Pretty soon, we may have 50-day weather forecasts!

WHAT'S NEXT?

Scientists in Japan have developed a waterproof material that's based on the molecular structure of *Morpho sulkowskyi*, a butterfly. Biologists have noticed for some time that butterfly wings repel water. The Japanese team discovered that the molecular structure that makes the wings water-repellant is also responsible for their bright colors. Get ready for the coolest-looking raincoats you've ever seen!

SCIENCE FAIR PROJECT #8

How Can Barometric Pressure Be Used to Predict the Weather?

Scientists use an instrument called a **barometer** to measure pressure in the atmosphere. Measuring pressure helps meteorologists predict changes in weather conditions. In this experiment, you will make your own barometer and use it to predict the weather.

YOU WILL NEED:

◎ Small, clean can (like a soup can or tuna fish can) with the top removed

◎ Large rubber balloon

◎ Drinking straw (just a plain one—NOT the kind that bends)

◎ Duct tape

◎ Clear tape

◎ Scissors

◎ Ruler

1. Cut a piece from the balloon large enough to cover the opening on the can.

2. Stretch the balloon tightly over the opening of the can and tape the edge all around with duct tape to make an airtight seal.

3. Cut one end of the straw so it comes to a point. Lay the straw flat across the top of the can so the uncut end of the straw is at the center of the balloon piece and the pointed end hangs over the edge of the can like a pointer. Use clear tape to

attach the uncut end of the straw to the center of the rubber balloon. Congratulations—you've just made a barometer!

YOUR BAROMETER

4. Find an indoor location for your barometer where it will not be disturbed. Your location should be next to a wall (or other vertical surface).

5. Tape the ruler vertically against the wall so you can measure how far up and down the straw on your barometer moves. Place the straw pointer of your barometer in front of the ruler.

6. Over a period of a few weeks, measure the location of your straw against the ruler twice a day. Observe the general weather condition (clear, partly cloudy, overcast, fog, rain, etc.). Record your barometer measurements and weather observations in a journal.

◎ What kinds of weather conditions occur when the barometer is high? What kinds of weather conditions occur when the barometer is low?

◎ See if you can accurately predict clear or stormy weather using your barometer.

CHAPTER 8

THE NATURE OF SCIENCE

Human beings have been curious about the world around them for millions of years. Without this curiosity, our distant ancestors would never have made the first stone axe, the first painting, or the first house. As the scientific method has evolved over time, we've started to understand some of the basic laws of the universe—gravity, motion, relativity . . . Let's take a look at a few of those universal laws now, and see how they apply to our everyday lives!

MOVIES ON
BRAINPOP.COM
- The Scientific
  Method
- Newton's Laws
- Gravity
- Relativity
- Atomic Model
- States of Matter
- The Periodic Table
- Pulleys
...and many more!

Brain
POP®

115

GRAVITY, NEWTON'S LAWS, AND RELATIVITY

Gravity

Scientists are constantly revising theories based on new information. Ideas about gravity have evolved and changed over time.

Gravity is the force that attracts two particles of matter together.

It exists everywhere in the universe—holding everything together, from atoms to galaxies. **Sir Isaac Newton's law of universal gravitation** (at right) guided physicists for centuries after he published it in the late 1600s. Newton's theory held up most of the time, but some of his predictions were off when it came to space and planetary movement. In 1915, Albert Einstein explained why Newton's theories didn't work 100 percent of the time with his **Theory of General Relativity** (▶▶ SEE P. 117). Einstein used really advanced math to prove his point, so relativity is a bit too complicated for most of us to understand.

Gravity, the force that causes an apple to fall from a tree, also keeps the planets in orbit around the Sun! The more massive an object, the more gravity it has. The Moon is less massive than Earth, which is why astronauts can bounce around on it—the Moon's gravity does not pull at them with the strength of Earth's. And the closer you are to an object, the more you'll feel its pull. Earth's gravity pulls on the Moon, keeping it in orbit!

ISAAC NEWTON

Gravity works by bending **space-time.** You can imagine space-time as a trampoline. Let something heavy, like a bowling ball, represent a star. Put the ball in the middle of the trampoline, and it curves the material. Place a golf ball on the trampoline and it "falls" towards the bowling ball. The universe works in a similar way—less massive objects, like the Moon, fall toward heavier ones, like Earth.

When he was on the Moon, Alan Shepard whacked a golf ball half a mile! That's because the only force acting on the ball was the Moon's weak gravity. If he had somehow hit the ball in outer space, that thing would still be going today, over 30 years later! (That is, unless it got too close to a planet or star or collided with one.)

ALBERT EINSTEIN

▶▶ SEE P. 118 FOR DEFINITION OF SPACE-TIME.

Relativity

Albert Einstein's **Theories of Relativity** sum up how the universe works, at least on a large scale. Einstein's **Theory of Special Relativity (1905)** is all about the relationships between speed, time, and distance. Special Relativity states that the speed of light stays the same no matter how fast you're moving toward or away from it. So check it out: if you're riding in a car going 60 mph (97 km/h), and another car is coming from the opposite direction going the same speed, how fast are you approaching each other? At a speed of 120 mph (193 km/h), right? Right.

Now here's where it gets weird.

Light travels at 186,000 miles/second (300,000 km/second). So let's say your car is moving at a whopping 10,000 miles/second (16,000 km/second). You turn on your headlights. How fast is the beam of light moving? At a speed of 196,000 miles/second (315,000 km/second), right? Wrong! It still goes 186,000 miles/second (300,000 km/second). The speed of light cannot be changed! Weird, huh?

Since the speed of light does not change, Einstein figured that time and distance must be able to change in order for the universe to make sense. The only way it makes sense for the speed of light to remain constant is if time moves slower the faster you go. That's why if you took a trip in a spaceship going the speed of light, you wouldn't age at all!

Did you know...

If you're going 60 mph (97 km/h) in your car, time moves a tiny bit slower for you than for someone on foot. It's such a small difference, like trillionths of a second, that it doesn't really matter.

Did you know...

When you're in an elevator, going up, there's a moment when you feel heavier, right? That's an example of acceleration making you feel like you're being pulled downward, toward the center of the Earth. And when pilots talk about "G"s, like, "Hey dude, I pulled three Gs in that flight this morning," they're just saying that their acceleration caused them to feel three times the pull of Earth's gravity. Now you can speak pilot lingo!

Einstein's Theory of General Relativity describes how massive objects distort the fabric of space-time. Einstein said that gravity was a property of space, not just a force between two objects. He found that matter actually causes a curve in space and that less dense objects "fall" towards more dense ones as a result, bending their path. Look at the planets' orbits—the Sun's gravity causes them to fall into a curved path. Light is bent by gravity too—black holes bend light so much that it can't escape! **▸▸ FOR MORE ON BLACK HOLES SEE P. 213.**

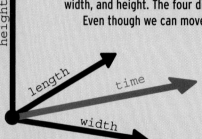

So what is space-time? Well, Einstein considered time a dimension, just like length, width, and height. The four dimensions in Einstein's physics are called space-time. Even though we can move around freely in three dimensions, we're sort of stuck in the fourth one, time. We're all moving forward, aging, along the time dimension.

If your brain is hurting, think of it this way: the universe from 1 second ago still exists. **You** from 1 second ago still exists; you just don't have the ability to move back and forth through time to check it out.

FAMOUS FACES

Isaac Newton is considered one of the greatest scientists of all time. He discovered that white light is actually made up of a spectrum of colors. He invented an entire branch of mathematics. You may have heard of it; it's called calculus. He constructed the first reflecting telescope. And his theories of gravity and motion hold up to this day. Now, is it true that he came up with his ideas on gravity after being hit on the head by a falling apple? Probably not, but he probably got his ideas by studying the world, and a falling apple may have helped clue him in to the mystery of gravity.

Despite being one of the most important physicists ever, **Albert Einstein** failed his entrance exam to engineering school! So don't give up hope next time you mess up on a test. Look at Einstein: he went on to develop the Special and General Theories of Relativity, which have continued to shape physics since they were published in the early 20th century.

Newton's Laws of Motion

Isaac Newton was a busy guy. On top of defining how scientists think about gravity, he came up with his three laws of motion. These laws describe how and why objects stop and go.

You might think the laws are obvious—we take most of them for granted every day—but back in 1687, none of this stuff was understood the way it is today. Until Newton's laws came along, that is.

Imagine a soccer ball lying on your bedroom floor. It's just sitting there. It won't move. And it'll stay there until you do something about it. Duh, right? Well, that's Newton's First Law of Motion.

NEWTON'S FIRST LAW: Unless some force acts on an object, its speed and direction will stay the same. If the object is not moving, it will not begin moving until some force acts upon it. This is also called inertia.

Now if you were to take the ball outside and kick it . . .

NEWTON'S SECOND LAW: When a force acts on an object, it will slow down, speed up, change direction, or some combination of the three. The greater the force, the greater the change. The greater the object's mass, the less the change.

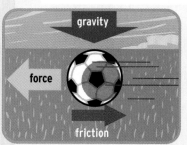

Your foot kicking the ball is a force. The harder you kick the ball, the greater the ball's velocity.

The ball keeps moving for a while, even after your foot's not touching it anymore. What makes it do that? Inertia again. That ball's going to keep going until something makes it stop.

So what makes the ball stop? Mainly friction and gravity acting against its movement. Friction is the energy created when two objects rub together. The soccer ball rolling over the grass creates friction, slowing it down to a stop. This is just another example of the Second Law. Friction is a force that changes the soccer ball's speed.

If you stay outside kicking soccer balls all day, you may notice your kicking foot gets a little sore. This is because of Newton's Third Law of Motion, which says that any time force is exerted on an object, it pushes right back.

NEWTON'S THIRD LAW: If you push or pull an object, the object pushes or pulls back with equal force.

THE PERIODIC TABLE

The periodic table is a list of all the known elements in the world. The one we use today was developed by a Russian teacher named **Dmitri Mendeleev** in 1869. Everything on Earth is made up of **matter** and matter is made up of elements. An **element** is a substance that contains only one kind of atom (see picture at right). Atoms with different numbers of protons in their nuclei behave differently.

The elements in the periodic table are organized by the way they look and act.

The elements are listed in order of increasing atomic number, which is the number of protons in one atom's nucleus.

The columns of the table are called groups. Each group contains elements whose atoms have the same number of electrons in their outer shells. Because of this, they behave in similar ways chemically.

| 1
H
HYDROGEN |

| 3
Li
LITHIUM | 4
Be
BERYLLIUM |

| 11
Na
SODIUM | 12
Mg
MAGNESIUM |

19 **K** POTASSIUM	20 **Ca** CALCIUM	21 **Sc** SCANDIUM	22 **Ti** TITANIUM	23 **V** VANADIUM	24 **Cr** CHROMIUM	25 **Mn** MANGANESE	26 **Fe** IRON	27 **Co** COBALT
37 **Rb** RUBIDIUM	38 **Sr** STRONTIUM	39 **Y** YTTRIUM	40 **Zr** ZIRCONIUM	41 **Nb** NIOBIUM	42 **Mo** MOLYBDENUM	43 **Tc** TECHNETIUM	44 **Ru** RUTHENIUM	45 **Rh** RHODIUM
55 **Cs** CESIUM	56 **Ba** BARIUM	57-71 **-**	72 **Hf** HAFNIUM	73 **Ta** TANTALUM	74 **W** TUNGSTEN	75 **Re** RHENIUM	76 **Os** OSMIUM	77 **Ir** IRIDIUM
87 **Fr** FRANCIUM	88 **Ra** RADIUM	89-103 **-**	104 **Rf** RUTHERFORDIUM	105 **Db** DUBNIUM	106 **Sg** SEABORGIUM	107 **Bh** BOHRIUM	108 **Hs** HASSIUM	109 **Mt** MEITNERIUM

▲ ALKALI METALS

▲ ALKALINE EARTH METALS

▲ TRANSITION METALS

▼ LANTHANIDES

The rows of the table are called periods. All elements in the same period have the same number of electron shells. (▶▶ SEE P. 122.)

57 **La** LANTHANUM	58 **Ce** CERIUM	59 **Pr** PRASEODYMIUM	60 **Nd** NEODYMIUM	61 **Pm** PROMETHIUM	62 **Sm** SAMARIUM
89 **Ac** ACTINIUM	90 **Th** THORIUM	91 **Pa** PROTACTINIUM	92 **U** URANIUM	93 **Np** NEPTUNIUM	94 **Pu** PLUTONIUM

▲ ACTINIDES

Each element in the table is described by its
- Actual name
- Atomic number (the number of protons in its nucleus)
- Shorthand symbol
- Atomic mass (this is the average mass of one atom of the element as compared to carbon-12)

Oxygen
8
O
15.9994

ELECTRON (-)

PROTON (+)

NEUTRON (Ø)

THE STRUCTURE OF AN ATOM

SEMIMETALS

NOBLE GASES ▶

2 **He** HELIUM

SEMIMETALS					
5 **B** BORON	6 **C** CARBON	7 **N** NITROGEN	8 **O** OXYGEN	9 **F** FLOURINE	10 **Ne** NEON
13 **Al** ALUMINUM	14 **Si** SILICON	15 **P** PHOSPHORUS	16 **S** SULFUR	17 **Cl** CHLORINE	18 **Ar** ARGON

28 **Ni** NICKEL	29 **Cu** COPPER	30 **Zn** ZINC	31 **Ga** GALLIUM	32 **Ge** GERMANIUM	33 **As** ARSENIC	34 **Se** SELENIUM	35 **Br** BROMINE	36 **Kr** KRYPTON
46 **Pd** PALLADIUM	47 **Ag** SILVER	48 **Cd** CADMIUM	49 **In** INDIUM	50 **Sn** TIN	51 **Sb** ANTIMONY	52 **Te** TELLURIUM	53 **I** IODINE	54 **Xe** XENON
78 **Pt** PLATINUM	79 **Au** GOLD	80 **Hg** MERCURY	81 **Tl** THALLIUM	82 **Pb** LEAD	83 **Bi** BISMUTH	84 **Po** POLONIUM	85 **At** ASTATINE	86 **Rn** RADON
110 **Ds** DARMSTADTIUM	111 **Uuu**	112 **Uub**	113 **Uut**	114 **Uuq**	115 **Uup**	116 **Uuh**	117 **Uus**	118 **Uuo**

▲ POOR METALS

▲ NONMETALS

63 **Eu** EUROPIUM	64 **Gd** GADOLINIUM	65 **Tb** TERBIUM	66 **Dy** DYSPROSIUM	67 **Ho** HOLMIUM	68 **Er** ERBIUM	69 **Tm** THULIUM	70 **Yb** YTTERBIUM	71 **Lu** LUTETIUM
95 **Am** AMERICIUM	96 **Cm** CURIUM	97 **Bk** BERKELIUM	98 **Cf** CALIFORNIUM	99 **Es** EINSTEINIUM	100 **Fm** FERMIUM	101 **Md** MENDELEVIUM	102 **No** NOBELIUM	103 **Lr** LAWRENCIUM

Atoms are not the smallest things around. Inside atoms there are even tinier particles called **electrons**, **protons**, and **neutrons**. Every element in the periodic table has a different configuration of these subatomic particles.

WHAT MAKES ATOMS REACT?

Inside atoms, electrons circle the nucleus in orbits that scientists imagine as shells (nobody has actually seen them). Atoms tend to "want" four or eight electrons in their outermost shell. The farther an atom is away from this goal, the more it reacts with other atoms. Atoms that "try" to lose their outer electrons in chemical reactions are called cations. Those that try to gain electrons in reactions are called anions. Once an atom has four or eight electrons in its outer shell, it becomes stable.

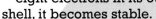

nucleus

electron

electron shell

argon

The **ALKALI METALS** are very reactive—that single electron in their outer shells is likely to "jump" to another atom. Sodium (Na) makes up half of the compound we call table salt, or **sodium chloride** (NaCl). But you wouldn't want to put plain old elemental sodium on your food—it'd burn your mouth!

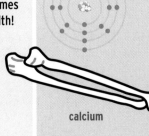

sodium

The **ALKALINE EARTH METALS** have two electrons in their outer shells, so they're not as reactive as the alkali metals. **Calcium** is an alkaline, and, as with sodium, it would be unsafe for you to eat calcium on its own. But when combined with chloride, it becomes an important mineral for your bones' health!

The **TRANSITION METALS** are strong, hard, and shiny. They conduct electricity and heat well. The transition metals include **gold** (Au) and **silver** (Ag) and many of the compounds they form are colored. Transition metals vary in how reactive they are, depending on their electron configurations.

calcium

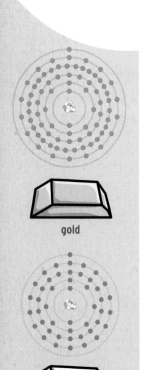

gold

silver

The **POOR METALS** are soft and weak with low melting points. **Aluminum** (Al) and **copper** (Cu) belong to this group. Poor metals are often mixed into alloys—bronze is an alloy made by combining **tin** (Sn) and copper. Poor metals are useful since they're so easy to melt and work with. For example, they're used in aluminum cans, airplane parts, and telephone wires.

The **SEMIMETALS** are hard to nail down—they have some properties of both metals and nonmetals. Elements like **silicon** (Si) and **germanium** (Ge) are used in semiconductors because they are capable of conducting electricity, but this conductivity can be controlled—the **diode** of a laser beam in a CD or DVD player uses a semimetal. ▶▶ FOR MORE ON CDs, SEE P. 177; FOR MORE ON DVDs, SEE P. 188.

The **NONMETALS** are mostly gases. They are very reactive, have low melting points, and do not make great conductors. **Fluorine** (F) combines with oxygen to make fluoride, an important mineral for teeth. **Carbon** (C) is probably the most important nonmetal—it can combine with many different elements to form compounds. It's also part of the carbon dioxide we breathe out, and the coal we burn for energy.

The **NOBLE GASES** are just the opposite of reactive: their electron shells are full, and they're not giving up any electrons without a fight. Scientists can force the noble gases to form compounds in a lab, but they won't normally react in nature. **Neon** (Ne) is a noble gas used to make lights.

The **LANTHANIDES** have so much in common that they're hard to tell apart. **Samarium** (Sm) is a lanthanide that's used to make powerful magnets.

The **ACTINIDES** are very radioactive elements. Some of them occur in nature; others have only been made in labs. **Uranium** (U) is an actinide that you've probably heard of—it's used in nuclear reactors.

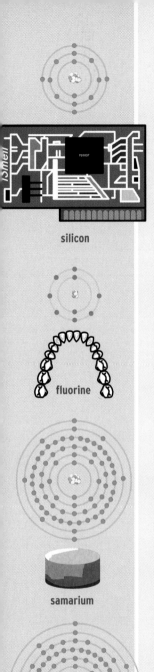

silicon

fluorine

samarium

uranium

aluminum

carbon

neon

MOVIES ON BRAINPOP.COM

Did you know...

Those fireworks you see on the Fourth of July light up the sky with the help of alkaline earth metals! The color of fireworks depends on packets of chemicals called "stars" that explode in the sky—magnesium or aluminum are used to make white, sodium salts are used for yellow, and copper salts are used for blue!

SIMPLE MACHINES

Ever wonder why pulleys are used to lift heavy objects? And how do the wheels on your car turn and turn? Thank goodness for simple machines.

MOVIES ON BRAINPOP.COM

Simple machines make **work** easier to do. Work is the amount of energy needed to move or change any object. Some simple machines magnify force, others distance. Even though they've been around since the first caveman used a stone axe as a wedge, simple machines can still be found in the latest technology. No matter how complex a machine is, it probably uses a simple machine in one place or another. Check it out!

SIMPLE MACHINE	HOW IT WORKS	WHERE YOU'LL FIND IT
SLOPES, or inclined planes, trade distance for force.	By increasing the distance an object travels from point A to point B, a slope decreases how much force is needed to move it at any given point.	**OLD SCHOOL:** staircase, ramp

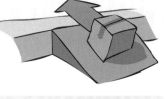

NEW SCHOOL: conveyor belt

A WEDGE is an inclined plane that you move, instead of moving objects over it.	It magnifies force by moving the object it's wedging a greater distance than it is moving.	**OLD SCHOOL:** axe, zipper

NEW SCHOOL: snowplow

SIMPLE MACHINE	HOW IT WORKS	WHERE YOU'LL FIND IT

A **SCREW** is just an inclined plane spiraling around a cylinder.

It moves a greater distance around in circles than it does forward and backward. So it trades circular distance to magnify back-and-forth force.

OLD SCHOOL: corkscrew, spiral stairs

NEW SCHOOL: electric garage-door opener

LEVERS are bars that balance or pivot on a **fulcrum**. Their **load** is the weight or resistance that has to be overcome for a lever to move. **Effort** is force that is applied to the lever in order to move it. A lever's effort, load, and fulcrum can be positioned differently:

A seesaw is a lever where the fulcrum is between the effort and the load.

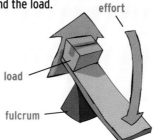

effort

load

fulcrum

In a wheelbarrow, the load is positioned between the effort and the fulcrum.

When you pinch a pair of tweezers, the effort comes between the load and the fulcrum.

WHEEL AND AXLE sets increase force by using the difference in each item's circumference.

The axle turns in a small circle, going a shorter distance but moving with a greater amount of force than the wheel around it.

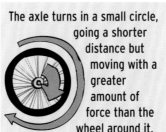

OLD SCHOOL: door knob, wagon
NEW SCHOOL: electric scooter

A **PULLEY** is a force magnifier used for lifting things straight up.

It works because the amount the load is lifted is a fraction of how much rope gets pulled.

OLD SCHOOL: dumbwaiter
NEW SCHOOL: elevator

What's Uup?

Looks like we might have to revise the periodic table of elements. On February 1, 2004, a team of Russian and American scientists reported that they had created two new elements: **Uut** and **Uup**. The team created the new elements by firing calcium (Ca) atoms at americium (Am) atoms. To do this, they used a cyclotron, a particle accelerator that makes atoms collide at very high speeds.

113	115
Uut	**Uup**

Each calcium nucleus contains 20 protons, and each americium nucleus contains 95. When the atoms collided, an element with 115 protons resulted. Within a fraction of a second, it decayed radioactively to an element with 113 protons. That one lasted 1.2 seconds.

Uut and Uup are just temporary names until other scientists can confirm the team's results. If that happens, the team can name the confirmed elements whatever they want. Who knows what weird properties these elements will have? They might lead to cool new inventions or ways to make existing stuff better.

The last new element was discovered in 1994. It's called darmstadtium, named for the city in Germany where it was discovered. It has 110 protons in its nucleus.

Want to go for a ride?

How do astronauts prepare for travel in space? Antigravity chambers, right? Nope. Right now there's no such thing. Astronauts have to take a sickening ride on the KC-135A, a jet nicknamed the Vomit Comet.

It flies in a big arc and then free-falls from the top of the curve. The people inside float for about the first 30 seconds of the descent. It's not really anti-gravity, but it's all they have.

SCIENCE FAIR PROJECT #8

Do Objects of Different Weights Fall at Different Speeds?

Gravity pulls downward on everything near Earth's surface. It pulls harder on heavy objects than it does on light ones. That's why heavy objects are harder to lift than light ones. Does that mean that heavy objects fall faster than light ones? In the 16th century, Galileo designed an experiment to test this idea. However, instead of dropping the objects, he rolled them down a long ramp so they would be easier to observe. You can easily re-create his famous experiment.

YOU WILL NEED:

◎ A 6-foot (1.8 m) piece of wood that has a long groove down the middle

◎ Several small balls of about the same size but different weights (a large plastic bead, a glass marble, and a metal ball will work nicely)

◎ Several books

◎ Two small wood blocks

◎ Duct tape

◎ Stopwatch

◎ Ruler

◎ Marker

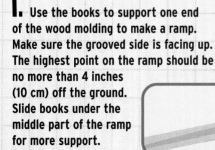

1. Use the books to support one end of the wood molding to make a ramp. Make sure the grooved side is facing up. The highest point on the ramp should be no more than 4 inches (10 cm) off the ground. Slide books under the middle part of the ramp for more support.

2. Use duct tape to attach one block on top of the molding at the bottom end of the ramp.

3. Use the marker to make a line across the molding about 2 inches (5 cm) from the top of the ramp.

4. Place the other block on the ramp so the top edge of the block is on the line you drew. Hold this block in place with your hand.

5. Place the first ball on the ramp just above the block you are holding.

6. Pick up the stopwatch. Pull the block off the ramp and start the stopwatch at the same time. Stop the stopwatch when the ball hits the block at the bottom of the ramp. Record the time.

7. Repeat steps 4 through 6 at least two more times for the same ball. Find the average time it takes for the ball to roll down the ramp.

8. Repeat steps 4 through 7 for each of the other balls you are testing.

◎ Which ball took the least amount of time to roll down the ramp? Does the weight of the ball affect the amount of time it takes the ball to roll down the ramp?

◎ Try starting the balls at different points on the ramp. Do you still see the same pattern you observed before?

CHAPTER 9

ENERGY

The world wouldn't work without energy! We wouldn't have heat or electricity, and there would be no using a computer or cellphone. Since the beginning of history, when early humans used fire to cook food and warm themselves, people have been hooked on energy. Today, in the United States, we use 840 million gallons of oil per day!

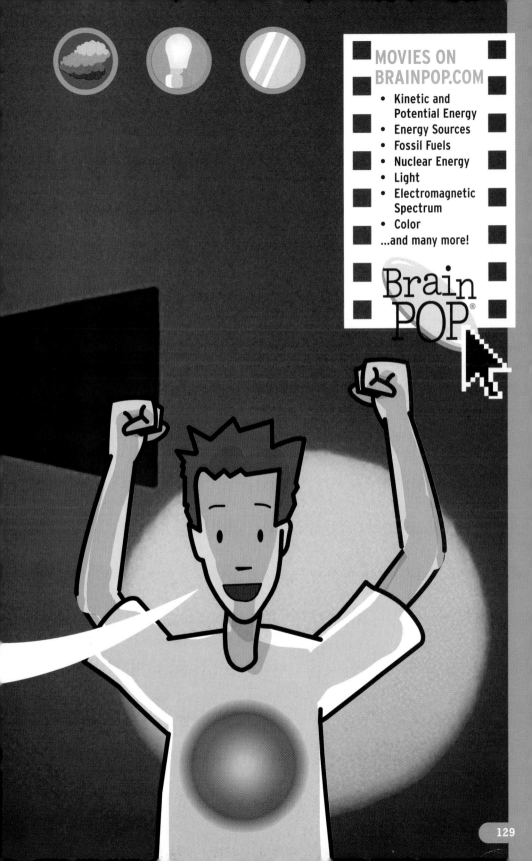

MOVIES ON
BRAINPOP.COM

- Kinetic and
  Potential Energy
- Energy Sources
- Fossil Fuels
- Nuclear Energy
- Light
- Electromagnetic
  Spectrum
- Color
...and many more!

Brain
POP®

WHAT IS ENERGY?

Energy makes change. It is the ability to do work. Work is the amount of effort or force used over the distance you have covered. If you ran very quickly up a very steep hill, you would expend a lot of effort and travel a short distance. If you slowly strolled to the top of the same hill by taking a path that zigzagged up the hillside, you would walk a much longer distance, but you would have done the same amount of work.

There are two kinds of energy: anything that's moving has **kinetic energy** (a.k.a. the energy of motion). That ball rolling across the street has kinetic energy. So do your fingers as they tap tap tap on the computer.

Potential energy is a different story. It's the possibility of kinetic energy. A skier at the top of a ski slope has a whole lot of potential energy. When he starts down the hill, that potential energy is released as kinetic energy. The food you eat contains chemical energy, another form of potential energy. Your body converts this chemical energy into kinetic energy.

People are always looking for ways to take the potential energy we find in nature (like oil, wood, sunlight, etc.) and turn it into kinetic energy.

Kinetic energy, the energy of motion

TYPES OF KINETIC ENERGY

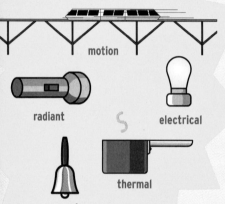

motion

radiant

electrical

thermal

sound

TYPES OF POTENTIAL ENERGY

chemical

mechanical

nuclear

gravitational

RENEWABLE/NONRENEWABLE

NONRENEWABLE ENERGY is limited in supply, and cannot be remade in a short period of time.

Oil

Gas

Coal

Nuclear

ENERGY SOURCES

Natural Energy Sources

Before we used fossil fuels, people burned wood to cook food, heat homes, and power steam engines.

Fossil fuels are composed mainly of carbon and hydrogen. All living things—plants and animals—are also carbon based. Therefore, scientists are certain that fossil fuels come from the decomposed remains of long-dead plants and animals.

All fossil fuels come from the broken-down remains of life forms that died millions of years ago.

FOSSIL FUELS

COAL is formed mainly from swampy forests that grew about 350 million years ago! When the forests died, they were slowly buried in sediment. Eventually, the pressure from that sediment buildup compressed the forest matter into the rock we call coal. ◄◄ SEE PP. 72-73 FOR MORE ON HOW SEDIMENT TURNS TO ROCK.

OIL comes from the remains of plants and animals who lived in ancient seas. Sediment covered their remains on the sea floor. Pressure and heat, like the kind that creates metamorphic rock, changed the remains into oil.

NATURAL GAS deposits come from the same ocean organisms that created oil. It is thought that natural gas formed when the deposits of dead matter reached very high temperatures.

RENEWABLE ENERGY refers to those sources of energy that occur naturally and repeatedly in the environment or energy made from clean technology that won't run out.

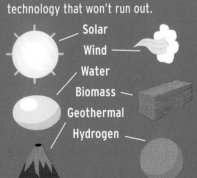

- Solar
- Wind
- Water
- Biomass
- Geothermal
- Hydrogen

RESERVES

People are worried about how much fossil fuel we have left. Based on **proven** reserves, current rates of consumption, and existing technology for extracting fules, here's how long supplies will last. Of course, discoveries of new fuel reserves could extend these deadlines.

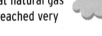

Oil–45 years

Natural Gas–63 years

Coal–230 years

OIL'S USES

You probably know that oil can be refined into gasoline, airplane fuel, and diesel gas. But did you know that oil is also used to make:

Plastics

Polyester

Pesticides and fertilizers

Styrofoam

Detergents

Paint base

Perfume base

WHAT COMES AROUND...

Burning wood and fossil fuels releases energy in the form of heat. But check this out: all of that energy originally comes from the Sun! Trees and other plants convert solar energy into chemical energy—that's how they eat and grow! So when animals eat plants, the energy they get from the food really comes from the Sun. And when animals eat other animals . . . well, you get the point. Even fossil fuels, which come from decayed plant and animal matter, are ultimately a form of solar energy.

FOSSIL FUEL POLLUTION

If oil and coal are natural, how come using them is so bad for the environment? Unfortunately, when fossil fuels burn, they release carbon dioxide and other polluting chemicals into the air. The process of refining fossil fuels into other products produces dangerous chemicals too. ◄◄ FOR MORE ON POLLUTION, SEE PP. 92-93.

OZONE causes throat and lung irritation when breathed, eventually leading to permanent scarring.

CARBON DIOXIDE contributes to the Greenhouse Effect, which most scientists think is causing global warming. ◄◄ FOR MORE ON GLOBAL WARMING, SEE PP. 90-91.

SULFUR DIOXIDE helps cause acid rain, which can harm plants, rivers, and lakes.

PARTICULATE MATTER, like ash and soot, can cause respiratory problems like asthma and bronchitis.

BENZENE, a highly flammable component of gasoline, evaporates easily into the air and water and can cause cancer, birth defects, and many other health problems.

CARBON MONOXIDE is a poison. In high enough concentrations, it can even kill you!

How Does an Object's Color Affect How It Absorbs Energy from Sunlight?

You may have noticed that objects of some colors seem to heat up differently than objects of other colors. In this experiment, you will find out how color affects the way an object gets energy from the Sun.

YOU WILL NEED:

- ◎ Thermometer (indoor/outdoor type is best)
- ◎ Construction paper of different colors (red, orange, yellow, green, blue, purple, black, white)
- ◎ Clear tape
- ◎ Lots of sunlight (if you can't get lots of sunlight, use a lamp with a 100-watt bulb)
- ◎ Watch or clock

1. Do this step in a shady place! Fold each piece of construction paper in half (so the short sides of the sheet meet each other). Tape two edges of each folded sheet closed so your paper makes a pocket.

2. Do this step in a shady place! Place your thermometer in the first paper pocket so the thermometer bulb is inside. Measure and record the temperature before placing it in the sun. Be sure to record the color of the paper.

3. Place the paper with the thermometer inside in direct sunlight for 15 minutes. Measure and record the temperature at the end of 15 minutes.

If you are using the lightbulb instead of sunlight, place the paper with the thermometer inside 5-10 inches away from the bulb. Measure this distance carefully and record it so you can use the same distance with the other colors.

4. Repeat steps 2 and 3 using the other colors of paper. Be sure to bring the thermometer into the shade and let it cool down before you put it into the next paper pocket.

5. Presenting your results on a chart or graph will make it easier to compare the different colors.

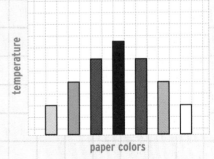

temperature

paper colors

- ◎ Which color heated up the most? Which color stayed coolest?

- ◎ What color or colors should you wear to stay cool on a sunny summer day? What colors are best to wear to keep warm?

Nuclear Power

energy = mass × speed of light² $(186,000 \text{ mps})^2$

$E=mc^2$. You've probably seen Einstein's equation a million times, but do you know what it means? It states that the energy (E) stored in any piece of matter is equal to its mass (m) times the speed of light (c) squared. Now, the speed of light is around 186,000 miles (299,337 km) per second. So even a small bit of matter contains huge amounts of energy!

Nuclear may sound like a scary word, but it actually refers to the energy stored in an atom's nucleus. Atoms are the smallest bits of elements.

NUCLEAR FISSION

Incredibly strong forces keep the particles in an atom's nucleus together. Normally, nothing can break it apart.

But scientists discovered that a neutron colliding with an atom can split open the nucleus, releasing some of the energy that holds it together.

Radioactive elements like uranium and plutonium are special. They release other high-speed neutrons when they are split apart.

These neutrons hit other nearby atoms, and split. This is called a **chain reaction**, and it's why nuclear fission releases so much energy.

nucleus

generic split

oxygen split

chain reaction

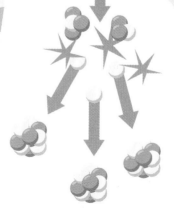

Did you know...

After a nuclear reaction, the mass of the matter you end up with is less than the mass you started out with. Why? Because some of that mass has been converted into energy: $E=mc^2$!

NUCLEAR POWER PLANTS

Nuclear power plants are like big steam engines, except instead of burning coal or wood to heat water into steam, a nuclear chain reaction is used. Here's how it works:

Pellets of uranium (or other radioactive material) are stored in fuel rods.

Fuel rods are packed together with control rods (made of materials such as boron or cadmium), which absorb neutrons and help slow the chain reaction. This keeps the nuclear reaction from getting out of control and causing a meltdown.

The fuel rods are immersed in fluid, and the nuclear reaction begins. The fluid picks up heat released by the reaction. The heat is transferred to water, and produces steam.

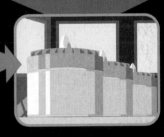

NUCLEAR WASTE

Nuclear fission produces highly radioactive waste. About 3 percent of the material left over from a fission reaction falls into this category. Exposure to even tiny amounts of radioactive waste can cause cancer and birth defects. That's because energy in the form of gamma rays is thrown off by this material. Gamma rays can easily penetrate our cells and damage our DNA. All the spent nuclear fuel in the world would cover a football field with 15 feet (4.6 m) of toxic junk.

There is no way to destroy radioactive material. You just have to wait for it to release all of its energy and become safe on its own. The problem is, this takes millions of years! So the only thing we can do with the waste is to keep it far away from where we live, like deep underground.

Did you know...

Some nuclear waste is so dangerous, it gets packed in glass cubes, in tiny little pieces! There are plans now to bury much of this high-level waste deep beneath Yucca Mountain, about 100 miles (160 km) from Las Vegas, Nevada.

Renewable Energy Sources

Because fossil fuels pollute the environment and will eventually run out, there's lots of research going into clean, renewable sources of energy. Here are a few promising leads.

SOLAR POWER

The Sun is an endless source of power. The energy from all the sunlight hitting Earth each year dwarfs the amount we create burning fossil fuels. The problem is how to harness that energy efficiently. Photovoltaic cells (solar cells) turn sunlight into electricity. Energy from the Sun drives electrons in solar cells from one atom to another, creating an electric current. But solar cells still don't create enough power to make them a good alternative to fossil fuel and nuclear energy, though they can be used to power houses. And they're still very expensive. Scientists are working constantly to make them cheaper and more efficient. Right now, these cells are used in calculators, watches, road signs, street lights, and navigation buoys in the ocean.

Electrons in photovoltaic cells hop from one atom to another when heated—a current!

WIND POWER

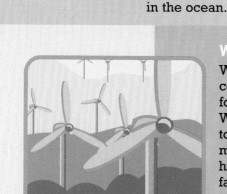

Wind power: the other solar energy

Windmills have been used for centuries to harness the wind's energy for pumping water and grinding corn. Windmills use the power of the wind to turn giant turbines, which convert motion into electricity. Driving on the highway, you may have seen wind farms—huge arrays of windmills close together. Since wind is created by differences in air temperature, wind power is actually a form of solar energy. Even though wind power is cheap, clean, and inexhaustible, it has a couple of big drawbacks:

- Wind farms take up a lot of room and can be an eyesore.
- They're very noisy.
- You have to wait for the wind to blow, something that's not under our control.

MOVIES ON BRAINPOP.COM

◀◀ FOR MORE ON WIND, SEE PP. 104-05.

WATER POWER

People have harnessed water power now for thousands of years. Grain-grinding mills used a paddle wheel in a river to turn their grinding stones. Using a very similar technology, hydro-electric plants use the flow of falling water to turn turbines. The movement of the turbines, which drive electrical generators, gets converted into electricity. Most hydroelectric plants are built on rivers as part of a dam, and they do affect the environment. Changing the flow of a river can permanently change or permanently destroy its ecosystem.

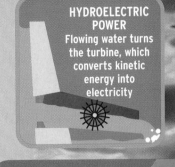

HYDROELECTRIC POWER
Flowing water turns the turbine, which converts kinetic energy into electricity

Did you know...

In France, there's a hydroelectric plant that runs on the ocean's tides. It's the first of its kind, and can power a city of 300,000 people!

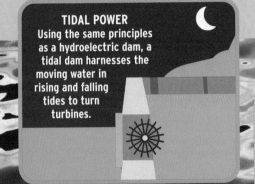

TIDAL POWER
Using the same principles as a hydroelectric dam, a tidal dam harnesses the moving water in rising and falling tides to turn turbines.

GEOTHERMAL POWER
Hot rock beneath Earth's surface heats water up, forcing it to the surface.

GEOTHERMAL POWER

Ever taken a dip in a hot spring? Or watched a geyser erupt? The same energy that heats these waters can be used to heat homes and generate electricity. Deep in Earth's crust, some areas of rock get close to 2,000°F (1,100°C). This energy sometimes comes to the surface as hot water or steam. Countries like Iceland, which have this natural resource, use geothermal energy for much of their power.

WHAT'S NEXT? The Hydrogen Economy

One of the most promising next-generation fuel sources is the hydrogen fuel cell. Hydrogen cells combine hydrogen and oxygen into water. The by-products of this reaction are heat and electricity. Hydrogen cells are nonpolluting and energy efficient and are powered by a completely renewable resource. There's no end to the supply of hydrogen in the world, unlike fossil fuels.

fuel cell

Hydrogen has a ways to go before it replaces fossil fuels. The biggest challenge right now is that hydrogen does not appear in pure form, and it currently requires more energy to create pure hydrogen than the hydrogen then delivers as fuel.

LIGHT

Light is a form of energy. As far as we know, nothing in the universe travels faster than light.

Light is still one of the biggest mysteries of science. Sometimes it acts like a wave, and sometimes it acts like a particle. Most scientists now accept that it is a little of both. This is called **quantum theory**.

Light is made when an atom's electron gains and then loses energy. This can happen in a number of different ways:

By **heating** something up, like the wick of a candle

When something gives off light even after the energy that caused the glow has been removed, that's phosphorescence. Dinoflagellates, a type of algae that live in the ocean, emit this type of light. A glowing watch dial is another example.

Through **chemical reactions**, like in bioluminescent fish

Through sonoluminescence, a little-understood process whereby objects emit light when struck by sound waves

RAINBOWS

The visible-light section of the electromagnetic spectrum looks white, but it's really a mixture of a whole bunch of colors: red, orange, yellow, green, blue, indigo, and violet. Mix all this light together, and you get white. Isaac Newton discovered this when he passed white light through a prism, a transparent, solid object with angles like a cut jewel. When white light passes through a prism, the colors of light bend differently, according to their wavelengths. The result is a splitting up of the white light into its component colors.

Rainbows show up when sunlight bounces off of water in the air. The droplets of water act as tiny prisms, splitting white light into colored light. The individual drops of water are tiny, but the overall effect is a huge-looking rainbow!

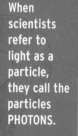

EM Spectrum

The visible light that we see all around us is just one part of the electromagnetic (EM) spectrum. The EM spectrum is just the name for a bunch of types of radiation organized by the amounts of energy they carry. Starting with the lowest energy level, the seven types of EM radiation are:

▶▶ FOR MORE ON RADIO WAVES, SEE PP. 172-73.

RADIO WAVES These low-energy waves are used to carry radio and television signals.

MICROWAVES The shortest of the radio waves, microwaves have the same frequency as water molecules. When food is zapped with microwaves, the water molecules inside it vibrate. The movement of the molecules heats up the food.

INFRARED LIGHT Anything that has a temperature gives off infrared waves.

VISIBLE LIGHT This is the only part of the electromagnetic spectrum that we can see.

ULTRAVIOLET LIGHT Ultraviolet light from the sun helps us process vitamin D, but too much can give you skin cancer!

X-RAYS X-rays carry enough energy to travel through skin and muscles, but they are stopped by bone. That's why we use them to take pictures of our skeleton.

GAMMA RAYS Radioactive materials like plutonium give off gamma rays. They can penetrate our cells and damage our DNA.

▶▶ FOR MORE ON HOW LIGHT IS CAPTURED IN PICTURES, SEE PP. 184-85.

LONG WAVELENGTH

SHORT WAVELENGTH

REFLECTION

We can see the Sun because it is a source of light. But what about things that don't give off light, like you and me? How can we see them? We can because light bounces off those objects. Everything you see either emits or reflects light.

Did you know...

You can never reach a rainbow, no matter how long you walk towards it. That's because a rainbow is sunlight coming from behind you bouncing off of water in the air in front of you. As you walk, the angle created by the Sun, the water droplets, and your head stays the same.

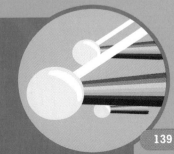

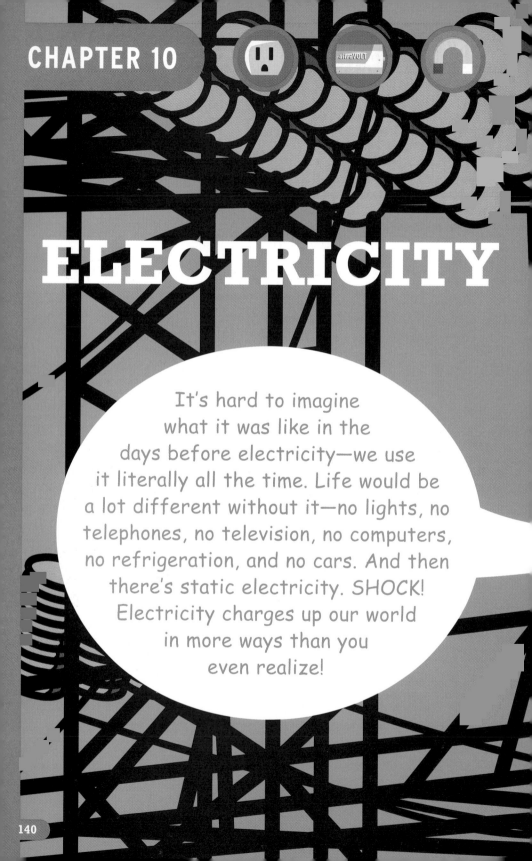

CHAPTER 10

ELECTRICITY

It's hard to imagine what it was like in the days before electricity—we use it literally all the time. Life would be a lot different without it—no lights, no telephones, no television, no computers, no refrigeration, and no cars. And then there's static electricity. SHOCK! Electricity charges up our world in more ways than you even realize!

MOVIES ON
BRAINPOP.COM

• Electricity
• Static Electricity
• Batteries
• Magnetism
...and many more!

Brain
POP®

ELECTRICITY

At the most basic level, electricity is all about the movement of electrons (those tiny, negatively charged particles that orbit an atom's nucleus a little bit like planets around a star). Atoms are the smallest complete bits of an element. Every atom has a nucleus of protons and neutrons that's usually surrounded by one or more electrons. Electricity is what we get when electrons move from one place to another.

Static Electricity

Ever get a shock when you touch someone else? Do you notice crackling noises and sparks when you pull off your favorite sweater? These are examples of **static electricity**. Despite its name (*static* means still), static electricity results from the *movement* of electrons from one surface to another.

Every atom is made up of a characteristic number of protons, neutrons, and electrons. Protons have a "positive" charge, electrons have a "negative" charge, and neutrons have no charge. The positive charge of ONE proton cancels out the negative charge of ONE electron. Typically, atoms are *neutral* (have no charge), because they tend to have the same number of protons and electrons.

Proton

Electron

HERE'S THE RUB

ADHESION, a bond that forms between two objects when they come into contact, causes atoms to lose electrons. When the objects are pulled apart, adhesion bonds can pull electrons from the surface of one object to the other. The objects now have an *electrostatic charge*. The object that lost electrons is positive, and the one that gained electrons is negative. These charges can last for hours and hours, which is where the *static* in static electricity comes from!

Conductors are materials that don't hold tight to their electrons and allow electrons to flow easily through them. Metals, like copper wire, are good conductors. Insulators, like a rubber

Atoms that pick up extra electrons carry a negative charge and are called **anions** (AN-eye-unz), or negatively charged ions. Atoms that have lost one or more electrons are called **cations** (KAT-eye-unz), or positively charged ions.

THE ZAP WHEN YOU TOUCH A DOORKNOB

Chances are, you just walked across a carpet. The rubber soles of your sneakers are insulators that picked up electrons from your carpet, another insulator. This gives your entire body a negative charge. Touching a conductor, like that metal doorknob, will neutralize the charge. The electrons will fly from your finger to the metal. ZAP!

Did you know...

Flip the lights off, look in the mirror, bite down on a wintergreen Life Saver, and you might see a spark!

balloon, hold their electrons tight and don't let them flow through easily.

You can see the effect of static electricity by taking an insulator, like a balloon, and rubbing it against another insulator, like your hair. The balloon picks up electrons from your hair, leaving your hair with a positive charge. The balloon gains negatively charged electrons, so it's left with an overall negative charge. The negatively charged balloon attracts the positively charged hairs, pulling them together. Opposites attract after all!

LIGHTNING

Lightning is a form of static electricity. A storm cloud tends to build up a strong positive charge at its top and a negative charge at the bottom. This negative charge is so big, it repels electrons from the ground, thousands of feet below, giving the ground a positive charge. Sometimes a huge flow of electrons (lightning) neutralizes the charge difference between the top and bottom of the cloud. Other times, lightning neutralizes the difference between the bottom of the cloud and the ground, which is when it gets dangerous to be outside!

FAMOUS FACE BENJAMIN FRANKLIN

Benjamin Franklin is known as the father of electricity. During a thunderstorm around 1750, Franklin flew a kite with a key tied to the string. (Do NOT try this at home—Franklin's experiment could have killed him!) The key picked up electrons from the charged air. When Franklin put his finger near the key, it produced a spark. That spark proved that clouds produce electricity that is carried to Earth by lightning. ▶▶ SEE P. 144 FOR MORE ON LIGHTNING RODS.

LIGHTNING RODS Lots of tall buildings use lightning rods to prevent damage from lightning. A lightning rod is a stick of metal attached to the high point of a building. A thick cable (made of a good conductor like copper or aluminum) runs from the bottom of the rod, down the building, connecting finally to a metal grid buried in the ground.

Lots of people think that lightning rods attract lightning, but that isn't true. Lightning rods exploit the fact that electrical charges like lightning tend to follow the *path of least resistance*. All that means is that lightning goes wherever it can move easily—water, for example, is a good conductor of electricity, so we're taught to stay away from the water during an electrical storm. Lightning rods are made of highly conductive metal (▶▶ SEE P. 142), providing a low-resistance path for the lightning to follow and guiding the electricity harmlessly into the ground. This prevents it from hitting the building and doing real damage.

EXPERIMENT
with Bob the Ex–Lab Rat

STATIC CLING

It's sort of tough to imagine that electrons actually get knocked loose from their atoms to cause static electricity. But you can see for yourself with this experiment.

YOU WILL NEED:
• two balloons
• a couple of yards of thread
• a mirror

STEP 1 Blow up each of the balloons and tie them off.

STEP 2 Tie one end of the thread to one balloon and the other end of the thread to the other balloon.

STEP 3 Rub each balloon against your hair. Make sure to keep the balloons as far away from each other as possible at all times.

STEP 4 Pick the thread up by the center, letting the balloons hang down at equal lengths. Notice how they repel each other? That's because they're both covered in electrons picked up from your hair. Like charges repel.

STEP 5 In front of the mirror, put either balloon close to your head. Your hair, positively charged from all those electrons it lost, sticks up to reach the negatively charged balloons. Opposite charges attract!

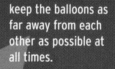

144

COPY MACHINES

One of the coolest ways we see static electricity at work has to be in copy machines. Here's how they do their job:

1. Using bright light, a positively charged copy drum is selectively neutralized to form an image out of cations (▶▶ SEE P. 142).

2. Negatively charged ink powder (toner) is attracted to the image on the drum.

3. Positively charged paper rolls across the drum, and the toner sticks to it in the form of the image.

4. Heated rollers melt the solid toner, making it stick to the paper as a permanent image.

Electric Currents

Electricity that flows along a metal wire or other conductor is called a current. Our homes are powered by electrical currents. The electricity that we have at home is an alternating current, or AC for short.

▲ Electric currents power our homes.

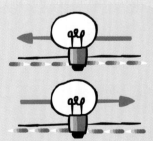

With AC, the current flows in one direction and then switches to go the other way. The switching happens so quickly that the filament inside a lightbulb doesn't have time to cool down and grow dim. If it did, AC current would make all of those lightbulbs in your house flicker. How annoying!

BASICS

Electricity can be measured with three basic units: amps, volts, and ohms (pronounced OAMZ). To understand what these units measure, it's helpful to think of electric currents like water flowing through a pipe—volts are equivalent to water pressure, amps would describe how many gallons per second are flowing, and ohms, which measure resistance to electrical flow, would be the pipe's diameter. The higher the resistance, the smaller the diameter. The relationship between these units is amps = volts/ohms.

So, AC is the type of current electricity that is fed into our homes. On the other hand, DC, or direct current, is usually battery powered. Check out the science behind AC and DC:

DC (DIRECT CURRENT)

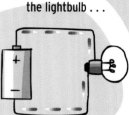

3. provide power to the lightbulb . . .

4. and are drawn to the positive terminal of the power source.

1. Electrons leave from the negative terminal of power source.

2. They flow along a conductor . . .

AC (ALTERNATING CURRENT)

1. Electrons flow through one prong in the plug . . .

5. and then the direction reverses along the same path!

2. and down one half of the wire . . .

3. They provde power to the television set . . .

4. flowing out of the television through the other wire and back into the wall . . .

SAFETY RULES

The AC current that comes out of your walls is powerful stuff. Keep it from harming you by following a few basic safety rules:

- **NEVER** touch a wall socket with anything but a plug!
- **NEVER** touch the metal part of a plug when you plug it in.
- Check cords to make sure they're not torn or frayed. **DON'T** use a cord that is torn or has a hole in it.
- **DON'T** pull the cord to remove a plug.
- **DON'T** overload a wall plug or extension cord with too many devices.
- Stay away from high-voltage cables and train rails.
- **NEVER** use electric devices when you are wet or standing in water.

Circuits

Current electricity usually flows along a circuit. Like its name suggests, a circuit is circular. Electrons flow from the power source to the electrical device and back to the power source again. Most circuits have at least three things in common:

A power source
A conductor (that's anything for the electricity to flow through, like a copper wire)
An electrical device

There are two basic types of circuits:

SERIES CIRCUITS

Series are the simplest types of circuits. In a series circuit, all the parts of the circuit must conduct electricity for the circuit to work. If any part of the circuit fails, the whole thing won't work. You've probably seen this happen with holiday lights—when one bulb blows, the whole string dies. Here's why: it's all one big loop. If just one of those lights blows, the circuit is broken and none of the lights will go on. That's why most quality light strings are hooked up in parallel.

1. Current flows from the power source . . .

3. and back to the power source.

2. through a wire to the lights . . .

Festive lights like these are connected in a series circuit.

PARALLEL CIRCUITS

Parallel lines never meet up; same with parallel circuits! In a parallel circuit, the current flows along more than one path. That way everything doesn't depend on everything else to work. A car's headlights are a good example of a parallel circuit. When one light goes out, the other still works.

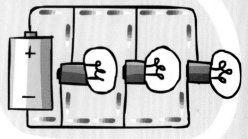

1. Current flows from the power source . . .

3. and each light has a separate wire leading back to the power source.

2. through a wire to the lights . . .

BATTERIES

MOVIES ON BRAINPOP.COM

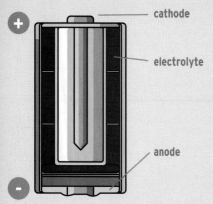

cathode

electrolyte

anode

Batteries produce electricity by changing stored chemical energy into electrical energy. The main parts of a battery are the **anode**, the **cathode**, and the **electrolyte**. The negative electrode, or anode, is usually a metal like zinc, which gives up electrons easily. The positive electrode, or cathode, is a material that tends to collect electrons, like carbon. And the electrolyte is a pasty mixture of chemicals that conducts electricity.

Batteries come in all sizes: as small as a pill or the size of a house. The AAA, AA, C, D, and 9-volt batteries that you use in your flashlights and radios are dry-cell, or alkaline, batteries. They're called "dry cells" because they have a paste or gel inside instead of the liquid that some other batteries use.

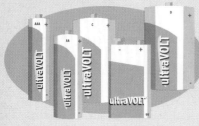

Batteries at Work

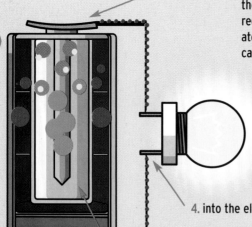

5. and back to the carbon cathode of the battery, combining with its molecules in a process called **reduction**. One of the things produced by the carbon rod's reduction is hydrogen. These hydrogen atoms tend to collect on the outside of the carbon rod, which would eventually prevent its uptake of more electrons. That's why the cathode is submerged in a carbon/manganese compound. The compound reacts with the hydrogen and keeps it off the cathode. Once there are no more free electrons for the anode to lose, the battery goes dead.

4. into the electrical device . . .

3. The electrons flow through the conducting wire . . .

1. The battery is connected to a circuit.

2. Chemicals in the electrolyte (ammonium chloride) react with the metal of the negative anode, causing it to lose electrons in a process called **oxidation**.

DIFFERENT TYPES OF BATTERIES

ALKALINE BATTERIES—The kind you use all the time. (Duracell, Energizer, etc.) The electrodes are zinc and carbon, with an alkaline electrolyte.

LITHIUM PHOTO BATTERIES—Good for use in cameras because of their ability to supply power surges, like the kind needed for a flash to go off!

LEAD-ACID BATTERIES (rechargeable)—Used in automobiles, these have electrodes made of lead and lead oxide and a strong acidic electrolyte.

LITHIUM-ION BATTERIES (rechargeable)—Small and powerful, these guys are often found in laptop computers and cell phones.

SILVER-ZINC BATTERIES—Used in planes because they are both powerful and lightweight.

EXPERIMENT
with Bob the Ex–Lab Rat

MAKE A POTATO BATTERY

Lemons and potatoes can make batteries! That's right. I once had a potato-powered clock going!

YOU WILL NEED:
- One potato
- Two pieces of different metals like zinc and tin or copper and nickel (you can use coins, silverware, jewelry, etc.)
- A few feet of copper wire
- One small torch bulb (available at hardware stores)

STEP 1 Attach a piece of copper wire to each of the different pieces of metal.

STEP 2 Push one piece of metal into one side of the potato and the other piece of metal (a different type) into the other side of the potato.

STEP 3 Touch the wires to the base of the lightbulb and it should light up!

Pretty cool, isn't it? You can try it with a lemon too!

THE POWER GRID
Almost every home and business in the US is connected by a giant power grid made up of more than 200,000 miles (322,000 km) of high-voltage wire. Much of this system was built quite a while ago, in the 1960s and '70s.

When one part of the grid fails, it can affect millions of people. Because of the automatic safety measure built into the system, other parts of the grid can shut down in response, just to be safe.

In August of 2003, there was a big blackout on the East Coast. It lasted several days in some areas and ended up costing $4–10 billion in damage.

MAGNETS

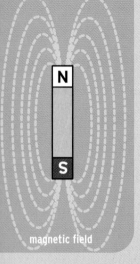

magnetic field

It's not called the electromagnetic spectrum for nothing. Magnetism and electricity behave in very similar ways. In fact, it is possible to create a magnet out of electricity and vice versa (▸▸ SEE P. 151).

Magnets get their name from a type of iron ore called magnetite that occurs naturally in the earth. A simple bar magnet has a north and south pole. An invisible area called a magnetic field extends out from these poles. A magnetic field is just an area where magnetic objects experience a force. Pour lots of iron shavings around a bar magnet, and you'll see the field.

If you put a north pole near a south pole, the two ends will attract each other. But two north poles or two south poles will repel each other.

Earth's Magnetic Field

So why are the ends of a magnet called north and south? Earth has its own magnetic field and its own magnetic north and south poles, slightly offset from the geographic poles. Some scientists think this is caused by the iron core at the center of the planet, but no one is really sure.

A magnet's north pole is naturally attracted to Earth's magnetic south, while its south pole is attracted to Earth's magnetic north.

A compass is a magnetized needle that's balanced on a pivot. Because it's light and suspended, the needle aligns itself with Earth's magnetic field. The part of the needle that points north is its south pole.

USES OF MAGNETISM

Lots of everyday technology uses magnetism, like:

 ◂ Audio tape

 ◂ Electric motors

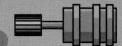 ◂ Generators

 ◂ Floppy disks

Electromagnetism

All electric currents produce magnetic fields. The strength of the field depends on the strength of the electric current.

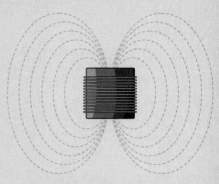

Even a single wire with a tiny bit of electricity running through it has a small magnetic field.

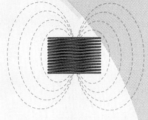

When you coil an electric wire, the field becomes stronger.

Winding that coil around an iron core produces an even stronger magnetic field.

USES OF ELECTROMAGNETS

Electromagnets are useful because they can be turned on and off with the flick of a switch. And you can vary the strength of an electromagnet by adding or subtracting electric current from it.

That means there's no limit to how strong an electromagnet can be. MRI (magnetic resonance imaging) machines use extremely strong electromagnets to create images of the inside of our bodies. The magnets are so strong that any metal containing iron in the room will fly towards the machine when it is on.

▲ The Meissner Motor is an electromagnetic motor that uses superconductors to run.

MOVIES ON BRAINPOP.COM

Did you know...

Sure, electric currents cause magnetic fields, but it works the other way too. If you move a regular magnet along a coil of wire, an electric current flows through the wire!

ELECTROMAGNETS ARE ALL AROUND YOU.
They're used in,

◄ Metal detectors

◄ Stereo speakers

Vending machines

▶ Doorbells

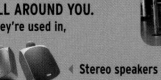

Electric motors

◄ Televisions

PLEASE RING

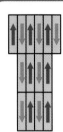

MAGNETIZING IRON

Not all metal is magnetic, but any piece of metal that contains iron has the potential to become a magnet. Metal containing iron has clusters of atoms called magnetic domains inside of it.

In unmagnetized iron, the poles of these domains are all jumbled up, so they pretty much cancel each other out.

But check out the domains inside a magnet! The alignment of the domains inside a magnet creates a magnetic field.

When you place a magnet next to a steel nail, the magnetic field is powerful enough to temporarily align domains in the nail. It becomes magnetized, and the two are attracted to each other. Pull the magnet away, and the nail's domains will go back to a random pattern.

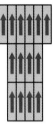

The magnetic domains in unmagnetized iron do not line up.

The magnetic domains in magnetized iron are alligned.

WHAT'S NEW?

What do cell phones, personal music players, handheld computers, palm pilots, and portable game devices all have in common? They allow you to communicate, learn, and have fun on the go. What else do they have in common? Rechargeable batteries power them. And each device usually comes with its own plug and/or special battery charger (which must also be plugged into the wall). Keeping everything powered up and ready to go can mean quite a tangle of cords near your wall outlet.

An English company called Splashpower is working on a solution to alleviate the hassle of finding room for all your electronic equipment's plugs. It is called the SplashPad™, which is a charging platform that plugs into the wall and uses high-frequency electromagnetic induction to transfer power from the SplashPad to any device fitted with a SplashModule™. Less than .04 inches (1 mm) thick, the SplashModule™ would be inserted into devices you currently own, and it would receive the electromagnetic field from the pad and convert it into usable power that would recharge the battery at the required voltage. The Splashpower team hopes their technology will become a built-in feature of future battery packs, handsets, and gadgets. Roughly the size of a place mat, the SplashPad™ can provide power for as many gizmos as you can fit on it.

Splashpower™ technology opens the door for future opportunities too. Imagine charging your desk lamp, wireless mouse, kitchen mixer, or house fan on a wireless charging pad. Picture SplashPads™ in public places, allowing you to recharge your batteries while you grab a slice of pizza or lounge in the park.

SCIENCE FAIR PROJECT #10

How Do Different Substances Affect How Water Conducts Electricity?

Pure water does not conduct electricity well. However, when certain substances are dissolved in the water, the mixture becomes an excellent conductor of electricity. These substances are called electrolytes. In this experiment, you will test different substances to find out if they are electrolytes.

YOU WILL NEED:

- ◎ 6-volt battery
- ◎ Insulated copper wire
- ◎ Miniature incandescent lightbulb
- ◎ Lightbulb holder (can be bought at a hardware store)
- ◎ Wire strippers
- ◎ Large glass or small glass bowl
- ◎ Distilled water (can be bought at a drug store)
- ◎ Substances to be tested (sugar, salt, baking soda, vinegar, etc.)

1. Cut three lengths of wire, each about 10 inches (25 cm) long. Strip the insulation off each end of the wire pieces.

2. Put the lightbulb in the lightbulb holder. (Both these items can be bought at a hardware or electronics store).

3. Connect one terminal of the battery to one terminal on the bulb holder with the first length of wire. Attach the second length of wire to the other terminal of the battery and the third length of wire to the other terminal of the bulb holder.

4. Touch the ends of the two loose pieces of wire together to make sure the bulb will light up.

5. To test how well a liquid conducts electricity, put some liquid in the glass. Put the ends of both loose pieces of wire into the liquid, but do not let the ends touch each other. If the liquid conducts electricity, the bulb will light up.

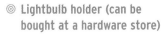

6. Test how well distilled water conducts electricity. Mix different substances with distilled water to see how well the mixtures conduct electricity. Be sure to rinse the glass after each new substance. Record your observations in a journal.

- ◎ How well did the distilled water conduct electricity? Which substances caused the water to conduct electricity?

- ◎ You can use the setup from this experiment to test how well other substances conduct electricity too!

COMPUTERS
AND
COMMUNICATION

What would our world be like without computers? It's hard to imagine. E-mail, Instant Messages, Internet searches, file storage...They've changed the way we think, work, and interact with friends, and they have made research a whole lot easier! Cellphones and wireless devices are so much a part of our daily habits that it's hard to remember what we did before they existed.

COMPUTER BASICS

A lot's going on beneath the casing of your computer. You can't see it, but everything that you do—from tapping a key to saving a file—means work for your computer's parts.

Binary

Computers think and communicate in a language of ones and zeros called **binary**. All the information in your computer is stored in binary. Sure, it may all look like files and folders and desktop patterns, but way down deep, it's just a bunch of ones and zeros. The keys you type, the movements of your mouse, even the sound of a recorded voice are all represented by binary code.

COUNTING IN BINARY

0, 1, 2, 3, 4, 5, 6, 7, 8, 9 . . . These are the numbers that most people use to count. It's a base-10 number system (because there are 10 symbols). Our numbering system probably turned out to be base-10 because we have 10 fingers to count on.

The binary system is base-2, using only two symbols, a zero and a one. Now why do you think that is? Well, one of the simplest electrical circuits is a switch—representing on and off, yes and no, empty and full, and one and zero.

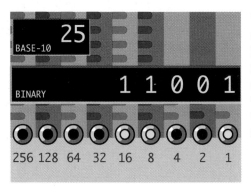

The number 1 in binary is 0001. That means there is one "1" in the number 1. How about the number 25? Using our number system, 25 would be described as two 10s and five 1s. But 25 in binary would look like this: 11001. That's one 16 (2^4), an 8 (2^3), no 4s (2^2), no 2s (2^1), and a 1 (2^0), or 16+8+1=25.

Each one or zero is called a binary digit or **bit**. It's the smallest unit of information.

BITS AND BYTES

So, just like a light switch, the circuits in a computer have two options: on and off. "On" is represented by the number "1", and "off" is represented by the number "0". When your computer stores information in its memory and on your disk drive, it stores only ones and zeros. So everything you do on your computer, from typing the letter "a" to saving a term paper, has a binary code.

Did you know...

If you typed "The small black cat ran from the big dog," saved it, and looked at how much disk space it took up, it would say 40 bytes. Now, if you count the letters and spaces in that sentence, you'll see that they add up to 40!

Since a bit can only be a zero or a one, there's not a whole lot of room for number combinations. There's only so much you can do when you limit your alphabet to two numbers. In the 1950s, computer engineers decided that they would group eight bits together to represent each letter of the alphabet. Eight bits grouped together are called a **byte**. There are 256 different possible combinations using eight zeros and ones. That's more than enough to cover the alphabet and other keyboard characters like * and %. This binary system sounds pretty complicated compared with the one we're all used to, but computers are so fast that they can handle it with no sweat.

Did you know...

The capital letter "A" is stored on your computer as **01000001**. The star symbol "*" is stored on your computer as **00101010**.

Hardware

Your computer comes with a lot of things built right in—the hard drive, the circuit board, and the **CPU**, for starters. There's also tons of stuff you can add to it, inside and out—a mouse, a printer, video cards, external hard drives, CD burners . . .

Every computer has a **CPU** (central processing unit). The CPU is like a brain—it handles most of the work that goes on, crunching numbers and telling the other parts what to do. A CPU's power (speed) is measured in hertz, or how many times a second it can process instructions. If a processor's speed is 100 megahertz (MHz), it can process 100 million instructions every second!

RAM AND ROM

Every computer has ROM and RAM chips inside. Computers use RAM and ROM to remember stuff.

ROM

- ROM stands for "read-only memory," and it holds onto information that the computer needs permanently.
- RAM is short for "random-access memory," and it's a more temporary type of storage.

RAM

The difference is like the long- and short-term memory used by your brain. If you were a computer, ROM is where you'd keep the stuff you need all the time, like your name and what your parents look like. RAM is where you'd store temporary stuff, like the items on a menu in a restaurant.

◄◄ FOR MORE ON MEMORY, SEE P. 25.

What's What on Your Computer

A **HARD DRIVE** is a box that contains several hard magnetic disks where all the information on your computer is stored in the form of bits. Back up your hard drive often because it contains a lot of important information! The hard drive is where your computer keeps your software, all the programs and games that you run, and all of the files you create. As long as you remember to save your work, it will be stored on your hard drive.

SOUND CARDS have analog/digital converters that can change bits into sound signals and back again. They let you play music, listen to the radio, record sound, and play video games!

Speaker grill and sound cards

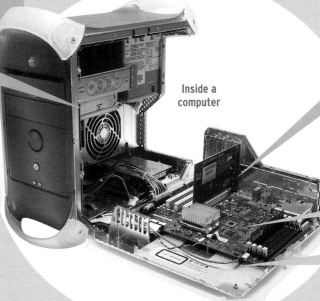

Inside a computer

Clickety, click, click. A **COMPUTER MOUSE** lets you move the cursor around your screen without touching the keyboard. Moving the mouse across a hard surface turns wheels inside the mouse. These wheels send signals to the computer. The signals determine how much, and in which direction, the cursor moves on the screen.

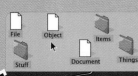

Did you know...

The roller ball mouse is not the only way to point: Nowadays, there are **OPTICAL MICE** that shine a light on the mousing surface to determine their position. A **TRACKBALL** is essentially an upside-down mouse, with the ball on top. With a **TRACKPAD**, your finger moves the pointer.

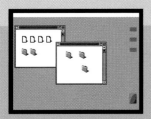

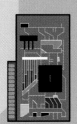

MAC VERSUS PC

Computer users divide over this one. PCs have way more users worldwide, but Macs (Apple brand computers) have cornered a niche in the graphics, design, and video arenas.

VIDEO CARDS turn data into the pictures you see on your monitor. They let you watch movies, see images, and view Web graphics.

MOVIES ON BRAINPOP.COM

Did you know...

Mac users get off easy when it comes to viruses—such a small percentage of the world uses Macs that you rarely see viruses made to affect them.

Most likely your **MODEM** is inside your computer. These days, there are a bunch of different kinds of modems, but the principle is usually the same. A modem sends these bits back and forth by serving as a bridge between your digital computer and an analog line, like your telephone.

The **CIRCUIT BOARD**, or **MOTHERBOARD**, ties all the parts of your computer together. External devices like keyboards, scanners, and printers are connected to the circuit board.

Electrical pathways called "buses" link up the internal stuff, like the ROM, RAM, and hard drive, as well as any other parts you might have in there, like a sound card or video card.

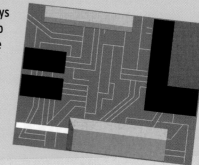

WHAT'S NEW? ▶ PDAs

Say good-bye to calendars and address books! PDA stands for personal digital assistant. It's basically a small computer that you can hold in one hand. In addition to organizing your life with built-in calendars, appointment schedules, sound alerts, and storage for all your addresses and phone numbers, a PDA can hold your downloaded e-mail and play music! Plus, they connect up to your computer, so you can transfer information back and forth from your PDA to your PC. Some PDAs have wireless service, allowing you to access the Internet in hot spots.

Ink-jet print head spraying ink on page

In an **ink-jet printer**, you've got a print head filled with ink-spraying nozzles that moves back and forth across the paper in lines. As it works its way across the page, the print head fires jets of quick-drying ink at your paper. Your computer sends electrical signals to the nozzles telling them whether or not to fire. So, ink-jet printouts are really a combination of dots and blank spaces.

Each nozzle in the print head contains a tube with a tiny heating device inside. The ink fed into the tube is heated up and a bubble of ink forms and expands until it finally shoots out onto the paper.

Color ink-jet printers work in much the same way, firing four different colors instead of just one.

▲ Printouts are made up of dots of the four colors of ink which combine to make every color imaginable.

▲ An ink-jet cartridge, ▼ and color laser printer

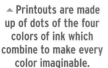

Printers

There are two main types of printers—ink-jets and lasers. They're both a great way to get what's on your computer onto paper, but they do the job in different ways.

Laser printers receive signals from a computer just like with the ink-jet, but that's where the similarity ends.

1. The signals are sent to a laser or other light emitting diode (LED) that fires pulses of light at a printing drum.

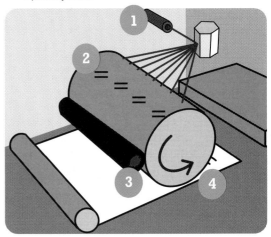

2. The drum is a heat-sensitive metal cylinder that is given a negative electrical charge at the beginning of each print cycle. The pulses of light neutralize the drum's negative charge in places where they strike it.

3. As the drum rotates, it passes over brushes containing a dark, positively charged powder called toner.

4. The paper that moves through a laser printer is given an even bigger negative charge than the drum. That charge causes the ink from the drum to be attracted to the paper. As a piece of paper rolls through, the drum's ink jumps to it. A heater seals the toner to the paper, giving you a "dry" print that feels warm to the touch. For a **color laser printer**, the drum gets toner powder in four colors instead of just black.

SCANNERS

Scanners work a lot like our eyes do. Inside the scanner, there is a CCD (charge-coupled device) that's made up of light-sensitive cells. When you press "scan" on your computer, a light bar moves across the object being scanned and that light is reflected to the CCD by a system of mirrors in the scanner. When the light hits the CCD, each cell gives off an electrical signal that corresponds to the strength of the light that hits it. These signals are converted into a binary number and sent to the computer. Darker parts of the scanned object reflect less light and are given lower numbers; brighter areas reflect more light and are given higher numbers.

Software

All of those programs that run on your computer—Photoshop, Word, Instant Messenger— they're software applications. You can add to them, delete them, modify them, and upgrade them. Software is any computer program that provides instructions that let the computer hardware do its job.

SYSTEM SOFTWARE, like Windows or MacOS, has the task of running your computer and allowing you to use it. Your system software is an interface that's made up of all the files, images, windows, and buttons that let you interact with your computer and access all the files and applications stored on it. System software lives on your hard drive, so it can be upgraded from time to time. Your computer can't operate without it, so this is one software application that you definitely don't want to delete!

APPLICATIONS SOFTWARE, like Word and Instant Messenger, gives your computer more to do and tells it how to carry out their specific functions. Applications software lives on your computer's hard drive, so you can add to and delete applications. You don't need applications software to use your computer, but all those programs sure are nice to have!

VIRUSES!

As the name suggests, viruses are bad news for your computer. They can wipe out your files, cause your system to malfunction, and generally wreak havoc. Each time the infected program runs, the virus runs too. It can reproduce (by attaching itself to other programs) and cause all sorts of problems.

Where do viruses come from? Often from e-mail downloads. When an e-mail virus arrives in your inbox, it replicates itself by automatically mailing itself to everyone in your address book. Viruses usually come in the form of attachments, so many people choose to delete e-mails from unknown addresses rather than risk opening them.

> A virus is a small piece of software that latches onto other programs.

Did you know...

Antivirus programs can help protect your computer, but they have to be updated often. New viruses can come along at any moment. If you don't download the updates, antivirus software can't do its job.

Mac logo   Windows logo

FAMOUS VIRUSES

In January of 2004, the Mydoom worm infected about a quarter of a million computers in a single day. In 2000, the ILOVEYOU virus mailed itself all over the world, crashing computers left and right. In March of 1999, the Melissa virus was so tricky that it caused Microsoft to turn off completely their e-mail systems until the virus could be contained.

TIMELINE OF **THE INTERNET**

The Internet didn't happen overnight. It took 14 years to get it up and running as we know it, and it's constantly growing.

1969 THE PENTAGON'S ADVANCED RESEARCH PROJECT AGENCY (ARPA) MAKES AN OPERATIONAL CHAIN OF FOUR COMPUTERS, STATIONED AT UNIVERSITIES TO TRY OUT ARPANET. THEY SEND THE LETTER **L**, AND THEN AN **O**, BUT THE SYSTEM CRASHES WHEN THEY TRY TO SEND A **G**.
(THEY WERE SPELLING "LOGIN.")

1971 THE FIRST E-MAIL, A.K.A. ELECTRONIC MAIL, IS SENT.

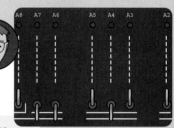

1975 BILL GATES DROPS OUT OF COLLEGE TO DEVELOP A VERSION OF **BASIC** COMPUTER LANGUAGE FOR THE FIRST COMMERCIALLY SUCCESS-FUL COMPUTER, THE "ALTAIR."

1976 APPLE COMPUTER GETS STARTED AS STEVEN WOZNIAK AND STEVE JOBS DEVELOP THE APPLE I COMPUTER.

1977 THE NUMBER OF ONLINE COMPUTERS BREAKS 100.

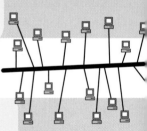

1981 THE IBM PC IS BORN, FEATUR-ING AN OPERATING SYSTEM CALLED MS-DOS, PRESENTED BY THAT BILL GATES GUY AND DEVELOPED BY TIM PATERSON.

1982 THE WORD "INTERNET" IS USED FOR THE FIRST TIME.

1984 APPLE MAKES A CUTE AND INCREDIBLY USER-FRIENDLY COMPUTER CALLED THE MACINTOSH.

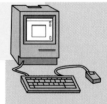

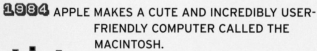

1987 ONE OF THE FIRST COMPUTER VIRUSES SPREADS ACROSS THE SERVERS, FORCING THE ENTIRE INTERNET TO SHUT DOWN FOR 24 HOURS.

1989 AMERICA ONLINE, PRODIGY, AND COMPUSERVE ALL OFFER INTERNET CON-NECTIONS FOR EVERYONE.

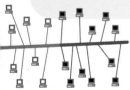

1990 HYPERTEXT TRANSFER PROTOCOL, OR HTTP, IS WRITTEN, CREATING A UNIVERSAL SEARCH-AND-DISPLAY MODE.

1990 IN SWITZERLAND, THE CORPORATION FOR RESEARCH AND EDUCATIONAL NETWORKING (CERN) CREATES THE WORLD WIDE WEB AND THE NUMBER OF SERVERS REACHES 1,236,000.

1994 THE WHITE HOUSE WEB SITE, WWW.WHITEHOUSE.GOV, IS LAUNCHED.

1994 PIZZA HUT TAKES THE FIRST ONLINE PIZZA ORDER.

1994 TWO COLLEGE GUYS NAMED JERRY YANG AND DAVID FILO CREATE AN INTERNET DIRECTORY AND CALL IT "YAHOO."

1998 APPLE COMPUTER CREATES THE IMAC, A COMPUTER DESIGNED FROM THE GROUND UP WITH THE INTERNET IN MIND.

1999 COLLEGE STUDENT SHAWN FANNING INVENTS "NAPSTER," SO THAT INTERNET USERS CAN SHARE AND TRADE MUSIC.

2001 CLOSE TO 10 BILLION E-MAILS FLY ACROSS THE NET EACH DAY!

2004 THE NUMBER OF INTERNET USERS WORLDWIDE IS EXPECTED TO REACH 700-945 MILLION!!

Internet

It's how you send e-mail, chat with friends, do research for school, play games, get your news and information . . . But what exactly *is* the Internet? Well, it's a network that connects computers all over the world so they can communicate with each other.

INTERNET SHORTHAND

Sometimes, it's just too time-consuming for tired fingers to tap out a whole phrase! IM and e-mail users have a short-hand to keep the messages coming and going, quickly!

CRACKING THE CODE:

2dA = today
2moro = tomorrow
b4 = before
bf/gf = boyfriend/girlfriend
bfn = bye for now
btw = by the way
brb = be right back
cm = call me
cul8r = see you later
f2f = face-to-face (in person)
fbi = i'll look into it
gr8 = great
gtg or g2g = gotta go
h2cus = hope to see you soon
idk = i don't know
j4f = just for fun
lol = laughing out loud
pir = parents in room
rotfl = rolling on the floor laughing
ruok = are you OK?
ttyl = talk to you later

HOOKED IN

When you dial up or log on, your computer is joining a network that's already in place. Large groups of computers called servers connect to one another. Our home computers connect to these servers using modems to join the network. This way, we get access to Internet stuff like e-mail and the World Wide Web.

WAYS TO GET THERE:

DIAL-UP uses your normal telephone line to access the Internet at speeds of up to 56 Kbps (kilobits per second). When your modem dials in to your service provider, the computer is connected to the Internet. When you log off, the modem disconnects and your phone line is free.

Did you know...

When it comes to the Internet, cookies have a whole new meaning. A cookie is actually a small file left behind on your computer by an Internet site.

The cookie contains information about you and your interaction with that Web site, like which pages you visited and what your e-mail address is (if you chose to enter it). When you return to that site, it can read the information in the cookie to give you content you'll like, and automatically log you in. Cookies sound like a good thing, but they can decrease the security of your computer. Your browser allows you to choose whether or not to accept cookies, so it's up to you. Just be aware that some sites can't work properly unless you say "yes" to cookies.

ISDN (Integrated Services Digital Network) also uses your phone line to access the Internet. Unlike dial-up, ISDN can reach speeds of up to 128 Kbps.

DSL (Digital Subscriber Line) uses your existing telephone line, but it combines regular phone service and Internet access using a special DSL hub. When you're hooked into DSL, your computer stays connected—there's no dialing-up involved. DSL speeds vary between 126 Kbps and 1.54 Mbps. Telecom companies keep looking for ways to increase the speed of DSL and cable.

CABLE INTERNET uses the same cables that bring you cable TV. The cable is "split" so that you can watch TV and be online at once. A cable modem is connected to your computer, and its average speed is about 708 Kbps (ranging from 500 Kbps to a few megabytes per second). The more people there are in your area using cable, the slower it gets.

A **T-1 line** is from the phone company, but it's not a regular telephone line. T-1 is a dedicated digital line divided into 24 channels. T-1 speeds can reach 1.54 Mbps, depending on the number of computers.

T-3 is the luxury car of Internet connections. It reaches speeds of 44.7 Mbps and is used by big corporations that have a lot of traffic on their servers.

WIRELESS speeds and services vary. Basically, an airport or wireless card inside your computer links up with one of the above networks, like DSL or T-1. ▶▶ FOR

MORE ON WIRELESS INTERNET, SEE P. 168.

COMMUNICATIONS

When it comes to keeping in touch, nothing beats the phone. (Except of course seeing someone face-to-face.) And what about cellphones? Some people don't even bother with landlines anymore. These days, cellphones let you talk, text, send pictures, play games, and even access the Internet!

Regular Phones

Okay, so, we still use them. No service issues, no weird echoes, no speech breaking up... not usually anyway. A traditional phone is actually a pretty simple gadget that changes sound energy into electrical energy, and then back into sound energy.

▲ local exchange

HERE'S HOW IT HAPPENS:

A **hook switch** connects your phone to the **jack** in your home that is linked to a network of wires. When you pick up the **handset**, an electric current flows through the line from your **local exchange**, where your call is routed to its destination. When the exchange is ready to deal with your call, you hear a dial tone.

▶ main exchanges

Each number or symbol on your phone's keypad sends out its own separate electrical signal to the exchange. The local exchange routes your call through a series of main and local exchanges. Before you even hear a ring, the receiving phone gets electrical signals from the local exchange and decodes them. The microphone in the mouthpiece turns the sound waves from your voice into an electric signal that is sent to the phone of the person you're calling. The speaker in their earpiece turns the electric signal from your phone back into sound waves.

▲ local exchanges

A device called a **duplex coil** blocks the sound of your own voice from coming back at you through the speaker. And you get to talk to your friends and family!

165

Cellphones

Cellular phones have a mouthpiece and earpiece like the phone in your house, but they're much more like sophisticated radios than telephones.

HOW CELLPHONES WORK

A **base station** is made up of a radio antenna and electronic equipment. Cellphone signals are sent and received through base stations.

Cellphone companies divide cities into grids of hexagon-shaped **cells**. Each cell is about 10 square miles (16 square km) in size, with a base station in the center.

CAN YOU HEAR ME NOW?

Base stations are connected through a system of exchanges. That's so you can talk to someone outside of your cell. When you cross from one cell to another, your phone connects automatically to that new base station. A base station transmits and receives radio waves. With cellphones, you speak on one channel and listen on another. This is called a duplex channel, and it lets you and the person you're calling talk at the same time.

Since each separate cell has its own base station, frequencies can be reused across the city, as long as two cells that are touching don't use the same frequency.

DIGITAL PHONES

Digital phones improve cellphone technology with much better sound quality, less interference, and the ability to roam farther away—even across the ocean! Digital phones look a lot like regular cellphones, but they work differently. Some digital phones connect to base stations just like the analog cellphone, but then instead of sending and receiving radio waves, they transmit sound information using bits and bytes. Bits and bytes are tiny, so the digital call signals can be compressed a lot—three digital calls can occupy the same channel at once. All-out digital services, like PCS (personal communications systems), have their own network of towers and frequencies. The PCS signal is much clearer, provides better coverage, and reduces the chance of call interference.

FAMOUS FACES: FROM PHONES TO CELLPHONES

Alexander Graham Bell invented the telephone in 1876. The radio was invented by Nikolai Tesla sometime in the 1880s. Cellphones combine these two technologies!

Satellites

How do reporters in remote areas communicate with the outside world? How is it possible to access the Internet in the middle of the desert or figure out your exact location when you're lost on top of a mountain? Orbiting 100 to roughly 22,000 miles (160–35,400 km) above Earth's surface, communications **satellites** can send and receive radio signals with devices such as computers, satellite phones, and Global Positioning System (GPS) receivers, making talking and e-mailing possible just about anywhere with the right gadget.

GPS

Don't leave home without a Global Positioning System (GPS) receiver—especially if you're not exactly sure where you're going.

Twenty-seven GPS satellites orbit about 12,500 miles (20,200 km) above Earth. (Twenty-four are in use, three are for backup.) Each sends out a signal that someone with a GPS receiver can use to determine their latitude, longitude, and altitude at any time. Twenty-four is the magic number for satellites, because at any given time and place, at least four satellites will always be above the horizon. Each GPS satellite transmits a special predetermined code via radio waves. The GPS receiver knows what the code should look like at any given time, so it can use this code to figure out how far away the satellite is.

With a GPS receiver, you can pinpoint your location on Earth at any time, in any place.

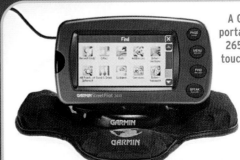

A Garmin portable GPS 2650 with touchscreen

If a child wears this Wherify Wireless GPS watch, his parents can pinpoint his location (to within a few feet) on a Web site.

WHAT'S NEW?

Satellite Phones

Some cellphone services are providing wide coverage by using satellites to transmit signals. This is good news for international users who move from continent to continent on a regular basis. **Mobile cellular phones** first look for service from land-based radio towers; in Europe and the United States, the phone is likely to find a signal. But, if no service is available, a mobile cellphone can switch to satellite operation. Your call is bounced from satellite to satellite until it reaches its destination. This is the way the coverage works in China and Japan.

Wireless Internet

Connect in cafes, at home, and at work—without wires! To make the connection, your computer accesses a signal from a base station (that's the cellphone radio tower). **Wi-Fi** (Wireless Fidelity) is the technology used to bring that signal to you. There are lots of places where you can connect to this service with your laptop, PDA or regular PC, provided they are equipped with an airport or wireless card.

Hotspots are places that offer wireless Internet access. You can take your laptop into any hotspot and get on the Internet, using their wireless signal. Sometimes, buildings and homes are equipped with wireless access, so that you can move from room to room with your computer and always be online.

BLACKBERRY

It's e-mail-on-the-go, mostly used by businesspeople who need to send and receive e-mails constantly. BlackBerry® handhelds are small and compact, giving you full access to e-mail, Web browser, and organizer functions. BlackBerry is also SMS-enabled (SMS stands for Short Messaging Service), which means it can exchange short text messages with other SMS-enabled devices, such as another BlackBerry or an SMS-enabled cellphone. And many BlackBerry models have integrated cellphones. You can access your existing mailbox wherever you are and it's constantly connected as long as a cellphone tower is nearby. At home or at work, BlackBerry allows you to wirelessly connect to your computer and synchronize any changes that were made to your e-mail and calendar while you were out and about.

SCIENCE FAIR PROJECT #11

How Do Magnetic Fields Affect Data on Computer Disks?

Magnets are sometimes used to record information on computer disks. The magnet creates a pattern that can be read later to retrieve the data. Unfortunately, a strong magnet can destroy the magnetic pattern on a disk, and the data that was saved can be lost. In this experiment, you will find out how different types of disks are affected by magnetic fields.

YOU WILL NEED:

◎ Personal computer with floppy disk and CD-ROM drives

◎ Floppy disk

◎ CD-ROM

◎ Magnet (the stronger the better)

WARNING!!! KEEP THE MAGNETS AWAY FROM YOUR COMPUTER AND ALL DISKS THAT ARE NOT PART OF THIS EXPERIMENT!

1. Save files (text files will probably work best) onto the floppy disk. Make a copy of the entire disk on your computer's hard drive. DO NOT USE A DISK THAT HAS VALUABLE DATA ON IT!

2. Save files on a CD-ROM. If your computer cannot save files onto a CD-ROM, try going to a film developing lab—most of them will "print" your pictures on a CD-ROM.

3. Make a copy of the entire CD-ROM on your computer's hard drive. DO NOT USE A DISK THAT HAS VALUABLE DATA ON IT!

4. Bring the floppy disk and the CD-ROM into ANOTHER ROOM. Rub the magnet slowly across the surface of the floppy disk once. Then, rub the magnet slowly across the surface of the CD-ROM once.

5. Bring the disks back to your computer. DO NOT BRING THE MAGNET NEAR YOUR COMPUTER!! Read the data that is on the disks. Compare the quality of the data to the quality before they were exposed to the magnets. Note and record any changes to the data on the disks.

6. Repeat steps 3 and 4 until there are significant changes in the data found on the disks.

◎ Which type of disk is damaged more by magnetic fields?

◎ You can also test how scratching the disk affects the quality of data. Scratch the surface of the disk with a pin or other sharp object. To scratch the surface of the floppy disk, you will need to open the metal shutter that protects the "floppy" part inside, which holds the data. You can even try punching a hole in the floppy disk and drilling a hole in the CD-ROM.

CHAPTER 12

SOUND AND MUSIC

Back in the old days, if you wanted to hear music, you had to go to a concert. Now, you just pop in a CD or download an MP3.

RADIO

Radio Waves

Like light waves, radio waves are part of the electromagnetic spectrum. (◀◀ SEE P. 139 FOR MORE ON THE EM SPECTRUM.) They can travel through space at the speed of light. And they're not just for radios! Radio waves bring us television pictures (▶▶ SEE PP. 192-93), cellphone calls (◀◀ SEE P. 166), and GPS satellite navigation (◀◀ SEE P. 167), to name just a few of the many ways they're used!

WHERE DOES SOUND COME FROM?

It's all in the waves. A sound wave is a chain of vibrating air molecules.

When objects vibrate, their movement causes the air molecules around them to vibrate too. Unlike radio waves, sound waves need to have something to vibrate in order to travel—they can't move through empty space.

Take clashing cymbals: As one cymbal pushes into the air, air molecules are packed tighter, creating a high-pressure area called a compression. When the cymbal pulls back, it creates a low-pressure area called a rarefaction. Put 'em together, and you get a cycle. These cycles form a longitudinal wave.
◀◀ SEE P. 28 FOR INFO ON HOW WE HEAR SOUND.

FREQUENCY Sound waves are measured by their frequency, or cycles per second. Humans can hear sounds from 20-20,000 cycles per second, or Hertz. How loud a sound is depends on the force of the compression, or the amplitude of the wave. A low amplitude produces a quiet sound; a high amplitude means LOUD NOISE! The pitch of a sound comes from the wave's frequency. High frequency waves make high-pitched sounds; low frequency waves make low-pitched sounds.

cymbal

SOUND WAVE

compression
rarefaction
compression

cymbal

compression
rarefaction

WHAT'S NEW? Satellite Radio

On road trips, you lose your favorite radio stations pretty quickly—98.7 FM in Washington, D.C., is not the same station as 98.7 FM in Detroit, Michigan.

Satellite radio, a.k.a. digital radio, is changing all that. Satellite radio signals are beamed from Earth up to satellites in space and then bounced back down to receivers on Earth's surface. Satellite radio signals can reach distances of about 20,000 miles (32,200 km). That means you can pick up a satellite radio station almost anywhere!

I Heard It on the Radio

Since its invention, the radio has enabled rapid communication and brought the world closer together. To get to your ears, radio waves have to make the journey from transmitter to receiver.

TRANSMISSION

Radio waves are made and sent out by a **transmitter**. Here's what goes on to get a wave on its way:

Did you know...

When you speak, your vocal chords vibrate to produce sound waves!

IN THE STUDIO Sound or music is fed into a microphone creating a sound signal to get the whole process rolling.

OSCILLATION Radio waves are generated by an electric circuit (◀◀ SEE P. 147), which oscillates back and forth to make a wave of alternating voltage called a carrier signal. A **carrier signal** wave has a steady frequency and amplitude.

MODULATION At this point, the carrier signal is an electromagnetic wave, with no sound component. In the modulator, the carrier signal gets combined with the **sound signal**, making one sound-carrying radio wave.

AMPLIFICATION The carrier signal is strengthened, increasing its energy so it can travel farther with less chance of interference. The amplified carrier signal is passed on to an **antenna** that broadcasts the signal in the form of radio waves.

RECEPTION The radio you have is actually a radio receiver. As the name suggests, a radio receiver uses an antenna to receive radio waves. and then basically undo all the work that the transmitter did. The receiver changes radio waves back into electric signals, picks out the frequency signal you've chosen, amplifies it, separates the sound signal from the carrier wave, and then sends sound through to the speakers.

AM radio waves

FM radio waves

AM/FM These are two different types of modulation. A carrier signal is steady, but the sound signal is not. Think about it— voices and music are loud, soft, mid-range... all over the place! For AM (amplitude modulation), the sound signal varies the carrier wave's amplitude, but keeps the frequency the same. In FM (frequency modulation), the sound signal varies the carrier wave's frequency, keeping the amplitude the same.

RECORDING AND PLAYING SOUND

In order to play a tape, CD, or MP3 file, you first have to record sound into a microphone.

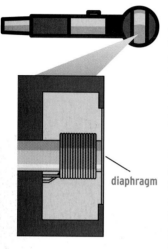

diaphragm

A **MICROPHONE** converts sound vibrations into electronic signals. There are lots of different kinds of microphones that do this in different ways. One of the most common types is the **dynamic** microphone. Inside a dynamic microphone's head, there's a very sensitive membrane, called a **diaphragm**). The diaphragm is attached to a metal coil inside a **magnetic field**.

When sound waves strike the diaphragm, it moves, and so does the coil. The coil's movement inside the magnet creates a small electric current. (◀◀ **FOR INFO ON ELECTROMAGNETISM, SEE P. 151.**) Tiny changes in the current reflect changes in the sound waves hitting the microphone. Since a particular electric current change corresponds to a particular change in sound, the current sent out by a microphone can be turned back into sound by a speaker.

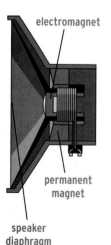

electromagnet

permanent magnet

speaker diaphragm

A **SPEAKER** works like a microphone in reverse, converting an electric signal into sound. If you look at the front of a speaker, you'll see a large cone, or diaphragm. This is just like the one in a microphone but much bigger. The back of the diaphragm is attached to an electromagnet. The electromagnet is surrounded by a doughnut-shaped, permanent magnet.

The way these two magnets interact with each other is the basis for how a speaker creates sound. A music playback device (CD player, record player, etc.) sends an electric current to the speaker's electromagnetic coil. Changes in the current cause the electromagnet's field strength to vary. Whenever the electromagnet's strength changes, it reacts with movement to the permanent magnet surrounding it. This movement causes the diaphragm to move too. The diaphragm's movement pushes air, which creates sound.

RECORDING: ANALOG AND DIGITAL

Analog and digital recording are two different ways to capture sound. Analog sound recording stores a complete sound wave. Digital recording stores parts of a sound wave. These parts are called "samples." Each method has advantages and disadvantages for producing recordings with the highest possible FIDELITY.

Fidelity is how close a recording comes to the original sound.

Analog Recording

The earliest analog recording machines captured sound by reproducing sound waves onto a solid object. Let's look at a vinyl record as an example.

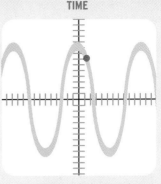

TIME

FREQUENCY

▲ Analog data is recorded as one smooth, continuous stream. The red circle represents one point in that stream.

VINYL RECORDS

A microphone picks up a sound and converts it into an electric signal. This signal is sent to a special speaker that has a needle instead of a diaphragm. The needle's point touches a spinning disc of warmed vinyl. Electric signals coming into the speaker's electromagnet cause the needle to move, which carves a physical representation of the sound wave into the vinyl.

A record player is just the opposite of the device that records the discs in the first place. A needle travels along the record's groove. This needle is attached to an electromagnet that is suspended in a permanent magnetic field. As the needle travels along the record groove, its movements vibrate the electromagnetic coil. The variations in distance between the coil and the permanent magnet create a current in the coil. This current is amplified and then sent to the speakers.

MAGNETIC TAPE

Another way to encode analog sound is onto magnetic tape. Magnetic tape is just a strip of plastic with an iron-oxide dust attached to its surface. Because it contains iron, this dust is magnetic. But unlike a paper clip or iron filings, the dust stays magnetized after you take the magnet away.

▼ An electric current magnetizes the iron coating on the tape.

Just as with a vinyl record, it all starts with a microphone which picks up a sound and converts it into an electric signal. This signal is sent to the tape recorder's **head**, a circular electromagnet with a small gap between its poles. Changes in the electric current create changes in the strength and polarity of the electromagnetic field. As the tape flows past the head, these changes are permanently recorded into its magnetic iron coating. ◀◀ FOR INFO ON ELECTROMAGNETISM, SEE P. 151.

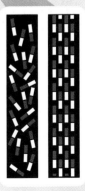

Digital Recording

There are tons of different formats for digital music, including CDs, MP3s, and DATs (digital audio tapes), to name just a few. But unlike with analog formats, all digital music is recorded in the same basic way: by converting sound waves into bytes (◀◀ FOR MORE ON BYTES, SEE PP. 156-57). The machine that does this is called an analog-to-digital converter, or ADC.

Just like analog recording, digital recording all starts with a microphone (◀◀ FOR INFO ON MICROPHONES, SEE P. 174). The microphone's analog electric signal is fed into the ADC. The ADC looks at the signal and stores samples of the analog wave as numbers. So what's a sample? It's just a number representing the frequency of a sound wave at any given point over time.

There are two factors that affect the fidelity of a digital recording: sampling rate and sampling precision.

The **sampling rate** is simply the number of samples taken per second. CD-quality sound takes 44,100 samples per second!

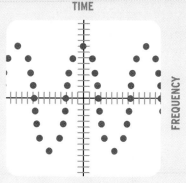

▲ Digital recording is not made up of one continuous sound stream. It is a series of individual sounds.

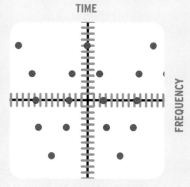

▲ Compared with the diagram above, this sample contains fewer points of information and is less precise so will not sound as rich.

Sampling precision refers to how fine a measurement each sample is. CD-quality recordings have a sampling precision of 65,536! That's like having 65,536 different colors to use in a drawing.

MP3s

An MP3 is just a smaller, "compressed" version of a CD-quality song file. The average song in CD format takes up about 30 megabytes (MB). An MP3 of the same song is only about 3 MB.

That's 10 times smaller than the CD version. Even though it contains 10 times less information, MP3 sounds very close to CD quality. That's because MP3s are made using **perceptual noise-shaping algorithms**. In plain English, that's just a computer program for erasing sound information that's unde-tectable to most human ears. A little bit of sound quality is lost when you convert from CD quality to MP3, but for many people, it's worth it. Your 1,000-song MP3 player could carry only about 100 CD-quality files!

CDs

The average CD can store 74 minutes of music, or 783 MB. How do they fit all that information on one 4.7–inch (12 cm) disc?

INSIDE A CD CDs start off as a simple piece of plastic. Digital music files (made up of millions of bytes) are stored on the plastic as a series of tiny bumps that spiral out from the center. The bumps are only 5 mm (5 millionths of a meter) wide! Remember that bytes can be broken down into patterns of ones and zeros. On a CD, zeros are stored as bumps, and ones are stored as flat areas. A thin sheet of aluminum is laid over the bumpy side of the plastic and coated with a layer of acrylic.

HOW CD PLAYERS READ CDs A CD player spins a disc around at up to 500 revolutions per minute. As the disc spins, the CD player's laser focuses a beam onto the disc's spiral track of microscopic bumps. Remember that the track is coated in aluminum, so it reflects the beam. The bumps reflect the beam much less than the spaces between. A special light-detection device can tell whether the laser is hitting a bump or not. It reads the flat areas as ones and the bumps as zeros. These numbers are assembled as bytes. The bytes are sent to a digital-to-analog converter (DAC), which turns bytes back into an analog music signal. ◀◀ FOR MORE ON BYTES, SEE PP. 156-57.

A laser in your CD player reads the bumps on the CD's surface.

1001001101

An **MP3 player** contains a decoder algorithm that reads the encoded file that an MP3 recorder creates. The bytes are then put through a DAC, and the resulting analog signal is sent through an **amplifier**. This boosts the amplitude (volume) of the signal. Finally, the signal is sent to the head-phones, which are just tiny versions of speakers (◀◀ FOR INFO ON HOW SPEAKERS WORK, SEE P. 174).

Some MP3 players store music using **flash memory**, which is contained on a microchip. The advantage of these players is that they are small and rugged. The disadvantage is that they can't hold that many songs. MP3 players that have hard drives, like Apple's iPod, are more fragile, but they can store lots more music.

▲ iPod, an MP3 player

DEBATE: MP3 downloads

Web sites like Emusic, MP3.com, and Kazaa have made it easy to download free music from the Web. This gives MP3 users a lot of options, and free options at that, but is it morally wrong and illegal to download music from these sites? Some say, yes. Record companies and music artists are not happy about the fact that their copyrighted music is being acquired for free. Why should people buy CDs when the music is free online? The record companies and artists are worried about losing money, and control of their product. So far, the law has come down on their side: in 2001, Napster was successfully sued by the Recording Industry Association of America (RIAA) to stop the transfer of copyrighted music over their network. And these days, it's not uncommon to read about individual file swappers getting sued by big record companies—and some of these users are as young as 12!

Supporters of file sharing argue that trading MP3s is no different from burning (see box below) one of your friends a music mix from your collection or making a copy of your favorite new CD. It's just that you've got thousands of friends' music collections to choose from all of a sudden. Thinking realistically, some record companies and computer makers have come up with ways to compromise. Apple's iTunes allows users to download tracks from its online store for 99 cents each. Those tracks can be burned to CD up to 100 times by the user. And after a few years out of service, Napster is back, offering music files again for a fee.

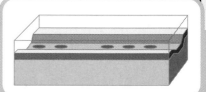

▲ CD-R surface

BURNING CDs

Most computers come with a CD-R or CD-RW drive, which lets you burn files, including MP3s, to a CD. But you can't just put any old CD in there and start recording. You have to use CD-Rs or CD-RWs. A CD-R (recordable CD) is a special type of disc that contains one more layer than a normal CD (◄◄ FOR INFO ON CDs, SEE P. 177). Above the reflective aluminum layer, there is a layer of dye. This dye is transparent, so the laser of a CD player can shine through it. A CD-R drive contains two different lasers: a read laser for playing CDs and a write laser for burning them. The write laser is much stronger. When you burn a CD-R, the write laser heats up parts of the dye and makes them opaque (not transparent). These opaque parts are unreflective, and act like the bumps on a normal CD.

A CD-RW (rewritable CD) contains a type of dye that can be turned from transparent to opaque, and from opaque back to transparent. The dye turns opaque when it's heated to one temperature, and turns transparent again when it's heated to another temperature. CD-RW drives have a write laser that can change temperature, so it can make the dye transparent or opaque as needed.

MOVIE SOUND

The movie industry has developed its own unique methods for getting sound onto film. The first "talking pictures" were introduced in the late 1920s, and they used an innovative optical sound encoding system—a thin, opaque strip along the film's edge. Within that strip is a clear line that varies in width. As the film moves along, a light in the projector reads this strip of sound and sends an electrical signal to the speakers.

Dolby Laboratories, RCA, and Eastman Kodak collaborated in the early '70s to bring stereo sound to optical soundtracks. Their technique was simple: in the space originally occupied by a single optical soundtrack, they placed two tracks, one for the left speaker and one for the right. In the late '70s, Dolby introduced optical surround sound. Surround sound uses two optical soundtracks to encode four tracks of sound: left, right, center, and rear. It's all in how the signals are interpreted by a special program. If the two soundtracks are identical, the sound signal is sent to the center speakers. If the two tracks are different, the signal is sent to the left and right stereo speakers. If the two tracks are out of phase (meaning they're not lined up), the signal is sent to the left, right, and rear speakers—surround sound!

Dolby Digital was introduced in 1992. It's an optical sound system, but encoded digitally as black dots representing ones and zeros. Dolby's digital reader interprets the black dots as ones and the clear parts as zeros. The binary code is actually encoded sound!

soundtracks

WHAT'S NEW?

Yamaha MusicCAST

Listening to music while you shower used to mean lugging a boom box into the bathroom. Now you can have music anywhere in your house, without stringing hundreds of feet of speaker wire. The Yamaha MusicCAST system has an 80GB hard drive, enough to store 1,000 hours of MP3 music. But here's the really cool part: it can beam the music to wireless speakers in any room in your home! Get a couple of small, wireless speakers, and you can take your music anyplace in your house.

WHAT'S NEXT?

FMD-ROM

If you're impressed with how many MP3s you can fit on your CD-Rs, check this out: in the next few years, special new discs may store up to 1 terabyte of data. That's 1 trillion bytes! Regular CDs store information only on their surfaces. The next generation is the Fluorescent Multilayer Disc (FMD-ROM), and it can store many layers of information on top of each other. The discs are clear, so a laser reading one of them can focus on one layer of information, while ignoring others. It's expected that eventually these discs will contain 100 layers of information—that's enough to store a terabyte of data and that means about 330,000 MP3s! ◀◀ FOR INFO ON CDs, SEE P. 177.

EXPERIMENT with Bob the Ex-Lab-Rat

MAKE YOUR OWN MUSIC

Musical instruments make sound by vibrating air–different amounts of air can make different sounds. You can make your own instrument and see how it works.

YOU WILL NEED:

• 5 glass bottles
• a pitcher of water
• food coloring

STEP 1 Drop some food coloring into the water so that it's tinted.

STEP 2 Line the bottles up in a row and pour the colored water into each bottle in graduated amounts so that the first bottle contains just a bit of water and the last one is almost full.

STEP 3 Blow across the top of a bottle. Now do the next one.

Do you notice a difference in the sounds? Blow across the whole line of bottles and see how that sounds. Try blowing across them in a random order and see if you can make some music!

SCIENCE FAIR PROJECT #12

Many people believe that listening to certain types of music can help you do better on tests. In this experiment, find out if it's really true!

YOU WILL NEED:

- ◎ At least 25 volunteers
- ◎ Recordings of different types of music
- ◎ CD or cassette player
- ◎ Copies of arithmetic problems for each volunteer

1. Write three different "tests" of arithmetic problems. Each test should be different, but should use the same type of problem (for example, multiplying 2-digit numbers by 1-digit numbers). Use 20 questions for each test. Label the tests A, B, and C.

2. Give each volunteer one of the tests. Make sure that some people have test A, some have test B, and some have test C. Have your volunteers finish the test without any music playing. Give them a time limit (10 minutes should be good).

3. Give each volunteer a test they haven't taken yet. Have your volunteers finish the second test while you play relaxing music. Give them the same time limit you used for the first test.

4. Give each volunteer a test they haven't taken yet. Have your volunteers finish the third test while you play loud, fast music. Give them the same time limit you used for the first test.

5. Grade the tests. Find the average score for your volunteers for each kind of music played.

◎ Compare the scores for your volunteers for each type of music. Which music helped them to do the best on the tests?

◎ You can try similar experiments by having your volunteers finish puzzles and timing how long it takes them to finish.

CHAPTER 13

PICTURES AND MOVING IMAGES

DVD, HDTV, digital cameras, special effects. They bring us our favorite movies and TV shows. But before there was digital, there was analog. Since pictures hit the big screen, we have demanded more—crisper sound, more realistic animation, instant pictures. See where visual entertainment came from and where it's going!

PICTURES

When visible light hits objects, most of it bounces off. Your eyes catch this reflected light and send information to your brain, and the brain tells you what you're looking at and what color it is! Your brain processes images the same way no matter what you're looking at. But the way images are captured and presented to you, as still photos, moving pictures, television broadcasts, animation, video, computer graphics, special effects, that's another story altogether.

ANALOG AND DIGITAL

What's the difference between videotape and a DVD? Okay, they look different, but the main difference is that the videotape is an analog way to store information and the DVD is a digital way. Analog media, like tapes, store an electronic version of sounds or images; digital media, like the DVD, convert analog information into bits and bytes. ◀◀ FOR MORE ON BITS AND BYTES, SEE PP. 156–57.

There are pluses and minuses to both analog and digital formats, but digital has a leg up—it's computer-ready, and we are increasingly reliant on our machines! Digital files can be compressed (shrunk) to very small sizes and they can be read directly by a computer.

▲ light enters the camera through the lens

▲ shutter closed

Photography: The Analog Way

It's easy to forget where we came from. Up until a few years ago, it was more common to take a roll of film to a lab for development than it was to download a photo. **Film is plastic coated with a layer of emulsion containing silver salt crystals that react chemically when they're exposed to light.** The traditional photography and film processes are still relevant—we haven't totally converted yet. And even when we do, film has its own look and feel that is not easy to duplicate.

MOVIES ON BRAINPOP.COM

STILL PHOTOS

Taking a black-and-white picture is a pretty simple process—you insert film into a camera, point the camera at your subject, and press a button that opens the shutter; light floods in to expose the film emulsion. If it's dark, light from a flash on your camera might help out. Then you have to get the film developed and have the picture printed.

EXPOSURE How much light gets through to the film is determined by your shutter speed (how long the shutter stays open when you "click")

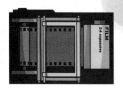

▲ shutter open, the film is exposed

Did you know...

Color film has three layers of emulsion—one sensitive to blue light, one to green, one to red. These three colors can be combined in different proportions to form any color in the world!

and the aperature of your lens (how wide the opening is). On a fully manual camera, you get to decide these things. Automatic cameras take care of the work for you. When light hits the emulsion, it causes a chemical change—the silver salts react and darken. The more light that hits the film, the darker it gets. The film is forming a negative image—the darker something is on your negative, the brighter it will be on your print!

DEVELOPMENT Expose a roll of film to light right when it's out of the camera and the whole thing will turn black in a matter of seconds. The emulsion is still ready to react. Development seals the deal—it washes away the unexposed emulsion and fixes the image into place. You're left with a dry negative.

PRINTING Printing is exposure all over again, but this time you're exposing paper coated with its own emulsion to light that is being shined through your negative.

HOW DOES THE IMAGE COME OUT LOOKING NORMAL? Well, the darkest parts of the negative (those were the lightest ones to begin with) let the least amount of light through to the paper's emulsion. So the most exposed parts of the film correspond to the least exposed parts of the paper, making your print look just like the original mix of light/dark! Just like film, photo paper is light sensitive. It has to be developed, and the image has to be fixed with chemicals in a dark space before it can be exposed to light.

Photography: **The Digital Way**

The camera may look similar—there's a lens, a flash, a shutter. But looks can be deceiving. There's no film on the inside, and with most digital cameras, there's no need even to look through a viewfinder—you can see your subject in a little screen on the camera's back! **A digital camera is really a camera with a computer right inside of it.** Since it doesn't need to house film and all the parts that move the film along, a digital camera can be really tiny. Some are nearly as thin as a credit card, or even built into your cellphone!

WHERE'S THE PICTURE?

Instead of exposing film, a digital camera converts the light waves bouncing off your subject into bits and bytes (◄◄ FOR MORE ON BITS AND BYTES, SEE PP. 156-57), and stores them as a computer does. A cable connects the camera to your computer so that images may be downloaded and saved to your computer, e-mailed to friends, uploaded to Web sites, or burned to CD. Photo-editing software helps you make changes to your images and prepares them for printing if you want a hard copy.

WHAT'S WITH RESOLUTION?

Digital images are made up of tiny dots called pixels. The resolution of an image, how much information is in it, is stated in megapixels (1,000,000 pixels = 1 megapixel). Digital cameras are measured by their megapixel capability—the higher the megapixel number, the more detail the camera will capture when you click and the sharper and richer the image will be.

MOVING IMAGES

Since 1895, when the Lumiere brothers sent a train barreling towards the audience with their "horror" flick, *Arrival of a Train at a Station*, movies have been messing with our sense of reality. And with technology like Imax and computerized special effects, they just keep getting reel-er!

Movies: The Analog Way

A moving picture is actually a series of still images that we see projected quickly enough that it fools our brains into thinking we are watching continuous movement. If a movie projector gets jammed while it's on, you see a still image on the screen—one **frame** of the filmstrip.

Persistence of vision is what makes the motion work. Our eyes sort of hang on to each still image until the next one arrives. When the still images move at 24 frames per second, our eyes see that as normal motion.

▲ Our brains hang on to still images so that we see continuous motion.

SHOOTING FILM

The film exposure and development process for moving images is the same as for still photos—filmstrips are just rolls of emulsion-coated plastic. Film is exposed, making a negative image, and developed to produce a positive image.

IN CAMERA Movie cameras have a motor that moves the film past the shutter. The motor's speed can be adjusted depending on the effect that's desired. A speed of 24 frames per second produces normal motion. Anything slower than that, say 12 frames per second, will be jerky, anything faster will deliver more detail and more closely match real life.

PROJECTING FILM

Projectors shine light through the positive film images, making them show up on a screen. The projector has a motor just like the movie camera. It also shows 24 frames per second, but the difference is that each individual picture is flashed twice so that our eyes don't see a flicker.

ANALOG VIDEO

There are still VHS tapes at your video store, but they may not be around much longer. With the superior quality of DVDs, videotapes may be a thing of the past pretty soon. The same goes for analog video cameras. Regular old video doesn't have the elegance of film or the computer compatibility and quality of digital video. For now, analog video is cheaper than digital (part of why it's still around), but that too will change in time!

SYNCING SOUND AND PICTURE

A movie's sound is recorded onto tape or digitally during shooting using separate microphones then added to the picture track. There are several ways that sound and picture can be brought together.
◄◄ FOR INFO ON DOLBY SOUND, SEE P. 179.

IMAX

Bigger is better. Imax (Image Maximum) theaters have enormous, larger-than-life screens that can be nearly 100 feet (30 m) high! Then there's the **Imax dome**, a rounded screen that literally surrounds you. A picture that big brings with it an overwhelming feeling—some people literally become nauseated by the motion of an Imax movie! Add to that the fact that some Imax screens display a 3-D image with six channels of sound, maybe more, and you're in for a whole new kind of picture!

HOW IMAX DOES IT

Extensive CG (computer graphics) work goes into building an Imax image. To make an image that big that's also sharp, you need a mighty big piece of film. Imax film is almost 10 times the size of the 35mm version you're used to seeing. The camera used to shoot Imax film is BIG, way too heavy for one person to hold. Then there's the issue of projection. Imax projectors are the most powerful in the world. And the Imax digital surround sound system delivers sound to the audience through tiny holes in the image screen. So the sound appears to be coming out of the picture!

TALKING PICTURES

What would it be like to watch a movie without any sound? When movies were first shown, they were silent, sort of. Some had music to accompany them, others had a commentator who read out what the characters were saying as people watched, and then subtitles were written across the bottom of the screen to give the characters words. All that changed when sound and picture were synced, playing at the same time so that characters could speak for themselves.

Movies: The Digital Way

Just like digital cameras, digital video cameras store images in binary code. DV (digital video) makes it cheaper and easier to capture moving images. You might even have a DV camera at home. DV does not look quite like film, but it's slowly making its way into movie theaters. In 2002, we got *Star Wars: Episode II, the Attack of the Clones*, the first big–budget studio feature shot entirely on DV! It doesn't look like film yet, but there are ways to make it come close!

SHOOTING DV

Most of the DV cameras you see are actually mini-DV cameras that record information onto digital cassette tapes. Video is shot at 29.97 frames per second. That's faster than the 24 frames per second we're used to seeing with film, and it makes a big difference in the way the image looks. DV images are created by interlacing, the way an image is formed on your TV screen. With interlacing, each frame of video is actually two sets of lines, scanned alternately so that they fit together to form a complete image.

▶▶ SEE PP. 192–93 FOR MORE ON TV.

DV is actually a lot sharper looking than film—there's none of the familiar blur and waviness that we're used to with movies.

▲ Sony Mavica, a digital video camera

DVD

DVDs (digital video discs) are a lot more like CDs (◄◄ SEE P. 177) than the VHS tapes they're replacing. That said, DVDs hold about seven times the information of CDs, making room for fun extras like commentary, cut scenes, and subtitles.

▲ CDs and DVDs look the same on the surface.

WHAT'S INSIDE DVDs are made mostly of plastic. As with a CD, the bits and bytes that make up the DVD image are stored as bumps on a spiral track of data. A laser beam in your DVD player moves across the disk, reading the bumps.

SO HOW DOES SOMETHING THE SAME SIZE HOLD SO MUCH MORE? The DVD player uses a thinner laser than the CD player, so the bumps on a DVD are smaller and closer together. That means more information stored in the same amount of space! And that's not all. There are dual-layer DVDs that hold up to 8 hours of footage!

▲ portable DVD player

MPEG2 COMPRESSION In another space-saving measure, DVD video is compressed using MPEG-2 software. Like MPEG-3 (MP3) for music, MPEG-2 shrinks the size of the video by only paying attention to the changes from one frame to the next. So if a person is standing in front of a stack of books and then takes a seat, MPEG-2 leaves the books alone and just adds in the new action.

> **LOOKS LIKE FILM...**
> There are exceptions to the 29.97 frames per second standard. Some DV cameras have the ability to shoot progressively, at 24 frames per second. A camera on its progressive setting acts like a film camera, shooting frame by frame without interlacing the image. The result is DV footage that looks a lot more like film.

Digital Video on-the-go

Watch DV anytime, anywhere, on your own portable player! It's like an MP3 player, but with video play capabilities added to the mix. Portable video players record and play back a compressed video format called MPEG-4. Like MP3 for music, MPEG-4 software compresses video files into a format that's small enough to carry, or, rather, fit on something you carry. It's not quite as easy as popping in your favorite DVD, but we're getting there. (First, you'd have to convert the DVD to the MPEG-4 format using software). And of course you can also store photos and music on your handheld video player—it's basically a mini–hard drive after all!

WHAT'S NEXT? The Blue Laser Disc

Blue-laser video players are coming along that will hold 3–5 times the content of your average DVD. The key is all in the color—of the laser, that is. Lasers used to read and write information on DVDs are normally red. The wavelength of the laser light determines how big a mark it makes on the disc and therefore how much data can fit. Blue light has a shorter wavelength than red light—the shorter the wavelength, the smaller the light spot on the disc's surface, and the more storage space on the disc. Hurray for blue!

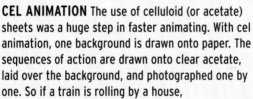

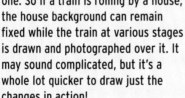
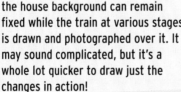

Gollum in *Lord of the Rings*, Shrek and Donkey. Animation has come a long way since the days of Mickey Mouse, when images were drawn frame by frame and painstakingly photographed with a **stop–motion film camera** (a film camera that can shoot one frame at a time). These days, some animated films are created entirely on computers. Others mix the traditional film medium with the new technology.

Animation: The Analog Way

A film camera records a series of images, one per frame. When they're projected one after the other, it looks like the image is moving.

INK ON PAPER

When animation began, every frame of the movie had to be drawn on a separate piece of paper, and then photographed one at a time by the camera. It was slow going—at 24 frames per second, 10 seconds of animation required 240 different pictures!

CEL ANIMATION The use of celluloid (or acetate) sheets was a huge step in faster animating. With cel animation, one background is drawn onto paper. The sequences of action are drawn onto clear acetate, laid over the background, and photographed one by one. So if a train is rolling by a house, the house background can remain fixed while the train at various stages is drawn and photographed over it. It may sound complicated, but it's a whole lot quicker to draw just the changes in action!

▶ The car's position changes, the house remains fixed.

Animation: The Digital Way

Computers have pretty much taken over animation land. With their speed and ease of use, it's hard for traditional animation to compete.

COMPUTER-ASSISTED ANIMATION

When the traditional animation process is moved to a computer, it becomes faster and easier. The need for photographing cels is gone, and there doesn't have to be a camera involved at any stage of the game. All of the usual drawing work can be done within layers of a computer program rather than layers of acetate. These virtual layers are eventually sandwiched together and then recorded to a strip of film, viewed online, or burned to a CD or DVD.

▲ In this sequence, only Moby's arm and the bowling bowl change position and therefore require re-drawing.

3-D GRAPHICS ANIMATION

Ever wonder how games like **Final Fantasy** manage to look so realistic? A lot of the 3-D animation you see in movies and video games is done with the help of sophisticated computer programs. Animators build realistic characters and scenery out of millions of polygons. The more shapes you use to create, say, a face, the smoother and more realistic that face will be. The 3-D animation programs also help create realistic surfaces, lighting effects, and depth. Without this software, your favorite PlayStation game would be a lot more boring.

▲ The addition of polygons creates greater detail.

BLUE SCREEN

Ever wonder how Superman flew through the air in the days before computerized animation? They shot him lying on sort of a shelf, arms outstretched, in a completely blue room. He probably looked pretty silly, but the bright blue color could later be separated from the figure and placed against an actual background—the city, the sky, outer space. Blue screen is still used to create special effects.

Did you know...

Live-action animation is when humans look like they're interacting with an animated character. It's a trick! For movies like **Lord of the Rings** and **Scooby-Doo**, actual live people stood in for Gollum and Scooby. The animated creatures were added later on.

WEB ANIMATION

These days, a Web site is hardly a Web site without some animation. But moving images take up more storage space than still ones, so how do they manage to load quickly over the Internet? A full-size animated movie like **Shrek** would take forever to stream, even with broadband. That's why Web sites use special Web animation programs, like Macromedia Flash. These applications compress animation to a size that's manageable over the Internet. Flash does this by "tweening" where the animator sets a start point and an end point for an image's movement and the software figures out the motion in between. This means the animation can contain fewer actual images, cutting down on file size. The animation created by programs like Flash is still basic compared with 3-D animation. But software designers are working on new programs that will put 3-D animation all over the Web!

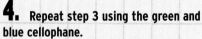

How Can Colored Filters Affect a Black-and-White Photograph?

Photographers often use colored filters when they take black-and-white pictures in order to change the way the pictures look. When the filter blocks a color of light from entering the camera, that part of the picture looks black. If the filter lets a color of light in, that part of the picture looks white. If a photographer knows how the filters will affect the picture, they can make the picture look exactly how they want it. In this project, you will learn how colored filters affect black-and-white pictures.

YOU WILL NEED:

- Digital camera with a black-and-white setting
- Pieces of colored cellophane (red, green, and blue at least)

1. A digital camera is best for this project. You can use a regular camera with black-and-white film, but you may waste a lot of film with pictures that don't come out quite right. Your school may have a camera that you can borrow or use with a teacher's supervision.

2. On a bright sunny day, take a color picture without any filters. Try to include lots of blue (sky) and green (trees or grass) in the picture. Include as many other colors (like red) as you can.

3. Hold a piece of red cellophane in front of the camera lens. You may need a double layer of cellophane. Be sure that your fingers do not block the lens. Take a color picture of the same scene using this red filter. Be sure to record the filter you used and the picture number in a journal.

4. Repeat step 3 using the green and blue cellophane.

5. Repeat steps 2 through 5 using the black-and-white setting on the camera.

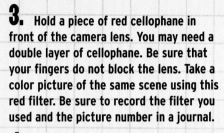

Compare the black-and-white pictures you took with the original color picture. Which colors looked black with each filter? Which colors looked white with each filter?

Many digital cameras include a histogram function. The histogram makes a graph that shows how much of each color of light reaches the camera. Compare the histograms when different filters are used. How does each filter affect the kind of light that enters the camera?

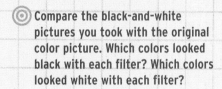

Take pictures of other scenes that contain other colors to see if the filters have the same effect. Try other colors of filters to see how they change the way your black-and-white pictures look.

Television

The TV programming you see on your screen starts off as film or tape in a camera. TV is normally shot on video tape—some of it is prerecorded, while other programming, like the news, is live feed. But how does TV programming get to you? The TV in your home receives signals over cable, satellite, maybe even still an antenna. Your TV has to read those signals, put a picture together, and reproduce sound. Here's how it's done:

MOVIES ON
BRAINPOP.COM

TV: The Analog Way

TRANSMISSION TV cameras turn the images they record into rows of tiny dots called **pixels**. Every pixel has a color and brightness. The video signal that gets sent to your TV is a combination of the pixel information and **horizontal and vertical sync**, so the TV knows how to arrange the pixels. The sound signal is separate, as is the synchronization information that tells the TV how to match up the sound with the picture. Video signals are broadcast as radio waves by a TV tower.

RECEIVING Analog TV can come to your home by antenna, cable, or satellite. When you pick a channel on your TV, the tuner selects the signal with the right frequency for that channel. A TV receives the video signal and breaks it down into its parts—the sound and synchronization signals are separated from the picture signal.

MAKING THE PICTURE COME TOGETHER The screen of a TV, like a computer screen, is made up of **pixels**. A **chrominance decoder** separates the picture signal into red, green, and blue light. These three color signals are sent to the **cathode ray tube**, or CRT. On the inside of your TV, the CRT scans red, green, or blue electron beams across a metal screen called a **shadow mask**. The TV screen is coated with strips of light-sensitive phosphors that light up red, green, or blue. The red electron beam

hits red phosphors to make them light up and so on with the green and the blue. Combinations of lit phosphors can create colors other than red, green, and blue. But every color you see on your TV is a combination of these three colors. Your screen is scanned in lines—first the odd-numbered lines, and then the even-numbered lines. This is called **interlacing**.

▲ Interlacing

SYNCING The sync signal ensures that the picture and sound stay in time.

ADDING SOUND The sound signal is fed out through the TV speakers.

TV: The Digital Way

Digital cable and digital satellite systems work with your existing TV. These services use the analog method of capturing an image and reproducing it; the difference is that the analog video signal is converted to digital format before it is sent. When your TV's digital box receives the signal, it has to convert it back to analog so the regular TV set can display it. Digitizing and compressing a regular analog signal, like digital cable and satellite companies do, lets them fit up to four channels in the space as one analog channel.

HDTV (high-definition television) is a whole different story. This is a fully digital TV system that gives you the best picture and sound quality of any TV around. The picture on an HDTV has a much higher resolution than the one we're used to—it displays up to 2 million pixels! That's 10 times what you get with a regular TV.

How does an HDTV signal fit so much more information into the same space as an analog TV signal? By using a compression technology called MPEG-2. The MPEG-2 software starts off by recording just enough of the picture to make your eyes see it as whole. Your brain fills in the rest and is fooled into thinking nothing's missing. In the next frame, the software only changes the parts of the image that have moved, leaving the rest of the image alone. So if someone stands up at a table, it would record that movement change, but not the rest of the room. A digital TV decodes the MPEG-2 signal and displays it in the same way that a computer monitor does.

CHAPTER 14

GETTING AROUND

Planning a trip? Two hundred years ago, traveling meant hopping on a horse-drawn stagecoach! Thanks to plenty of work by inventors and engineers, moving around is much less complicated these days. Planes, trains, and automobiles make it a whole lot easier to get where you're going.

NX-74205

195

ENGINES AND TRANSPORTATION

What's up under the hood? It's more than just a whole mess of metal. There are different engines that serve many different purposes. The one in your car is an internal combustion engine.

Internal Combustion Engines

They're not that complicated. Basically, in an internal combustion engine, the combustion or explosion that powers the car happens on the inside of the engine. Of all the internal combustion engines, the one we see most often is the **reciprocating, four-stroke, spark-ignition gasoline engine**. That's quite a mouthful. The key to this engine is a cylinder that contains a piston. The engine follows a cycle of four movements (strokes) that work by burning gasoline and air inside a closed cylinder. When gasoline is burned, it expands and builds pressure inside the cylinder. This explosive pressure forces the piston down and provides the energy for the wheels to turn.

◀ Lift the hood of a car and you'll find the engine, battery, oil container, and most of the other parts that make the car run!

Did you know...

Engine exhaust is bad for our environment. That's why cars have a device called a catalytic converter that changes exhaust gases like carbon monoxide into less harmful gases like carbon dioxide.

Diesel Engines

A diesel engine is an internal combustion engine that works without a spark plug. Inside its cylinder, the rising piston compresses the air so that it gets really hot. Diesel fuel is injected into the cylinder, and the hot air causes the fuel to ignite. So the compression itself creates the ignition. Diesel fuel requires less refining, but it also pollutes more. The diesel engine can create a lot of power. That's why a diesel engine is often used to move heavier vehicles like buses, trucks, and tractors.

THE DEAL WITH DRIVING

When you turn on a car by turning the key in the ignition, the ignition system tells the engine to get started. Here's how a cylinder in a four-stroke engine works:

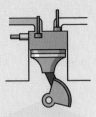 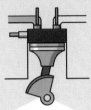 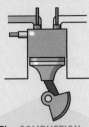 

Engine at rest.

The engine begins with the INTAKE STROKE. The intake valve on the cylinder opens up, and the piston moves down to let the engine take in a big gulp of air and fuel.

In the COMPRESSION STROKE, the piston moves back up to compress this fuel and air mixture while both the valves are closed. This makes for a powerful explosion.

The COMBUSTION STROKE happens when the piston reaches the top of its upward stroke. The spark plug makes a spark to light the fuel on fire and the gasoline in the cylinder explodes, pushing the piston down again.

The EXHAUST STROKE is the final action in this cycle. The piston moves back up again, and the exhaust valve opens to get rid of the burned fuel left over from the explosion. The exhaust gets pushed out of the cylinder and through the tailpipe.

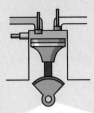

This whole process moves the piston up and down again and again, so that there's one power stroke per four strokes of the piston. The up-and-down motion of the pistons pushes the drive shaft around. The **drive shaft**, or **crankshaft**, turns the wheels, and the car moves!

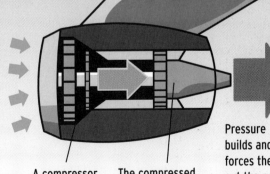

Fans at the front of a jet engine suck air inside.

Pressure builds and forces the air out the nozzle at the back of the engine, thrusting the plane forward.

Jet Engines

A jet engine is a type of internal combustion engine called a gas turbine engine. (These guys are used to power airplanes.)

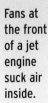

A compressor in the engine increases the pressure of the air.

The compressed air is forced into a combustion chamber, where burning fuel is added to the mix.

PLANES

It's a Bird. No. It's a PLANE!

It seems like magic when a huge plane with hundreds of people lifts into the sky. Actually, it's basic physics at work. Birds and bugs can fly by flapping their wings because their bodies are so light. Airplanes are too big for that, and they need to rely on a different technique. Flying involves four essential forces: lift, thrust, drag, and weight.

LIFT is just what it sounds like—an upward sucking or pushing that keeps the plane in the air.

THRUST is a forward push (that aerodynamic force that a plane must have in order to overcome the drag).

DRAG is the force that resists the plane's forward momentum. (If you stick your hand out the car window while you're moving along, you know what drag feels like.)

WEIGHT means the same thing for an airplane that it does for a person—it's the measure of the force of gravity pulling something toward Earth. In the case of a 747, it's about 870,000 pounds (395,000 kg)!

FLYING HIGH

In order for a plane to maintain a level path through the sky, the thrust has to exceed the drag and the lift has to exceed the weight. So where does lift come from?

net upward lift

air

Planes, like birds, bees, and most things that fly, have wings. The structure of a plane's wings helps give it the lift that allows it to overcome its weight. A speeding wing compresses the approaching air and splits it into two streams. One stream gets sucked up and over the wing. The other slows down and gets pulled under the wing. The net result is more pressure pointing up than down, so the wing is lifted.

Scratching your head? Don't worry. Lift is a very complex effect, although the physics behind it is well understood.

Often, airplane wings are built in a shape called an **airfoil**, similar to a bird's wing.

Did you know...

Leonardo Da Vinci drew a picture of a flying machine—the ornithopter—in 1485. He never built it, but the design of the first helicopter was based upon this drawing.

SO, WHAT'S THE PILOT DOING UP THERE IN THE COCKPIT?

Inside the cockpit, a pilot's job is to control all the parts of the plane that make it climb, dive, and turn. The pilot holds on to a control column that's connected to the plane's ailerons and elevators.

Flaps on the edges and tops of the wings are adjusted to change the shape of the wings during take-off, landing, and during flight. For take-off, the pilot raises the flaps, so air pushes against them and the nose of the plane turns upwards. For landing, the flaps are lowered, so the plane's nose drops. The pilot uses pedals to activate the plane's rudder (the vertical part of the tail that controls side-to-side motion). Together, the rudder and ailerons control turns. So when the plane needs to go up, down, left, right, or maybe even upside down, the pilot uses the control column to make these things happen.

Ailerons are hinged sections of the wings that bend opposite ways to bank the plane left and right.

Elevators are hinged sections of the tail that control up-and-down motion when the plane is in the air.

FAMOUS FACES

ORVILLE AND WILBUR WRIGHT owned a bicycle shop in Dayton, Ohio. But they weren't content to stay on two wheels. In 1903, the brothers succeeded in doing what humans had been attempting since ancient times. They built and flew the first powered vehicle that was heavier than air. Since then, we've reaped the rewards. A trip that once took months by stagecoach now takes only a few hours by plane. But the Wright brothers didn't simply hop in their new plane and head across the country. The first flight was only about 12 seconds, only about 1 foot (30 cm) off the ground, and a distance of only about 120 feet (37 m). Not very impressive by today's standards. The Wright Brothers sold the rights to the Wright Flyer to the US Government.

A BRIEF HISTORY OF FLIGHT

While innovators like the Wright brothers continued with some experiments of their own, World War I and World War II brought about the greatest advances in flight. In 1926, Ford introduced one of the first covered passenger airlines used commercially. It was called the Ford Trimotor. This plane held 8-13 passengers, depending on the model, and was covered with just a thin sheet of metal. With no climate control, the plane was hot in the summer and cold in the winter. It could only fly at an elevation of 6,000 feet (1,829 m). With all the passengers losing their lunch over the turbulence, and the smell of hot oil, the plane was less than cozy. At the same time, Boeing had created a similar passenger plane called the Boeing 80. These planes flew slightly higher, 14,000 feet (4,267 m), and had better climate control, plus hot and cold running water. As technology advanced, planes flew higher and higher and became more and more commonplace. World War II led to still further developments in aviation. Then, in 1969, came the Boeing 747, the largest passenger plane to date, which brought plane travel into the mainstream.

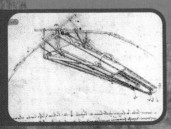

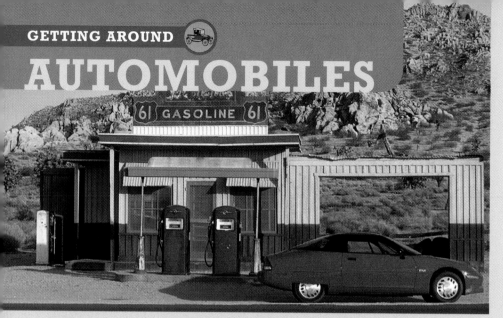

AUTOMOBILES

Cars

What would our lives be like without 'em? In 1769, the "car" was invented by Nicolas Joseph Cugnot. The **Steam Dray** was a three-wheeler powered by a steam engine. It had to stop every 10 minutes to build up enough steam to continue and it could only go 2 mph (3.2 km/h). Then, in 1885, Karl Benz designed the first car as we know it. The **Benz three-wheeler**, later known as the **Motorwagon**, was powered by an internal combustion engine and traveled at a max speed of 16 mph (26 km/h).

In 1896, **Henry Ford** built and sold his first car, the four-wheeled **Quadricycle**. The auto industry hit its stride in the early 1900s as Ford began producing car after car in his assembly plants. The momentum has continued ever since.

▲ Henry Ford

The Present and Future of Cars

Cars roll along the highways and roads every day. They get us from place to place, but they also pollute the environment and use up fossil fuels. In an effort to save our resources and protect our air, engineers and car manufacturers have worked out some possible solutions in electric and hybrid cars. ◀◀ FOR MORE ON GAS AND OTHER ENERGY SOURCES, SEE CH. 9, PP. 128–39.

ELECTRIC CARS From the outside, an electric car looks just like any other car. Wheels, windows, headlights, the works. But under the hood, it's a whole different story. **Instead of having an engine that burns fuel, the electric car runs on batteries.** This means there's no radiator, no transmission, no hoses, not a lot of what we expect from a car engine. The rechargeable batteries store the power for the engine. **The electric-powered car pollutes about 97 percent less than the**

internal combustion car. Its engine is much more efficient, and the fuel ends up costing about half as much. You may be thinking, "Sounds great! I can't wait to ride in one!" Well, unfortunately, there are still some problems with the electric car.

▲ Electric car drivers have charging systems like this one at home to repower the car's batteries.

OVER BEFORE IT STARTED? Because they are not mass-produced, these cars are still really expensive. They can also only run 100–140 miles (161–225 km), at the most, before they run out of juice, and then it takes about 8 hours to recharge the batteries. Then again, the average city driver puts in less than 50 miles (80 km) per day, making the electric car sensible for city driving.

If everybody bought an electric car, we could probably overcome issues like cost, but it may be too late. It looks like car makers could be bowing out of the electric car camp. As of 2004, several major manufacturers have stopped making and leasing electric cars, not wanting to maintain vehicles that such a small percentage of drivers actually use. With newer hybrid cars looking more promising, the electric car may have met its end before it even got going.

▲ In an electric car, a large battery replaces the engine.

WHAT'S NEW? Hybrid cars, the wave of the future

The next step in cleaner cars combines gas and electric power into a hybrid. **With hybrids, the work of running the car is divided between a battery-powered electric motor and a gasoline-fed internal combustion engine.** Hybrids give you a lot of the environmental benefits of an electric car, with the added power of a gas-fed engine that allows the car to travel farther, refuel, and recharge its batteries. It's not as "clean" as the totally electric car, but the fact that it doesn't need to be plugged in is a big plus. There are two ways that a hybrid car can operate:

- In a PARALLEL HYBRID, a gas engine and an electric motor work together to share the work of powering the car.
- In a SERIES HYBRID, a gas engine gives power to a generator, and then the generator gives power either to the electric motor that powers the car itself or to the batteries.

The Honda Insight and Toyota Prius are the two hybrids you're most likely to see cruising around town, but get ready to see a lot more hybrids in the years to come!

TRAINS

► Artist's rendering of a maglev train developed by Sandia National Laboratories in Albuquerque, NM.

Faster than a Speeding Bullet?

You didn't have to be Superman to outrun the first train. It was powered by steam engine and could travel at the rate of about 8 mph (13 km/h). The first commercial train doubled that speed, but still, that's pretty much a snail's pace.

Today, the average train is powered by a combination of electricity and a diesel engine, and it can run about as fast as a car. But trains are getting faster and faster! Now there are over 350 high-speed trains in existence. Amtrak's commuter train, the **Acela**, travels at a rate of about 150 mph (241 km/h). Japan's **Bullet Trains** speed along at rates up to about 170 mph (274 km/h), and European trains like the **TGV** in France can go up to 220 mph (354 km/h).

The name **maglev** is an abbreviation for Magnetic Levitation.

▲ Munich Airport Link in Germany, currently under development.

▼ Shanghai Transrapid began scheduled operations on December 29, 2003.

MAGLEV

The most exciting ride to hit the rails, or, more accurately, to hover above them, is the maglev train. Maglevs move by electromagnetic force. A maglev train has magnets on its bottom, and its track, or guideway, has a set of magnetized coils running along it. If you've held the positively charged sides of two magnets together, you can get an idea of what puts

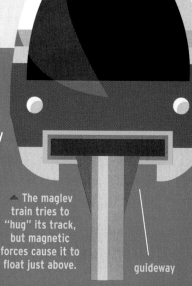

▲ The maglev train tries to "hug" its track, but magnetic forces cause it to float just above.

guideway

the "lev" in maglev. With an electric charge given to the track, the train's magnets and the coils in the guideway push away from one another, creating a cushion of air that makes the train float about 0.4-4 inches (1-10 cm) above the track. (It's practically flying!) The guideway coils move the train by constantly changing the polarity in the train's magnets. The area in front of the train attracts the magnets, pulling it forward, while the area behind helps out, pushing it along. The train is not touching the guideway, so there is almost no friction to slow it down, and that means high speeds!

Plans are underway for maglevs around the world. Currently, the Shanghai Transrapid soars from downtown Shanghai to the Pudong International Airport at 267 mph (430 km/h)! And an unmanned maglev train in Japan has zipped along to a new world-record speed of more than 343 mph (552 km/h).

CITY TRAVEL

In order to reduce automobile traffic in the early 20th century, many cities began underground transit systems or **subways**. Boston's subway system, nicknamed the "T," opened in 1904. New York and Philadelphia opened similar travel systems between 1905 and 1908. In the late '40s, people began to favor the automobile once again. But the '70s brought about a renaissance inspired by the building of San Francisco's Bay Area Transit (or BART). Today, the subway system remains a crucial part of many cities.

▼ Passengers on a New York City subway

SEGWAY™ HUMAN TRANSPORTER

The Segway Human Transporter was unveiled to the world in December 2001 and everyone was talking about it. Dean Kamen, its inventor, believed it was sure to change the way people travel. It hasn't accomplished that yet. But it's still pretty exciting.

Segway riders cruise a city sidewalk alongside pedestrians.

The Segway HT is self-balancing. It responds to the small shifts of its rider. To move forward, the rider leans forward; to reverse, he leans back. Moving right or left is as easy as twisting a grip on the handlebars.

How is all this accomplished? The Segway HT uses special solid-state gyroscopes and tilt sensors to balance. Conventional gyroscopes are spinning objects inside solid frames. They resist changes to their axis by applied force. That way, each time you apply force, that is, shift your weight, the small virtual gyroscopes counterbalance for you.

What's good about a Segway HT? It doesn't need gas, just electricity. It can be carried inside, so it doesn't require a special parking space. And it's a lot less expensive than an automobile, though with prices starting in the $4,000 range, it's not yet widely affordable.

COOL TRANSPORT

Helicopters

They're not as common as airplanes, but helicopters are the most versatile vehicles ever invented. The can fly up, down, forwards, backwards, and sideways. They can even hover! Flying a helicopter is really hard—it takes lots of training and lots of coordination. Here's how a helicopter takes to the air:

The main rotor on top of the helicopter spins, pushing air down and lifting the helicopter. But its spinning force makes the helicopter body want to spin too! That's why all helicopters have a tail rotor: these vertically oriented blades produce a sideways thrust, counteracting the spinning effect of the main rotor.

To move forward, the pilot tilts the nose of the helicopter down. This transfers some of the main rotor's downward force into a backward force that thrusts the helicopter forward. The farther down the nose is tilted, the faster the helicopter will go!

TIMELINE OF **TRANSPORTATION**

6500 B.C. THE WHEEL IS INVENTED BY THE SUMERIANS.

3000 B.C. RIVERBOATS FLOAT ALONG WITH THE HELP OF OARS.

2000 B.C. HORSES ARE DOMESTICATED AND USED FOR TRANSPORTATION.

1620 THE FIRST SUBMARINE COMES ALONG—IT'S A HUMAN-OARED SUBMERSIBLE.

1662 BLAISE PASCAL INVENTS THE FIRST PUBLIC BUS, OPERATING IN FRANCE.

1783 THE MONTGOLFIER BROTHERS INVENT THE FIRST HOT-AIR BALLOONS.

1787 THE FIRST SUCCESSFUL STEAM ENGINE IS INVENTED IN AMERICA.

1814 GEORGE STEPHENSON INVENTS THE FIRST PRACTICAL STEAM POWERED RAILROAD LOCOMOTIVE.

Submarines

A submarine is a vehicle designed to function deep below the ocean's surface. Inside every sub is a system of hollow spaces called ballast tanks that can be filled with either air or water. When they're empty, the sub is less dense than water, so it floats. When a submarine needs to dive, water is pumped into the ballast tanks, making the sub denser than seawater. Fins on the side of the sub, called hydroplanes, steer the sub downward. The sub's propeller moves it forward into a dive.

When it's time to go back up, the sub's ballast tanks are filled with air, causing its overall density to be lower than that of the surrounding water. Since the sub is less dense than the water, it starts to float up.

Conventional submarines run using a combination of diesel combustion engines and electric batteries. Nuclear submarines run using an internal reactor, and they can travel up to 398,000 miles (640,000 km) without refueling! Submarines are used mainly for military purposes.

HOT-AIR BALLOONS

They may not be practical, but hot-air balloons take the cake when it comes to fun. The way they rise and fall is pretty simple: warm air is less dense than cold air, so propane fuel is burned, filling the balloon **envelope** (the interior space) with hot air and making it less dense than the surrounding air, so that it rises. When the air inside the envelope cools, the balloon sinks. To keep the balloon on the up-and-up, the air inside the envelope has to be reheated. Balloon passengers travel in a basket attached below the envelope. Steering a hot-air balloon is a pretty inexact science. Pilots raise and lower the balloon to take advantage of wind currents, but if a strong gust or storm comes along, you're basically blowing with the wind.

1819 BICYCLES (WITHOUT PEDALS) ARE INVENTED; BICYCLES WITH PEDALS FOLLOW IN THE 1860S.

1832 HORSE-DRAWN STREETCAR APPEARS IN NEW YORK CITY.

1863 FIRST SUBWAY OPENS IN LONDON.

1869 STEAM-POWERED MOTORCYCLE INVENTED.

1873 SAN FRANCISCO CABLE CARS START MOVING.

1885 KARL BENZ BUILDS THE FIRST CAR POWERED BY AN INTERNAL COMBUSTION ENGINE.

1885 GASOLINE-POWERED MOTORCYCLES FIRST APPEAR.

1903 THE WRIGHT BROTHERS INVENT AND FLY THE FIRST ENGINE-POWERED AIRPLANE.

1908 HENRY FORD PRODUCES THE MODEL T FORD.

1939 FIRST SUCCESSFUL HELICOPTER FLIGHT TAKES PLACE.

1947 FIRST SUPERSONIC JET FLIGHT.

1970 FIRST JUMBO JET FLIES THE SKY.

1981 THE SPACE SHUTTLE **COLUMBIA** IS LAUNCHED.

The Air-Breathing Space Plane

In March 2004, NASA's newest plane, the X43A, reached a record-setting flight speed of about 5,000 mph (8,000 km/h). That's seven times the speed of sound! The X43A uses scramjet (supersonic-combustion ramjet) technology with an air-breathing engine to blast to its incredible speed.

▲ The X43A is mounted to NASA's NB-52B carrier aircraft for a systems test.

Scramjet engines work by sucking up oxygen from the atmosphere and blasting it into a combustion chamber, where it mixes with fuel, explodes, and powers the jet. This reduces the need to carry oxygen onboard the plane, making it lighter and faster. The catch? The plane needs to be moving at about five times the speed of sound in order for the engine to work. To get up to that crucial speed from the get-go, the X43A has to be boosted by rocket at takeoff.

This test mission was unmanned, and the plane flew for 11 seconds before a planned crash into the ocean. Look out for the X-43A as a space travel vehicle in years to come! ◀◀ FOR INFO ON SPACE TECHNOLOGY, SEE PP. 222-26.

▲ You might one day fly in the E-Plane!

WHAT'S NEXT?

E-Plane—Whew-wee!

Get ready for a little plane that's powered by an electric motor. Massachusetts researchers are hard at work on the E-Plane, a two-seater powered by Toyota Prius batteries and a 100 hp motor. The plane won't get you far, yet. Its range is only about 75 miles (120 km). But plans are already underway for a souped-up version, powered by a hydrogen-oxygen fuel cell. In its third stage, the plane is expected to fly on a fuel cell alone—which would expand the plane's range to distances over 500 miles! In addition to being more efficient than jet fuel–powered engines, the fuel cell makes for a much quieter ride.

SCIENCE FAIR PROJECT #14

When engineers design a car, they carefully test its shape to find out how easily air will move past it. Choosing a shape that is aero-dynamic makes it easier for the car to move at high speeds. In this experiment, you will test different shapes for a car to see which one will go fastest.

YOU WILL NEED:

- ◉ Wood board (about 6 feet (1.8 m) long and at least 3 inches (7.6 cm) wide)
- ◉ Several books
- ◉ Two small wood blocks
- ◉ Matchbox-type car
- ◉ Several index cards
- ◉ Scissors
- ◉ Clear tape
- ◉ Ruler
- ◉ Stopwatch
- ◉ Felt-tip marker
- ◉ Duct tape

1. Use the books to support one end of the board to make a ramp. The highest point on the ramp should be no more than 4 inches (10 cm) off the ground. Slide other books under the middle of the ramp to give more support.

2. Use duct tape to tape one of the wood blocks on the ramp at the bottom end.

3. Use the felt-tip marker to draw a line across the board about 3 inches (7.6 cm) from the top of the ramp.

4. Cut two rectangles of the same size from an index card. The rectangles should be the same length and height as the car. Attach the rectangles to the car with the clear tape. Cut other rectangular pieces to cover the front and top of the car and attach them with tape. Make sure the car rolls freely.

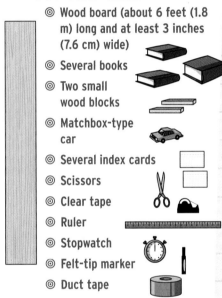

5. Place the other block on the ramp so the top of the block is on the line you drew. Hold the block in place with your hand. Put the car at the top of the ramp so it rests against the block you are holding.

6. Pick up the stopwatch. Pull the block away and start the stopwatch at the same time. Stop it when the car hits the block at the bottom of the ramp. Record the time.

7. Repeat steps 5 and 6 at least two more times. Find the average time it takes the car to roll down the ramp. Remove the index card pieces from the car when you are finished.

8. Cut new shapes from the index cards. Try a long, thin triangle, with the short side facing the back of the car. Try rounded sides with a curved top. Try making a sail for the top of the car. Make up your own car shapes to test. Repeat steps 5 through 7 with the new shapes. Be certain each time to check that the car can roll freely.

◎ Try placing a fan at the bottom of the ramp blowing upwards to add more wind resistance. What shapes help the car to go the fastest?

CHAPTER 15

SPACE

What's up in the sky? The universe is full of weird mysteries and cool stuff that we're just beginning to understand. Black holes and distant planets may not seem that important to life here on Earth. But solving riddles of the distant universe can tell us a lot about our own home too.

MOVIES ON
BRAINPOP.COM

- The Big Bang
- The Life Cycle of Stars
- The Sun
- Planets of the Solar System
- The Moon
- The International Space Station

...and many more!

Brain
POP®

HOW THE UNIVERSE BEGAN

No one knows for sure how the universe was created. A lot of scientists think that the **big bang theory** is the most likely explanation. It goes like this:

About 13.7 billion years ago, all the matter in the universe as we know it was packed together in one superhot, dense point called a **singularity**. No one is really sure why, but this singularity began a dramatic expansion, an event that filled all of space with all the particles of the embryonic universe rushing away from each other and that also marked the beginning of time. The universe began to cool as it expanded—about 3 minutes after the big bang, it had cooled from 100 million trillion trillion degrees **Kelvin** to 10 billion K (18 billion°F). And as it cooled, matter formed and, later, galaxies.

Scientists measure temperature using the **Kelvin** scale, which has no negative numbers. Zero on the Kelvin scale is called "absolute zero," the point at which molecules stop moving. To convert Celsius into Kelvin, simply add 273.15 to the Celsius temperature. **◀◀ TO CONVERT CELSIUS INTO FAHRENHEIT, SEE THE FORMULA ON P. 102.**

Did you know...
A cosmologist is a scientist who studies the origin and structure of the universe.

TIMELINE OF THE BIG BANG

 BIG BANG
SPACE FORMS AND
TIME BEGINS

 LESS THAN 1 SECOND
GRAVITY FORMS

 MINUTES
HYDROGEN AND
HELIUM GASES FORM;
ENTIRE UNIVERSE IS MADE
OF 75 PERCENT HYDROGEN
AND 25 PERCENT HELIUM

200 MILLION YEARS
THE FIRST STARS ARE FORMED

 1 BILLION YEARS
THE MILKY WAY, OUR GALAXY,
BEGINS TO TAKE SHAPE

10 BILLION YEARS
THE SUN EMERGES

 13.7 BILLION YEARS
HUMANS ARE BORN

MOVIES ON
BRAINPOP.COM

THE SUN AND STARS

They light up the sky, but what are they made of? Every star you see in the sky is a gigantic ball of superheated gas. Our sun is a medium-sized star that happens to be close by. From another star, the Sun would look like just another light in the night sky!

But even though they're made of gases (usually hydrogen and helium), stars are very dense. Stars are so dense that nuclear fusion takes place in their cores. That's what gives them all their heat and energy! ◀◀ SEE NUCLEAR POWER ON P. 134.

Life Cycle of Stars

Stars change throughout their lives just like we do. But you probably won't see these changes happening in your favorite star—a star's life cycle is billions of years long.

Stars start out as clouds of gas and dust drifting through space.

The force of gravity slowly pulls these clouds closer together, causing clumps to form. If a clump, or **protostar**, gets large enough, the pressure caused by the force of gravity begins to generate heat.

This heat and pressure build until **nuclear fusion** reactions begin to take place in the core. Gravity pulls the hydrogen atoms together, smashing and fusing them into heavier helium atoms.

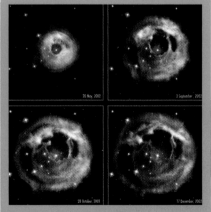

Expanding Star. These sequential images taken by the Hubble Space Telescope show an expanding supergiant star called V838 Monocerotis, located about 20,000 light-years away.

All that energy causes the star to ignite, entering its **main sequence**. THIS IS WHERE OUR STAR, THE SUN, IS RIGHT NOW, ABOUT HALFWAY THROUGH ITS 10-BILLION-YEAR-LONG MAIN SEQUENCE.

211

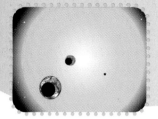

Eventually, our sun will use up all of its hydrogen. When that happens, the core will be so hot that the star will expand, growing to many times its current size.

That giant sun will engulf the inner planets, burning them to cinders. Stars in this stage of their life are called **red giants**, because their surface cools to glow red.

The star is burning helium now, fusing it into even heavier elements. Since these reactions aren't nearly as powerful as burning hydrogen, the star will begin to collapse.

What happens next depends on the mass of the star:

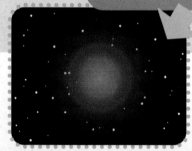

A star the size of our sun will enter its **Cepheid phase**, expanding and contracting, losing its outer layers in the process. The star will eventually collapse into a superdense ball of matter called a **white dwarf**. After milions of years as a white dwarf, it will cool off and end its life as a **black dwarf**. That's the route our sun will take, but there are different ways that a star can die.

Stars much bigger than our sun will collapse so quickly that they explode into a **supernova**, scattering stellar material far and wide.

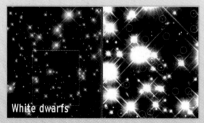

White dwarfs

White dwarf stars in the Milky Way Galaxy, as viewed from the Hubble Space Telescope. At 12–13 billion years, they are the oldest burned-out stars in our galaxy.

Supernova

The white bubbles are supernova blasts in nearby galaxy NGC 1569, as viewed from the Hubble Space Telescope. New stars can form out of this gas and dust!

Black hole

Did you know...

No light can escape a black hole. So how do scientists know that they're there at all? Dust particles in space heat up so much near a black hole that they emit X-rays, and the X-rays can be detected by special X-ray telescopes. In 2004, scientists using the space-based X-ray telescopes Chandra and XMM-Newton detected a black hole literally tearing an entire star apart!

◄ This is a composite X-ray (blue and green) and optical (red) image of galaxy NGC 1068. The elongated white spot is a cloud of gas and dust surrounding a central massive black hole.

Galaxies

Galaxies are huge collections of stars. They are held together by the massive gravity exerted by all those big stars. We live in the Milky Way galaxy, a spiral-shaped group of at least 200 billion stars, including our sun!

▶ An edge-on view of the Milky Way galaxy. The Milky Way galaxy is a spiral-shaped galaxy. Other types of galaxies noted by astronomers are elliptical galaxies, which are more common, and irregular galaxies, which are rare and exhibit a wide variety of shapes.

Milky Way galaxy

Did you know...

Our solar system revolves around the center of the Milky Way once every 220 million years. That means the last time we were at this point in the galaxy, dinosaurs walked Earth!

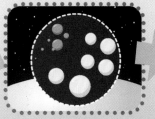

The core that's left over after a supernova explosion is so dense that the protons and electrons are crushed into neutrons. What you get then is a **neutron star**.

Some neutron stars spin rapidly, emitting pulses of radio waves. These neutron stars are also called **pulsars**.

If the leftover core is above a certain critical mass, it will continue to collapse in on itself, eventually forming a theoretical area of infinite density called a singularity. We call this a **black hole**, and its gravity is so powerful that nothing within range can escape it.

The Sun

Our sun formed about 4.6 billion years ago. It's a middle-aged star.

The Sun is 93 million miles (150 million km) from Earth, on average.

Like many other stars, the Sun converts hydrogen into helium and energy through a process called nuclear fusion. This is made possible by the extreme pressure and high temperature in the Sun's core—an incredible 27 million°F (15 million K; 15 million°C).

Energy from the Sun makes plants grow; animals eat the plants and are in turn eaten by other animals.

MOVIES ON BRAINPOP.COM

▲ X-ray photographs of the Sun taken from the Skylab space station in 1973. (Skylab fell to Earth in 1979.) These images show a boot-shaped coronal hole that rotated with the Sun. When the coronal hole was near the center of the Sun, it directed high-velocity solar winds toward Earth that distorted Earth's magnetic field.

Did you know...

Solar winds are streams of electrically charged particles, called ions, that flow out of the Sun at speeds of up to 2 million miles per hour (3.2 million km/h).

Did you know...

The Sun's mass is 333,000 times Earth's mass.

The tilt of Earth causes sunlight to strike it at different angles throughout the year, causing seasons.

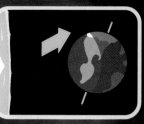

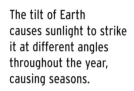

Take away the Sun, and Earth would quickly become a frozen ball of life-less rock. Still, guess how much of the Sun's total energy the Earth receives . . . only one-billionth!

JUPITER

SATURN

NEPTUNE

URANUS

THE SUN

The Sun makes up 99 percent of all the mass in the solar system, including all the planets!

MERCURY   VENUS   EARTH   MARS   PLUTO

The Sun isn't all brightness. There are cooler, darker parts called sunspots on the surface.

Did you know...

Eruptions on the surface of the Sun, called solar flares, can mess up radio and cellphone signals for days here on Earth!

THE PLANETS

Planets travel in orbits around stars such as our sun. They are smaller than stars and typically have hot cores. The nine planets in our solar system are made up of matter left over from the Sun's formation.

EARTH
93 million miles (150 million km) to Sun
7,926 miles (12,756 km) in diameter
• Earth's atmosphere protects the planet's surface.

MARS
142 million miles (228 million km) to Sun
4,222 miles (6,794 km) in diameter
• Mars has lots of craters, the tallest mountain in the solar system, and two moons! Rust gives Mars its reddish color.

VENUS
67 million miles (108 million km) to Sun
7,521 miles (12,103 km) in diameter
• Venus is almost the same size as Earth. Temperatures on Venus can reach 900°F (580°C), hot enough to melt metal!

MERCURY
36 million miles (58 million km) to Sun
3,032 miles (4,880 km) in diameter
• Mercury is like a ball of metal; 70 percent of it is iron and nickel.

1 2 3 4

Earth

Mars

THE GAS GIANTS
Jupiter, Saturn, Uranus, and Neptune are known as gas giants. They are not primarily rocky bodies like the other five planets. Instead, they're essentially huge balls of gas—mainly hydrogen and helium—wrapped around relatively small rocky cores.

   Mercury   Venus

JUPITER
484 million miles (778 million km) to Sun
88,846 miles (142,983 km) in diameter
• Jupiter's volume is 1,300 times Earth's. It has more than 60 moons and a giant storm on its surface called the Great Red Spot.

SATURN
0.89 billion miles (1.4 billion km) to Sun
74,898 miles (120,536 km) in diameter
• Saturn has at least 31 moons and thousands of rings made of ice and rock.

NEPTUNE
2.9 billion miles (4.5 billion km) to Sun
30,778 miles (49,532 km) in diameter
• Neptune takes 165 Earth-years to orbit the Sun. There's a stormy Great Dark Spot on Neptune that's kind of like the Great Red Spot on Jupiter.

PLUTO
3.7 billion miles (5.9 billion km) to Sun
1,413 miles (2,274 km) in diameter
• Pluto is the smallest planet in the solar system, and also the farthest out. It has a highly elliptical orbit, and some-times moves inside Neptune's orbit.

URANUS
1.8 billion miles (2.9 billion km) to Sun
31,763 miles (51,118 km) in diameter
• Uranus is so tilted that it looks like it's lying on its side!

5

6

8

9

7

Pluto

Jupiter

Saturn

PLANET DETAILS Although only Earth, with its liquid water and warm temperature, has proved to be suitable for life, each planet in the solar system has its own unique characteristics.

Uranus

Neptune

THE MOON

The Moon is basically a ball of igneous rock with a small core of iron and sulfur. The pale rocks of the highlands consist of aluminum and calcium and the darker **maria** have basalt rock. We see the Moon as the second brightest object in the sky, next to the Sun. But, unlike the Sun, the Moon doesn't actually make any light of its own.

The dark patches you see on the Moon's face are sunken plains called seas, or **maria**, which is Latin for "oceans." There's no liquid water on the Moon though.

The Moon goes through phases, which determine its appearance to observers on Earth. Sunlight strikes the Moon at different angles throughout its journey around Earth. The way the Moon looks to us depends on how much of its illuminated side is visible to us at the time.

▲ North pole of the Moon. This unusual view, taken by the interplanetary probe **Mariner 10**, shows portions of the Moon not viewable from Earth.

The Moon's brightness is actually light from the Sun, reflecting off the surface of the Moon.

The Moon takes 27.3 days to orbit Earth, but the time from one full moon to the next is 29.5 days because Earth is also moving in relation to the Sun. We call this period from one full moon to the next a LUNAR MONTH, by the way.

As the Moon rotates around Earth, we see more or less of it depending on its position relative to both Earth and the Sun.

When the Moon is growing, it is **waxing**. When it is shrinking, it is **waning**.

1 new moon — what you see

2 waxing crescent — what you see

3 first quarter — what you see

4 waxing gibbous — what you see

5 full moon — what you see

6 waning gibbous — what you see

7 last quarter — what you see

8 waning crescent — what you see

ORIGIN OF THE MOON

There's a lot of debate as to how the Moon got where it is in the first place.

The leading theory suggests that the Moon was the result of a collision between Earth and a rogue planet roughly the size of Mars.

The collision knocked off material from Earth that—along with fragments of the shattered object that struck Earth—formed the Moon.

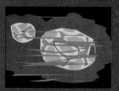

Other scientists believe that the Moon may have just formed along with Earth from the initial cloud of gas and dust that formed our solar system.

Another theory is that the Moon may have been just floating through the solar system, and got captured by Earth's gravity.

Solar and Lunar Eclipses

If you hear there's going to be an eclipse in your area, that means the light from either the Sun or Moon is going to be blocked out for a period of time.

Lunar eclipses happen more often, and you've probably seen one. They can only occur during full moons, when Earth is directly between the Sun and the Moon, and then only during those full moons when Earth's orbit around the Sun and the Moon's orbit around Earth—which is tilted by 5 degrees compared with Earth's orbit around the Sun—perfectly coincide. During a lunar eclipse, the bright lunar disk turns dark for up to an hour.

Lunar eclipses are pretty cool to see, but they're nothing compared with a **solar eclipse**! For a short time, the Moon blocks our view of the Sun. You'll see the Sun's corona spill out from behind the dark Moon.

▼ SOLAR ECLIPSE. Seen during the day when the Moon passes directly between the Sun and Earth.

▲ LUNAR ECLIPSE Viewed at night when the Sun and the Moon are on opposite sides of Earth.

▲ The Moon is about 239,000 miles (385,000 km) from Earth, which is pretty close when you're talking about space.

SOLAR ECLIPSE ALERT!

There'll be a few partial solar eclipses in 2005. Check NASA's eclipse homepage to see if your part of the world will get to see them: sunearth.gsfc.nasa.gov/eclipse/solar.html
DON'T FORGET: Never, ever stare at a solar eclipse without a proper viewing device—you could go blind!

ASTEROIDS, COMETS, AND METEORS

There's lots of stuff flying around in space and not all of it is as well behaved as Earth!

Asteroids

Asteroid Belt

Asteroids are rocks and boulders that are made up of the solar system's leftover matter. Thousands of asteroids orbit the Sun along with the nine planets. The smallest are less than a mile in diameter; others are a few hundred miles wide! Most of these rocks travel around the Sun in an orbit between Mars and Jupiter. This is called the **asteroid belt**.

Comets

Comet

Outside Pluto's orbit, at the edge of our solar system, are billions of icy clumps called comets. Sometimes, one of these clumps breaks away and gets sucked into the Sun by gravity. It can take thousands of revolutions around the Sun before it finally crashes into it. But along the way, bits of dust and ice break off and are vaporized.

The space probe *Giotto* flew by the most famous comet of all, Halley's comet, in 1986. It sent pictures back to Earth confirming what scientists had long theorized: that comets are just big, dirty snowballs.

Cataclysmic Asteroid

Comet Hale-Bopp

Did you know...

The Hale-Bopp comet passed close to Earth in 1997. Because of its very large orbit, it won't be viewable from Earth for another 2,347 years!

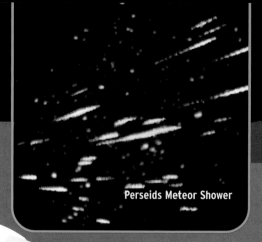
Perseids Meteor Shower

METEOR SHOWERS

METEOR SHOWERS

When Earth's orbit passes through the dust and ice shed by a comet, the particles burn up in our atmosphere. This is a meteor shower. Every August, Earth passes through the debris left behind by the Swift-Tuttle comet, giving us the Perseids meteor shower. The Swift-Tuttle comet itself takes 128 years to orbit the Sun and won't pass near Earth for more than another 100 years.

METEORITES A meteorite is any interplanetary rock—including asteroids and comets—that makes it through our atmosphere without burning up completely and crashes into Earth. By the time they reach Earth's surface, most meteorites are no larger than a grain of sand and don't do a lot of damage, but meteorites close to a mile across have landed here before. In 1908, a meteorite 200 feet (60 m) in diameter crashed into Siberia and wiped out 770 square miles (2,000 square km) of forest; it was seen by people as far as 466 miles (750 km) away.

Asteroids

Asteroid Ida with moon

NEAR-EARTH ASTEROIDS

Earth has had close calls with some big asteroids in the last couple of decades. If a big enough asteroid crossed our orbit, it could be disastrous for life on Earth. That's why NASA tries to keep an eye on any big asteroids that might intersect with us. In 2001, an asteroid called 2001 YB5, which measured 1,000-1,300 feet (300-400 m) in diameter, came within 375,000 miles (600,000 km) of Earth. That may seem like a long, long way, but in terms of space travel, it's right next door.

Did you know...

Some scientists think a giant meteorite may have caused the death of the dinosaurs by kicking up dust into the air and blocking the Sun for a long, long time.

SPACE TECHNOLOGY

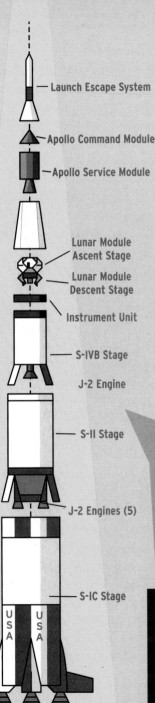

- Launch Escape System

- Apollo Command Module

- Apollo Service Module

Lunar Module
Ascent Stage

Lunar Module
Descent Stage

Instrument Unit

— S-IVB Stage

J-2 Engine

— S-II Stage

J-2 Engines (5)

— S-IC Stage

USA   USA

— F-1 Engines (5)

222

Humans are curious. We've devoted a lot of time and energy to learning more about space, and we've created technology that allows us to travel to and view far-off worlds.

Rockets

If you throw a ball up in the air, Earth's gravity will pull it back down. In order for that ball to escape our planet's gravity and make it into space, it has to reach what is known as *escape velocity*. What is our planet's escape velocity? 24,840 mph (40,000 km/h)!

To reach that incredible speed, rockets need to burn lots of fuel. Rockets are mainly big fuel tanks—the part of the ship where the satellite or astronauts go is pretty small. It takes a big explosion to even get 1 pound of matter away from Earth's gravity!

Once rocket fuel starts burning, there's no stopping it. That's why rockets have different stages. A stage is basically a separate tank of fuel. Once one stage burns through all its fuel, it drops off the rocket and back to Earth. Then the mission controllers or astronauts can ignite the next stage whenever they want.

SATURN V FACTS
The largest rocket ever launched, Saturn V was used by NASA between 1967 and 1972 to carry astronauts to the Moon. The overall height complete with Apollo spacecraft and launch escape system was 363 feet (over twice as tall as a space shuttle and its launch support components). The liftoff weight was 6.4 million pounds (2.9 million kg). The launch thrust of the five F-1 first-stage engines was 7.6 million pounds (3.5 million kg).

FAMOUS FACE
The first person to step on the Moon was Neil Armstrong, on July 20, 1969. The entire country watched it on live television.

No one has returned to the Moon since the **Apollo 17** mission in 1972, but the Chinese government has announced its intention to land people on the Moon in the next few years and the US plans to return to the Moon by 2020 for an "extended" human expedition.

MOON MISSIONS

Only the United States has landed humans on the Moon. In fact, six of the missions of NASA's Apollo space program landed men on the Moon's surface.

▷ Geologist-Astronaut Harrison Schmitt on the Moon's surface during **Apollo 17**'s mission in 1972, the final lunar landing by the United States.

SPACE SHUTTLE

The space shuttle is the world's first reusable spacecraft. Before it, astronauts would be launched into space in capsules on top of rockets and return to Earth by splashing into the ocean or dropping down in a field. The capsule could only be used once. The space shuttle uses disposable fuel stages, but the orbiter lands like a plane and can go up into space over and over again.

▲ Space shuttle **Columbia** blasts off on its 18th mission on October 20, 1995. NASA used the space shuttle for all kinds of missions, including satellite launches, satellite repairs, and scientific experiments. Tragically, **Columbia** broke apart on its reentry approach to Kennedy Space Center in February 2003, killing the crew of seven.

▷ Space shuttle **Atlantis** docks with the Russian space station Mir in 1995.

SPACE STATIONS

Trips to space on rockets usually last only a few days, and the typical shuttle voyage lasts seven days. Space stations let astronauts stay in Earth's orbit for months at a time. This allows scientists to study the long-term effect on humans of living and working in space. What they learn will help in the planning for future missions that may last a long time.

The International Space Station, which has been under construction in space since 1998, is a joint effort among 16 nations, including the US, Russia, Japan, and the member nations of the European Space Agency. When it is completed, it will be the largest space structure ever built—nearly as large as two football fields side by side.

▲ An astronaut works on the Unity Module, the US-built node at the top of the International Space Station.

International Space Station

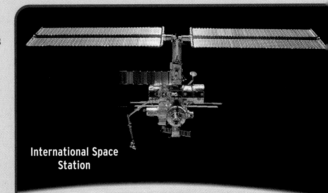

International Space Station

LIVING IN SPACE

The human body has not evolved to live in the weightlessness of space. Astronauts closely monitor their bodies to make sure they're staying healthy during space missions. Some of the health dangers of prolonged space travel include:

★ Weakened muscles
★ Brittle bones
★ Nausea
★ Slowed heartbeat

When Russian cosmonaut Sergei Krikalev returned to Earth after a particularly long stay of 313 days in the Mir Space Station, he was so weak he could barely stand and had to be given smelling salts!

▲ Astronauts train for weightlessness aboard a high-flying NASA aircraft called the "vomit comet"!

Mars Exploration

The year 2004 was a big year for Mars. The NASA rovers *Spirit* and *Opportunity* successfully landed on different parts of the planet and sent back amazing pictures and discoveries. In February 2004, experiments conducted by *Opportunity* achieved one of its main objectives: confirming that Mars once had liquid water. This was a huge discovery, since water is a necessary ingredient for all life on Earth.

Here are some of the cool tools on board these robot rovers:

PANORAMIC CAMERA (PANCAM) can take high-resolution pictures at different light wavelengths.

MICROSCOPIC IMAGER takes microscopic pictures of rocks and soil.

MINIATURE THERMAL EMISSION SPECTROMETER (MINI-TES) can determine the makeup of rocks and soil from a distance.

ALPHA PARTICLE X-RAY SPECTROMETER (APXS) detects X-rays emitted by rocks and soil.

ROCK ABRASION TOOL (RAT) is a powerful grinder, able to bore a hole 1.8 inches (45 mm) into rock.

ROVER'S "ARM" (ALSO CALLED THE INSTRUMENT DEPLOYMENT DEVICE, OR IDD) holds and maneuvers instruments.

Exploration rover

New Planet

Is Sedna the solar system's 10th planet? Maybe not, but it is certainly the most distant object in the solar system yet discovered. It was spotted on November 14, 2003, by astronomers using a powerful ground-based telescope at the California Institute of Technology's Palomar Observatory. Sedna is about 8 billion miles (12.8 billion km) from Earth—that's more than three times farther away from Earth than Pluto. It seems to be made of ice and rock and it has a diameter of less than 1,000 miles (1,700 km), making it even smaller than Pluto. Researchers say that it takes Sedna 10,500 years to orbit the Sun. For the next 72 years it will be relatively close to Earth, but then it will begin its long voyage to the outer limits of the solar system.

Did you know...

Sedna is the Inuit goddess who created the sea creatures of the Arctic.

WHAT'S NEXT?

Telescope Tech

Now that scientists have spotted a Jupiter-like planet circling a Sun-like star a mere 90 light-years away, the race is on to see if any Earth-like objects exist nearby. Problem is, we'll need some advances in technology before we can see any Earth-size objects that far away. Thankfully, a whole new range of high-tech telescopes are coming our way:

2006 The French space-based telescope Corot, which is scheduled to launch in early 2006, will search for rocky planets outside our solar system by monitoring the shadows planets cast on the faces of stars.

2007 The mission of NASA's **Kepler** spacecraft, scheduled for launch in October 2007, is to detect rocky, Earth-size planets around other stars. **Kepler**'s instruments will let scientists size up planets as they block out starlight from their parent stars.

NASA's SIM

2009 NASA's SIM (Space Interferometry Mission) will cut through the glare of stars and bring obscured objects into focus.

2015 NASA's Terrestrial Planet Finder is a system of synchronized, space-based observatories that will study and take pictures of planets outside our solar system.

Terrestrial Planet Finder

DEBATE: Is There Life on Other Planets?

The truth is, no one really knows. People have long wondered if there might be life on other planets. There are plenty of good arguments for and against it. You can weigh the facts:

Scientists estimate that there about 100 billion galaxies in the universe, each with an average of 100 billion stars.

Life needs more than stars, it needs planets. Images from the Hubble Space Telescope show that other stars are likely to have planets around them.

NASA's Mars rover *Opportunity* confirmed in February of 2004 that Mars once had liquid water, a necessary ingredient for life (at least on Earth it is).

There has been no scientific evidence to date of life as we know it on other planets.

Life arose on Earth because of a bunch of very specific conditions: it was warm, it had liquid water, and it had plenty of carbon, the element at the center of all life on our planet. The chances for these conditions occurring on any given planet are quite small.

Maybe we're only searching for life as we know it . . . There could be other types of life in the universe!

SCIENCE FAIR PROJECT #15

How Does the Sun's Position in the Sky Change?

Every day, the Sun appears to move across the sky because Earth is rotating on its axis. However, the Sun's path across the sky is different each day because Earth is orbiting the Sun. Since looking directly at the Sun can hurt your eyes, you are going to observe the shadow cast by an object to find the position of the Sun. In order to do this project, you will need to make observations over several weeks.

YOU WILL NEED:

◎ Pencil (or other small, straight, pointed stick)

◎ Large pieces of white paper

◎ Small block of wood with a pencil-size hole drilled in it

◎ Permanent marker

◎ Wristwatch

◎ Magnetic compass

1. Find a flat, outdoor location that is sunny all day.

2. Early in the morning, place a large sheet of paper on the ground in your sunny location. Make a mark in the center of the paper with your marker. Label one corner of the paper with the date of your observations. Use your compass to find north and draw a small arrow on your paper labeled "North."

3. Place the eraser end of the pencil into the hole in your block of wood. Then set the block down on the center mark on your paper so the point of the pencil sticks straight up.

4. Use your marker to mark the place where the shadow of the pencil's tip falls on the paper. Label this mark with the time of your observation. Make a note of the Sun's location in the sky compared with the shadow. Record this observation in a journal.

5. Repeat step 4 regularly throughout the day. Every hour on the hour is suggested, but you can observe the shadow more often if you like.

6. Repeat steps 2 through 5 on another day using a new sheet of paper. You will need to wait at least a week or two in order to see any real change in the locations of the shadows. Collect data on at least three or four different days so you can compare your results.

◎ How did the location of the shadow change each day? What does this tell you about the location of the Sun in the sky?

◎ How do the locations of the shadows look different on different days? What does this tell you about the location of the Sun on those days?

People have been using the position of the Sun as a way to tell time for thousands of years. How could you use your observations to tell the time? How could you use what you learned from this project to make your own sundial?

CHAPTER 16

BUILDING THE WORLD

How were the Pyramids built without the help of modern tools? How does a skyscraper stand so tall? How can bridges support the weight of so many cars? The answer is a matter of math, physics, design, engineering, and years of trial and error. Civilizations have left a mark on the world through their buildings. What will we leave behind?

BUILDING BASICS

Humans have always needed shelter. Where a building is placed, how it's shaped, and what materials are used to build it, tell us a lot about the civilization it came from and its solutions to the basic problems of designing and engineering a structure.

The Problem of Gravity

Since building began, humans have fought against the force of **gravity**. Earth's gravity pulls every **mass** on its surface toward the center of Earth. An object's **weight** is actually the amount of force with which gravity pulls that mass. That means that any structure we erect has to resist a force that wants to pull it down.

COMPRESSION AND TENSION

We're talking about pushing and pulling. No matter what kind of structure you're looking at, compression and tension are at work. For a structure to stay up, it has to have the necessary support to keep these forces in check.

COMPRESSION IS A FORCE THAT SQUEEZES MATTER TOGETHER. As a result, compressed material gets shorter. (Press on both ends of a loaf of bread at once and you'll see compression at work.) The buildings we see every day have to handle the force of compression from the weight of the structure. For example, the columns of a skyscraper are constantly being squeezed together by the load above.
▸▸ FOR MORE ON SKYSCRAPERS, SEE PP. 236-37.

TENSION IS THE OPPOSITE OF COMPRESSION—it's a force that pulls material apart. When matter is in tension, it gets longer. (Pull a rubber band apart and the rubber is under tension.) The cables of a suspension bridge are always being pulled at and stretched by the weight of cars on the roadway they carry.

POST AND LINTEL

One of the most basic examples of a structure that stands up to the test of time (and weight) is the post and lintel.

Two vertical columns support a horizontal beam. When weight is applied to the beam, it starts to bend, compressing the columns, and the whole thing works together to support the weight of the load. Simple, right? Of course there are variables that could make the structure unsound: builders have to use beams that are the right length, columns that are the right height, and building materials that are strong for the construction to work.

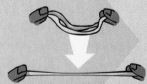

Did you know...

Every doorway in your home has a post and lintel! Take a look.

EXPERIMENT with Bob the Ex-Lab Rat

I'm making my favorite spaghetti dinner, waiting for the water to boil…This is a tense situation. Get it? Okay, maybe not funny, but try this and then make dinner!

YOU WILL NEED:
A box of dry spaghetti

STEP 1. Take about half the spaghetti out of the box and hold it in your hands.

STEP 2. Start to bend it.

STEP 3. Keep at the bending until the spaghetti starts to break apart.

Notice what breaks first? The outer pieces, right? That's because those pieces were in tension. The inner pieces were in compression. They were getting pulled apart by the force you applied with your hands. Brittle materials, like stone, break first at the area of tension, not the area of compression. If a stone beam in a post-and-lintel structure carries too much load, it will break first in the same way as the spaghetti.

forces of tension on the outer curve

compression on the inner curve

Back to Blocks

You most likely ran into the gravity dilemma playing with wooden blocks when you were small.

Stack one block on top of another, no problem. Add a third block, and the structure starts to wobble. You have to adjust the block's position to make the tower stand. Add a fourth block and . . . it falls over.

Why? Well, that bottom block has to support the weight of everything on top of it and it can't hack it alone. If you add a second block to the base, you'll find that you can build higher. Distributing the weight of those upper blocks onto a two-block base helps to stabilize the structure. That's the principle behind **pyramids**—wide base, narrow top. At some point, building outward becomes impractical. Think about how much space the **Great Pyramid** would take up if its height were doubled!

THE WONDERS OF THE WORLD

Architects and engineers have been dazzling us with their designs for centuries. Check out some of the major accomplishments in structures past and present.

Ancient Wonders

The Seven Wonders of the Ancient World are important monuments that can be traced back to the sixth century B.C.

1 THE GREAT PYRAMID

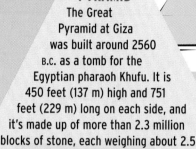

The Great Pyramid at Giza was built around 2560 B.C. as a tomb for the Egyptian pharaoh Khufu. It is 450 feet (137 m) high and 751 feet (229 m) long on each side, and it's made up of more than 2.3 million blocks of stone, each weighing about 2.5 tons (2,300 kg).

HOW DID THEY BUILD IT?

Without the help of sophisticated tools, computers, bulldozers, or cranes! Historians believe that it took a force of tens of thousands of slaves or peasants about 20-30 years to build the Pyramid. The blocks were cut from rock quarries using stone and copper tools and moved from the quarries to the Pyramid site along the water using barges or on land using wooden sleds. We're not exactly sure how the heavy blocks were raised high above the ground, but ramps made of dirt, brick, and rubble were used in part of the construction. They were built up as the Pyramid was raised and broken apart as it was finished. (◀◀ SEE P. 124 FOR MORE ON RAMPS OR INCLINED PLANES.)

WHY STONE, AND WHY THAT SHAPE?

Stone is strong. It can withstand a lot of compression, but not a lot of tension. As stones are stacked, the downward force of gravity compresses them. You can't even fit a piece of cardboard between those stones! The stones in the Great Pyramid have no problem handling that heavy compression. But remember the spaghetti experiment?

How do the Pyramid's stones handle all the tension created by such a heavy load? The answer lies in the shape. The lowest level has the most stones, spread over the largest area. The next level up has fewer stones, spread over a slightly smaller area, and so on to the top, which has only one stone. Each "level" of the Pyramid is lighter and smaller than the one below it, so the tension it exerts on the level below is manageable.

For a pyramid to stand, each of its four sides has to slope up and towards the others at the same exact angle so that they meet in a point. Each triangular face of the Great Pyramid is slanted at an angle of 51.5 degrees. The pyramid was built in levels, from the bottom up, so the builders had to check their work often, to make sure they were on course to meet at a point. The teeniest mistake in building and the sides would not match up at the top! Engineers probably made their accurate pyramids by running ropes from the outer corners up to the proposed meeting point. The Pyramids were also aligned north, south, east, and west, with one corner at each point of the compass.

2 THE HANGING GARDENS OF BABYLON were terraced gardens located in what is now Iraq. They were probably built by King Nebuchadnezzar II in the sixth century B.C. How did those gardens grow? Babylon rarely got any rain, so engineers had to come up with a way to water these spectacular gardens. Water from the local Euphrates River would have had to be lifted very high into the air to reach each level of the terrace. Some historians think a chain pump was used. A chain pump is made of two big wheels, one above the other, connected by a chain. Buckets hang on the chain, and a handle allows for a person to crank the chain in circles, sending the buckets down to a pool to pick up water and then up to the terrace to irrigate the gardens.

3 THE STATUE OF ZEUS AT OLYMPIA in Greece was built around 450 B.C. in celebration of the Olympic Games, held in Zeus' honor. Sculpted by Phidias, the statue was made of gold and ivory, showed Zeus seated on a magnificent throne, and stood 40 feet (12.2 m) tall.

4 THE TEMPLE OF ARTEMIS AT EPHESUS in what is now Turkey was finished around 550 B.C. after more than a century of construction. The temple was made of marble and contained a total of 127 60-foot (18 m) columns.

5 THE MAUSOLEUM AT HALICARNASSUS, now Bodrum, Turkey, was built by King Mausolus (this is where we get the word "mausoleum") and completed a few years after his death in 353 B.C. The rectangular tomb supported a colonnade with a pyramidal roof and a sculpture of four horses pulling a chariot on top.

6 THE COLOSSUS AT RHODES was a 105-foot (32 m) high bronze statue of the god Helios. Inside the statue were several stone columns, which acted as main supports. The Colossus stood for 56 years but then collapsed when an earthquake hit.

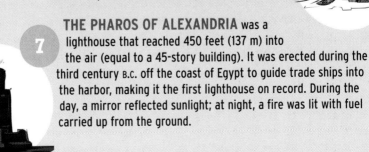

7 THE PHAROS OF ALEXANDRIA was a lighthouse that reached 450 feet (137 m) into the air (equal to a 45-story building). It was erected during the third century B.C. off the coast of Egypt to guide trade ships into the harbor, making it the first lighthouse on record. During the day, a mirror reflected sunlight; at night, a fire was lit with fuel carried up from the ground.

TIMELINE OF ARCHITECTURE

Ancient architects were able to take basic principles like post-and-lintel construction and simple geometry to make some pretty complex buildings. Here's a quick look at how their ideas were expanded on in the centuries to come.

ROMAN ARCHITECTURE
(fifth century B.C. to 5th century A.D.)
Greek and Egyptian buildings made spectacular use of straight lines. Roman builders were masters of the curve, incorporating **vaults** (curved roofs) and **domes** into their structures.

BYZANTINE CHURCHES/MOSQUES (400–800)
Going the Roman style one better, the architecture of Byzantium (what is now Turkey) added **pedentive domes** to the mix. These are domes built on top of square bases instead of cylinders. The strength of this structure allowed for more windows and therefore more interior light. The mosques of Istanbul remain some of the most beautiful buildings in the world.

▲ The Pantheon, Rome. Built in 25 B.C., destroyed by fire in 80 A.D., rebuilt in 125 A.D.

ROMANESQUE AND GOTHIC (1000–1400)
Around 1000 A.D., European architects began to build churches and castles that improved on the techniques of Byzantium. One of their major advances was the **flying buttress**, a support structure built on the outside of a building instead of the inside. The improved techniques of the Gothic period allowed for much larger windows, allowing churches of this time to incorporate huge stained glass windows into their walls.

▲ Hagia Sophia, Istanbul, Turkey. Built in the sixth century A.D.

RENAISSANCE (1400–1700)
The Renaissance (French for "rebirth") was a period of great artistic and scientific achievement in Europe. Architects made buildings that were more complex, brighter, and "lighter" looking than the heavy Gothic architecture from before.

▲ Cathedral of Notre Dame, Paris. Built from 1163 to 1250.

▼ St. Peter's of Rome. Built from 1546 to 1564.

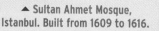

▲ Sultan Ahmet Mosque, Istanbul. Built from 1609 to 1616.

SCIENCE FAIR PROJECT #16

What Shapes Are the Most Stable for Building?

When engineers design structures that need to hold a lot of weight, they use certain shapes in their design that they know are stable. In this experiment, you will compare different shapes to see which one is able to hold the most weight.

YOU WILL NEED:

- ◎ Toothpicks (different sizes)
- ◎ Hot glue gun
- ◎ Coffee can
- ◎ Sand
- ◎ Measuring cup
- ◎ Safety goggles

1. Lay out toothpicks in two perfect squares and glue the corners together using the hot glue gun. Be careful: GLUE GUNS CAN GET HOT! Use four more toothpicks to connect these squares into a cube.

2. Make two more cubes just like the one you made in step 1. Set the first cube aside.

3. On the second cube, glue a toothpick across each face of the cube, dividing the square face into two rectangles.

4. On the third cube, glue two of the longer toothpicks across each face of the cube, dividing each square face into four triangles.

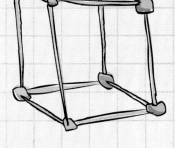

5. Allow the glue to dry on your structures before you test them.

6. Test the amount of weight each structure can hold. WEAR SAFETY GOGGLES WHILE TESTING YOUR STRUCTURES! Place an empty coffee can on top of the cube. Fill the measuring cup to the top line with sand. SLOWLY pour the sand into the coffee can until the cube breaks. Measure the amount of sand left in the measuring cup. Subtract the amount left in the cup from the amount you started with to find how much sand you added to the can. Record the amount of sand each cube could hold.

◎ Which shape gave the best support? Why do you think the other shapes didn't support the weight as well?

◎ Now that you have a stable shape for building, use that shape to design a bridge or tower. See how much weight your design can hold. Try comparing bridges or towers that use different shapes.

BIG BUILDINGS

What a building is made of is part of what dictates how sturdy it is and how long it will last.

The Importance of Steel

Until the late 19th century, most buildings had load-bearing walls made of stone or bricks and mortar (a mixture of cement, lime, or plaster with sand and water that is used as a bonding material). Load-bearing walls have to support their own weight, along with the roof, the floors, and everything else in the building. The thicker a load-bearing wall is, the more weight it can take. Until steel came along you didn't see buildings that were more than about 10 stories tall.

Steel has changed the way we build, strengthening our structures and decreasing their weight. Steel beams make it possible to reach higher and higher, without making a building's walls thicker. This metal is great at withstanding tension, making it ideal for building tall structures, like skyscrapers, and structures under extreme tension, like suspension bridges.

Scraping the Sky

How do they stand so tall? Well, at the heart of skyscraper engineering is a skeleton made of steel.

A steel skeleton, also called a superstructure, is actually a grid of beams and columns that supports a tall building against the forces that would bring it down—gravity, compression, wind, earthquakes.

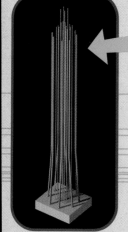

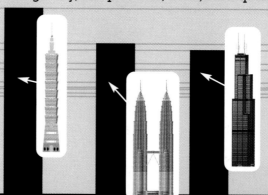

TALL, TALLER ... TALLEST!
See how the world's tallest buildings measure up when you stand them side by side!

| Taipei 101, Taipei, 2004, 1,667 feet (508 m) | Petronas Towers, Kuala Lumpur, 1998, 1,483 feet (452 m) | Sears Tower, Chicago, 1974, 1,450 feet (442 m) | Jin Mao Tower, Shanghai, 1998, 1,381 feet (421 m) |

At each level of the building, vertical columns are braced by horizontal beams called girders. Many buildings also have diagonal beams running between the girders for even more support.

HOW THE SUPER-STRUCTURE WORKS

The steel columns take on the load of the building. They are in compression. The girders binding them keep tension from pulling the skeleton apart and prevent forces like wind from damaging the structure. Even so, all that downward force needs somewhere to go. It's the job of the building's foundation to distribute that force without sinking into the ground.

With a steel skeleton in place, the building's structural work is accounted for. The exterior walls don't have to support weight or resist tension. As a result, they can be filled with windows or form a decorative lattice, for example. The job of the building's exterior simply becomes to keep the weather out and let light shine in.

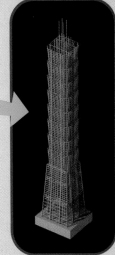

International Finance Centre, Hong Kong, 2003, 1,352 feet (412 m)

CITIC Plaza, Guangzhou, China, 1996, 1,283 feet (391 m)

Shun Hing Square, Shenzhen, China, 1996, 1,260 feet (384 m)

Empire State Building, New York City, 1931, 1,250 feet (381 m)

Central Plaza, Hong Kong, 1992, 1,227 feet (374 m)

Bank of China Tower, Hong Kong, 1990, 1,209 feet (369 m)

▷ Shanghai World Financial Center, 1,614 feet (492 m), is expected to be complete in 2007.

Disaster Proofing

Protecting our buildings and the people within them from the threat of wind, fire, earthquakes, and unknown impact is the job of every structural engineer.

WIND is more of a problem for taller buildings. Skyscrapers are built to sway a little bit in the wind, absorb the shock of that movement, and then snap back into position. It's a delicate balance—the structure needs to move with the wind and be flexible but not so flexible that it buckles under the stress.

EARTHQUAKES send out waves of energy, so structures have to be built with materials that bend but don't crack. It's often the parts that connect columns and girders in skyscrapers that take on most of the stress caused by earthquake movement. Older bridges and tall buildings are reinforced to prevent damage from the seismic waves of earthquakes.

FIRE Fire-proofing material is a part of every building design, to minimize the potential that the structure will weaken from burning. Escape routes are planned and incorporated into the design of buildings so that people can safely escape in the event of a fire.

IMPACT Buildings and bridges are built and strengthened so that they can withstand the impact of an automobile or, in some cases, a plane slamming into the structure.

THE TWIN TOWERS

Completed in 1971, the Twin Towers, or World Trade Center, stood as a New York City landmark for nearly 30 years. To reach a never-before-seen height (1,368 feet) and maximize the space inside, Minoru Yamasaki's plan was different from those of other skyscrapers in that it did not rely on an interior steel skeleton. The bulk of the building's strength was in its exterior walls.

Closely laced grid walls of vertical columns and horizontal beams supported the building's weight and protected it against high winds. The grid allowed for the steel columns and beams to be thinner and lighter than those used in a superstructure. Shock absorbers between the support columns and floor trusses allowed the towers to sway a little and then snap back to their original position.

The towers were built to withstand the impact of a large plane, but not the temperatures of its burning fuel. When planes crashed into the World Trade Center on September 11, 2001, the towers initially withstood the impact. But the intense heat of the fire, which reached temperatures of up to 1,500°F (800°C) as thousands of gallons of jet fuel burned, weakened the steel to a point where it could no longer support the weight of the structure.

▶ A fireman with rubble from the World Trade Center

WHAT'S NEW? Stronger Than Steel!

Steel-reinforced concrete is nothing new, but architects are using it in new ways, making buildings stronger and taller than was ever possible before. This combination of materials handles shock well, and it's strong. By putting steel bars inside concrete, you increase its ability to bend and flex (the concrete protects the steel against fire too). This is also important when it comes to buildings and bridges dealing with the shock of earthquakes and wind. Thanks to steel-reinforced concrete, we're building better structures and we're able to strengthen older ones that might be in danger of collapse some day. And using this material (instead of plain steel) as a building's structure lets architects design even taller skyscrapers.

Computer-Designed Structures

The precision required in building modern structures, like cable-stayed bridges (▶ SEE P. 243), is only possible with the help of computer design programs. Really, really exact calculations are best left to machines. But computer design programs do more than complicated math. With the help of the computer, architects no longer have to spend days and days drafting with a pencil and paper. Designs can be changed in seconds using any number of software packages without the need for massive redesigning. And the computer can even render a photorealistic 3-D building model, so the architect's end result can be visualized before building even begins!

Turning Green

Green building is architecture that strives to create energy-saving structures. A green building might be built with recycled materials or with careful use of skylights and windows so that less electricity is used to light the interior. Or it might include a plan to make use of alternative energy sources, like wind turbines to harness wind or maybe a method for catching and reusing rainwater.

▶ WHAT'S NEXT?

Green Plans for Skyscrapers

One of the most exciting uses for green building is seen in skyscrapers. These two are on their way up in New York City:

• **THE NEW WORLD TRADE CENTER (EXPECTED COMPLETION 2009)** Architects Daniel Libeskind and David Childs are collaborating on the design of the site. The high point of their plan will be the 1,776-foot (431 m) Freedom Tower. Even more impressive than the tower's height, is the way in which the architects are planning to use it to generate electricity. Propeller-driven wind turbines on the tower will harness energy and deliver as much as 20 percent of the building's electricity!

• **7 WORLD TRADE (EXPECTED COMPLETION 2005)** This eco-friendly building is already under construction. One of the buildings that fell on September 11th, 7 World Trade is being rebuilt with floor-to-ceiling windows of coated glass to allow sunlight in while keeping out heat and solar glare. The building is even going to catch rainwater and reuse it! Rainwater that's collected on the roof will be used to help cool the building and water a park next door. To keep the people inside warm, the building will use renewable and recycled resources like the husks of sunflower seeds to provide insulation.

MAKING THEIR MARK

The past 200 years have brought about some amazing structures by truly talented architects. Here's who's been up to what:

LOUIS SULLIVAN
(US, 1856-1924) One of the fathers of the modern skyscraper, Sullivan also trained one of the giants of 20th century architecture, Frank Lloyd Wright.
▲ 1891 Wainwright Building, St. Louis, MO

FRANK LLOYD WRIGHT
(US, 1869-1959) Over 400 of his buildings were completed. Wright wanted to "destroy the box" in favor of open-floor plans, and he liked the idea of integrating architecture into environment.
▲ 1936 Fallingwater, Ohiopyle, PA
He also designed the Guggenheim Museum in New York (1956).

R. BUCKMINSTER FULLER (US, 1895-1983)
Developed the Dymaxion principle, which called for using the least possible amount of material and energy in construction and manufacturing. He created the geodesic dome.
▶ 1967 Geodesic Dome, Montreal, Canada (designed for the US Pavilion at the 1967 Montreal Exposition)

LE CORBUSIER
(SWITZERLAND, 1887–1965)

Thought of buildings as "machines for living." Thought design should proceed from function (form follows function).

> 1929 Villa Savoye, Poissy, France

He also designed the Maison d'homme in Zurich (1967). Additionally, his work is widely seen as the inspiration for the planned city of Brasilia, which was inaugurated as the new capital of Brazil in 1960.

FRANK GEHRY
(CANADA, 1929–)

Gehry's swirly buildings can be seen around the world. Using a variety of unusual materials, including corrugated metal, titanium, chain-link fencing, and glass shards, his surreal, organic buildings are proof that architecture is art.

▲ 2003 The Richard B. Fisher Center for the Performing Arts at Bard College, Annandale-on-Hudson, NY

He also designed the Guggenheim Museum in Bilbao, Spain (1997).

SANTIAGO CALATRAVA
(SPAIN, 1951–) Calatrava's flowing, sculpture-like forms are found in cities all over the world. He is most famous for his bridges, though his next project will be the transit hub at the new proposed World Trade Center site.

◄ 2001 Reiman Bridge and Quadracci Pavilion, Milwaukee Museum of Art, Milwaukee, WI

BRIDGES

Golden Gate Bridge,
San Francisco, CA

Today's bridges range from footbridges meant to support pedestrians to colossal suspension bridges that can support hundreds of cars at once!

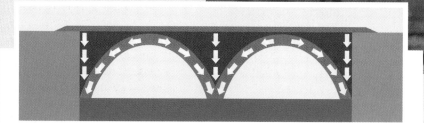

ARCHES An arch bridge doesn't need help from supports or cables. Arch bridges have great natural strength—they're always under compression. Compression pushes outward along the arch curve into the supports at each end called abutments. Abutments carry the load on the arch and keep the ends of the bridge from spreading out.

One of the most revolutionary arch bridges in recent years is the Natchez Trace Bridge in Franklin, Tennessee, which opened in 1994. It's the first American arch bridge to be constructed from segments of pre-cast concrete, a highly economical material. Unlike most arch bridges of its type, the Natchez does not rely on vertical supports to carry the load of cars and its own weight. Most of the bridge's load rests on the top of the two arches, flattened a bit to provide better support.

◀ The Rock Point Arch Bridge spans the Rogue River and the Old Pacific Highway in Gold Hill, OR.

Did you know...

A steel cable only 0.1 inch thick can support over half a ton without breaking.

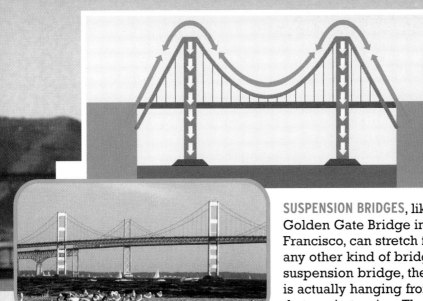

SUSPENSION BRIDGES, like the Golden Gate Bridge in San Francisco, can stretch farther than any other kind of bridge. In a suspension bridge, the roadway is actually hanging from cables that are in tension. The cables are strung through towers into concrete anchorages secured in rock at either end of the bridge. Most of the weight or load of the bridge is carried by the cables to the anchorages.

▲ Maryland's 4.3-mile (6.9 km) Chesapeake Bay Bridge connects Annapolis to the Eastern Shore.

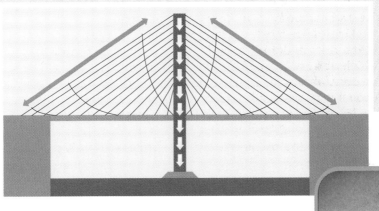

CABLE-STAYED A-shaped cable-stayed bridges are a close relative of M-shaped suspension bridges, except that they use less material. Looking at them, it's hard to see how the cable-stays stay up.

In an A-shaped bridge, there are a series of cables in tension that attach directly to the roadway, through the tower. Since the tension-filled cables feed into the roadway, both the roadway and the tower are in compression. Cable-stayed bridges require such precision in construction that they are not possible to make without the aid of computer design programs.

▲ The Pasco-Kennewick Bridge spans the Columbia River in Washington State.

243

INDEX

AC (alternating current), 145, 146
actinides, 123
Adams, Thomas, 50
adhesion, 142
AIDS, 34, 36
air pressure, 103-4, 111, 113
airplanes, 197, 198-99, 205, 206
allergies, 43
alternative medicine, 37
aluminum, 123, 144, 218
amber, 75
America Online, 162
amnesia, 25
amplification, amplifier, 173, 177
analog, 174, 175, 176, 177, 184-85, 186,
  189, 192-93
animals, 54-67
  cloning of, 62, 65, 66
  endangered, 60-61, 66
  extinct, 62-63
  genetically altered, 46
  kingdoms of, 56-57
  sun and, 214
  see also sea creatures; specific
    animals
animation, 189-90
anions, 122, 142
Antarctica, 88, 93, 102
antibiotics, 35, 37, 46
Apple Computer, 159, 162, 163, 177, 178
architecture, timeline of, 234
  see also buildings
Arctic, 91, 225
Armstrong, Neil, 222
ascorbic acid (vitamin C), 49
asteroids, 220, 221
astronauts, 126, 219, 222, 223, 224
atoms, 120, 121, 122-23, 126, 134, 136,
  138, 142, 148, 152
audio tape, 150, 175, 176
automobiles, 149, 200-201, 205
axle, 125

babies, 8, 10, 18, 21, 32, 33, 35
  see also infants
Bacon, Sir Francis, 71
bacteria, 4, 17, 21, 22, 23, 34-35, 36,
  48, 49, 52
balance, 28
balloons, hot-air, 204, 205
barometers, 103, 113
basalt, 80, 218
batteries, 148-49, 152, 200, 201, 205,
  206
bears, 60, 61, 91
Bell, Alexander Graham, 166
belly button, 8
Benz, Karl, 200, 205
benzene, 132

bicycles, 205
big bang theory, 210
binary code, 156, 179, 187
bioengineering, 46-47
biomass, 136
biomes, land, 86-89
birds, 5, 56, 63, 67, 92
birth, birth defects, 8, 132, 135
bison, 88
bits, 156-57, 158, 159, 166, 184, 185,
  188
Black Death, 36
black holes, 118, 213
BlackBerry®, 168
blackheads, 23
blackout of 2003, 149
bladder, 19
blood, 17, 19, 20, 21, 22
blood pressure, 24, 26
blue laser video players, 188
blue screen, 190
body, human, 14-39
Boeing, 199
bones, 21
boogers, 22
botulism, 48
brain, 16, 17, 24-26, 28, 29, 38, 39
Brainpop.com, movies on
  animals, 55
  buildings, 229
  communication, 155
  computers, 155
  Earth, 69
  electricity, 141
  energy, 129
  environment, 85
  food, 41
  human beings, 3
  human body, 15
  moving images, 183
  music, 171
  pictures, 183
  science, 115
  sound, 171
  space, 209
  transportation, 195
  weather, 99
bread, 42, 45
bridges, 230, 236, 238, 241, 242-43
broccoli, 51
bronze, 123
bubonic plague, 36
buffalo, 88
buildings, 228-43
burps, burping, 22
bus, 204
butterflies, butterfly garden, 59, 112
bytes, 156-57, 166, 176, 177, 180, 184,
  185, 188

cable, 164, 192
cable cars, 205
cactus, 88
Calatrava, Santiago, 241
calcium, 42, 43, 44, 45, 122, 218
calculus, 118
calendar, electronic, 159, 168
calories, 44, 51

camels, 88
cameras, 149, 184-85, 186, 187, 188,
  189, 191, 192
cancer
  breast, 33
  broccoli and, 51
  from benzene, 132
  from radioactive waste, 135
  skin, 93, 139
capillaries, 20
carbohydrates, 18, 42, 44, 51
carbon dioxide, 19, 50, 90, 91, 123,
  132, 196
carbon monoxide, 132, 196
carbon, carbonization, 75, 123, 131,
  148, 149, 226
carbon-14 dating, 12
carrageenan, 51
cars, 149, 200-201, 205
cartridge, ink-jet, 160
cast, and mold, 13, 75
catalytic converter, 196
cathode, cathode ray tube (CRT), 148,
  192
cations, 122, 142
cats, 58, 66
CDs (compact discs), 123, 176, 177, 178,
  185, 188, 189
cellphones, 149, 166, 168, 172, 185,
  215
Celsius scale, 102
cereal, 42, 45, 53
CFCs (chlorofluorocarbons), 93
chain reaction, nuclear, 134, 135
chat room, 163
cheese, 42, 48
chemicals, 92, 94, 96, 123, 132, 148
Childs, David, 239
chiropractic, 37
chlorophyll, 56
cholera, 34, 36, 47
cholesterol, 44, 50
circuit board, 159
circuits, electric, 147
circulatory system, 20
clouds, 100-101, 103, 104, 106, 107,
  109, 143
coal, 72, 75, 130, 131
colds, 34, 50
colors, 39, 133, 184, 185, 191, 192-93
comets, 220, 221
communication, computers and,
  154-69
compass, 150
composting, 95
compression, 230, 232, 236, 237, 242,
  243
Compuserve, 162
computers, 149, 154-69, 185, 187,
  189-90, 239, 243
concrete, 238, 242
conductors, 142, 143, 146, 147
continental drift, 70
continental shelves, 76
cookies, Internet, 164
copper, 123, 142, 144, 147, 232
coral reefs, 76, 90
Coriolis force, 105

corn, 47, 51, 96, 136
cosmologist, 210
Cousteau, Jacques, 76
cows, 46, 58
CPU, 157
cross-pollination, 47
cryonic research, 12
Cugnot, Nicolas Joseph, 200
cyclones, 101
cyclotron, 126

Dallenbach, Karl, 24
dandruff, 22
darmstadtium, 126
DC (direct current), 146
DDT, 60
deafness, 28
death, 9
deserts, 88
detergents, 132
dew point, 100
diabetes, 45
dial-up service, 164
diamonds, 72, 73
diesel, 196, 202, 205
digestive system, 18, 22, 42
digital, 164, 166, 174, 176, 177, 184, 185,
    187–88, 189–90, 193
    see also DVDs; PDA
dinosaurs, 5, 62–63, 71, 75, 213, 221
disasters, natural, 80–83, 238
diseases, 8, 34–36
    see also specific diseases
distance, 117, 124, 125
dizziness, 28
DNA (deoxyribonucleic acid), 4, 9, 32,
    57, 62, 135, 139
dogs, 58, 59, 66
Dolby sound, 179
dough, cookie, 48
dreaming, 26
droughts, 111
drugs (pharmaceuticals), 47
DSL (Digital Subscriber Line), 164
duplex coil, 165
Dust Bowl, 111
DVDs (digital video discs), 123, 184,
    186, 188, 189
Dymaxion principle, 240

e-mail, 159, 161, 162, 163, 164, 167, 168,
    185
E. coli, 48
eagle, bald, 60
earlobes, 33
ears, 21, 23, 28, 103
Earth, 68–83
    as planet, 216, 217, 218, 219, 221
    astronauts in orbit around, 224
    gravity of, 222
    heating up of, 90–91
    layers of, 68
    rotation of, 105
    Sun and, 227
    timeline of life on, 5
    water on, 225
earthquakes, 71, 81–83, 236, 238
eclipses, 219

ecosystem, 86
effort, 125, 130
eggs, 42, 46, 48, 49, 62, 63, 65
Einstein, Albert, 116, 117, 118, 134
elderly, 35
electricity, 91, 137, 140–53, 202, 239
    see also cars
electrolytes, 148, 149, 153
electromagnetism, 151, 175, 202
electron shells, 120, 122, 123
electrons, 121, 122, 123, 136, 138, 142,
    143, 146, 147, 148, 213
elements, 120–21
elevators
    airplane, 199
    in buildings, 117
Elizabeth II, queen of England, 79
EM (electromagnetic) spectrum, 139,
    172
embryo, 8, 19, 33, 65
emotions, 31
emulsifiers, 49
endocrine system, 17
energy, 42, 44, 128–39, 214, 239
engines, 196–97, 200–201, 202, 204,
    205, 206, 222
environment, 32, 46, 47, 84–97, 200,
    201, 239, 240
    see also pollution
EPA (Environmental Protection
    Agency), 93
epidemics, 34, 36
Eriksson, Leif, 12
escape velocity, 222
estrogen, 30
Etna, Mount, 80
Everest, Mount, 71, 79
evolution, 4–7
experiments
    battery, 149
    butterfly garden, 59
    composting, 95
    music, 180
    static cling, 144
    tension and compression, 231
    tornado in a bottle, 108
    volcanoes, 81
eyes, 23, 27, 32, 33, 93, 186
    see also eyes

fabric, waterproof, 112
Fahrenheit scale, 102
fallopian tubes, 19
Fanning, Shawn, 163
farts, farting, 22
fat(s), 18, 21, 42, 44, 51
fault, 83
fertilizers, 97, 132
fetus, human, 8
    see also embryo
fidelity, 174, 176
film, 184, 186
Filo, David, 163
fire proofing, 238
fireworks, 123
fish
    as food, 42, 48
    coral reefs and, 90

glow-in-the-dark, 66
    light and, 138
    pollution and, 92
Flat-Faced Man of Kenya, 6
Fleming, Alexander, 35
flight, history of, 199
flu, 35, 36
fluorine, 123
flying buttress, 234
FMD-ROM (Fluorescent Multilayer
    Disc), 180
fog, 100
food(s), 40–53
    canned, 48, 49
    enriched, 45
    fast, 51
    fortified, 45
    freeze-dried, 51
    genetically altered, 46–47
    irradiated, 46, 49
    junk, 45
    natural, 46
    of birds, 67
    organic, 46
    poisoning, 48
    preservation of, 48–49
    pyramid, 42
    space, 51
    spoilage of, 47, 48, 49
    terrorism and, 52
    vacuum-packed, 49, 51
force, 119, 124, 125, 130, 230, 237
Ford Corporation, 199
Ford, Henry, 200, 205
forests, temperate, 87
fossils, 6, 12, 63, 71, 75
Franklin, Benjamin, 143
Freedom Tower, 239
frequency, 172
Freud, Sigmund, 26
friction, 119
frog, California red-legged, 60
fruit(s), 42, 47, 48
fuel(s)
    cells, hydrogen-oxygen, 206
    fossil, 91, 96, 131–32, 136, 137, 200
    jet, 238
    rocket, 222
fulcrum, 125
Fuller, R. Buckminster, 240

galaxies, 210, 213, 226
Galileo, 127
gamma rays, 135, 139
garbage, 94–95
garlic, 37, 50
gas
    as fuel, 91, 130, 131, 132, 201
    atmospheric, 123
    burping and farting and, 22
    in soda, 50
Gates, Bill, 162
Gehry, Frank, 241
genes, genetics, 32–33, 34, 35, 46–47
geothermal power, 137
germanium, 123
germs, 17, 21
glaciers, 91, 96

glands, 17, 30
glucose, 42, 44
goiter, 45
gold, 122
GPS (Global Positioning System), 167
graphics, 159, 187, 190
grasslands, 88
gravitation, law of universal, 116
gravity
    building and, 230, 231, 232, 236
    comets and, 220
    Einstein on, 116, 118
    formation of, 210
    Newton on, 116, 118
    of black hole, 213
    on the Moon, 219
    rockets and, 222
    science fair project on, 127
    stars and, 211
greenhouse effect, 90–91, 132
gum, chewing, 50

hail, 107
hair, 21, 42
hands, washing, 48
hard drive, 158, 159, 161
hardware, 157–61
HDTV (high-definition television), 193
hearing, 28
    see also ears
heart, heart disease, 20, 21, 38, 45
helicopters, 198, 204, 205
helium, 210, 211, 212, 214, 216
heredity, 32–33
Hillary, Sir Edmund, 79
HIV (human immuno-deficiency virus),
    34, 36
homeopathy, 37
Homo sapiens, 2–13
hormones, 30, 31, 46
horses, 204
hotspots, 168
http (hypertext transfer protocol),
    163
human beings, 2–13, 210, 224
humidity, relative, 100
hurricanes, 109–10
hybrid cars, 200, 201
hydroelectric power, 137
hydrogen, 131, 137, 148, 206, 210, 211,
    212, 214, 216
    see also water

ice ages, 91
ice cream, instant, 52
IMAX, 187
immune system, 17, 34, 35, 50, 93
incinerators, 94
inertia, 119
infants, 38, 48
    see also babies
infection, 21, 48
influenza, 35, 36

insects, 54, 56, 75
instant messenger (IM), 163
insulators, 142–43
integumentary system, 21
interbreeding, 47
interlacing, 187, 193
internal combustion, 196, 197, 200,
    201, 205
Internet, 159, 162–64, 167, 168, 190
intestines, 18, 21, 22, 48, 56
iodine, 45
ions, 142, 214
iPod, 177
iron, 42, 44, 45, 53, 150, 151, 152, 175,
    216, 218
ISDN (Integrated Services Digital
    Network), 164
IVF (in vitro fertilization), 33

jackrabbit, 88
Jenkins, John, 24
Jenner, Edward, 35
jets, 197, 205, 238
Jobs, Steve, 162
Johanson, Donald, 6
juice, 45, 48
Jung, Carl, 26
Jupiter, 217
Jurassic period, 5

Kamen, Dean, 203
Kelvin scale, 210
keratin, 21
keyboard, 159
kidneys, 19
Knight, Nancy, 107
Krikalev, Sergei, 224

landfills, 94
Landsteiner, Karl, 20
lanthanides, 123
laser eye surgery, 27
lava, 72, 80, 81
Le Corbusier, 241
lead, 149
Leakey, Maeve, 6
lecithin, 49
Leonardo da Vinci, 198
levers, 125
Libby, Willard, 12
Libeskind, Daniel, 239
life span, 8–9
ligaments, 21
light, 138–39
    colors of, 118
    speed of, 117, 134, 138, 172
lightbulbs, 145, 146, 147
lightning, lightning rods, 101, 109–10,
    143–44
load, 125
Lucy, 6, 7
lunar month, 218
lungs, 19, 20
lymphatic system, 21

Mac (Macintosh), 159, 162, 163
machines, simple, 124–25
magma, 71, 72, 73, 79, 80

magnesium, 43, 123
magnetic field, 150, 152, 169, 214
magnetic tape, 175
magnets, 123, 150–52, 169, 202
mammals, 5, 56, 57, 64, 65, 88, 89
man, prehistoric, 4–7
manatee, 60
manganese, 148
maria, 218
Mariana Trench, 77
Mars, 216, 225, 226
mathematics, 118
matter, 120
measles, 36, 47
meat, 42, 46, 48, 49, 62, 63
megapixels, 185
memory
    computer, 157, 159
    human, 24–25, 26
Mendeleev, Dmitri, 120
menstruation, 19, 30
mercury, 92, 102, 103
Mercury (planet), 216
metal(s), 122–23, 142, 143, 144, 145,
    148, 151, 152
meteorites, 221
microphone, 174, 175, 176
microwaves, 139
milk, 42, 43, 45, 46, 48, 64
Milky Way, 210, 212, 213
minerals, 42, 43, 44, 45, 53, 72, 75
    see also specific minerals
Missyplicity Project, 66
mobile cellular phone. see cell phone
modem, 159, 164
modulation, 173
mold, and cast, 75, 13
monitoring, body, 38
Montgolfier brothers, 204
Moon, 101, 218–19, 222–23
mortar, 236
motherboard, 159
motion, laws of, 119
motorcycle, 205
motors, 150, 151, 206
mountains, 71, 78–79
mouse, computer, 158
mouth, 18, 19, 29
moving images, 182–93
MP3, MP3 player, 176, 177, 178
MPEG-2, MPEG-4, 188, 193
MRI (magnetic resonance imaging),
    151
mucus, 17, 22, 29, 50
mummies, 9
muscular system, 21, 31
music, 163, 170–81

nails, 21
Napster, 163, 178
NASA (National Aeronautics and
    Space Administration), 219, 221,
    222, 223, 225, 226
Nebuchadnezzar II, king of Babylon,
    233
neon, 123
Neptune, 217
nervous system, 16, 21

neutrons, 121, 122, 134, 135, 142, 213
neutrophils, 50
Newton, Sir Isaac, 116, 118, 119, 138
noise, 28, 172
Norgay, Tenzing, 79
nose, 19, 29
nuclear fusion, 134, 211, 214
nuclear power, 130, 134–35, 205
nucleus, 122, 126, 134, 142
nuée ardente, 80
nutrition, 42–45
nuts, 42

obesity, 45
oceans, 76–77, 90, 131, 219
    see also sea creatures
odors, 29
oil(s)
    and water, 50, 92
    as fuel, 128, 130, 131
    in food, 42
    other uses of, 132
oscillation, 173
osteopathy, 37
otters, 92
ovaries, 17, 19, 30, 33
oxidation, 148
oxygen, 4, 19, 79, 91, 93, 123, 137, 206
ozone layer, 93, 132

paints, 132
paleontologists, 6, 7, 63, 71
pancreas, 49
Pangaea, 70, 71
paralysis, 29
parasites, 48
Pascal, Blaise, 204
pasta, 42, 45
Paterson, Tim, 162
pathogens, 17, 35
PC (personal computer), 159, 162, 168
PCBs (polychlorinated biphenyls), 92
PCS (personal communications
    systems), 166
PDA (personal digital assistant), 159,
    168
penicillin, 9, 35
penis, 18
perfumes, 132
period, menstrual, 19
periodic table, 120–21, 122, 126
permafrost, 89
pesticides, 46, 60, 132
petrification, 75
pets, 58
PGD (pre-implantation genetic
    diagnosis), 33
pharm crops, 47
phone. see cellphones; telephone
phosphorescence, 138
phosphorus, 43
photography, 184–85
photons, 138
photosynthesis, 56
photovoltaic cells, 136
pictures, 182–91
pimples, 23

pixels, 185, 192, 193
Pizza Hut, 163
planes. see airplanes
planes, inclined, 124
planets, 215, 216–17, 225, 226
plants, 5, 56, 214
plastics, 96, 132
plate tectonics, 70–71
    see also tectonic plates
Pluto, 217, 220, 225
plutonium, 134, 139
polio, 36
pollution, 92–93, 97, 132, 200–201
polyester, 132
popcorn, 51
population explosion, 10–11
pores, clogged, 23
post and lintel, 230
potassium, 43
poultry, 42, 46, 48
power grid, 149
prairies, 88
precipitation, 103, 104, 106–7
    see also rain
pregnancy, 8, 33, 92
preservation, unaltered, 75
preservatives, 48–49
printers, computer, 159, 160
Prodigy, 162
progesterone, 30
projectors, 186, 187
prostate gland, 18
protein, 18, 21, 42, 44, 47
protons, 121, 122, 126, 142, 213
protostar, 211
puberty, 19, 23, 30–31
pulley, 125
pulsars, 213
pus, 22
pyramids, 231, 232
pyroclastic flows, 80

quantum theory, 138

radiation, 90, 93, 139
radio, radio waves, 139, 148, 158, 166,
    172–73, 215
rain, 92, 97, 100, 101, 103, 106, 132,
    239
    see also precipitation
rainbows, 138–39
rainforests, 87
RAM (random-access memory), 157,
    159
ramps, 124
recording, 174–79
Recording Industry Association of
    America (RIAA), 178
records, record player, 175
recycling, 91, 94, 239
reflection, 139
reflexology, 37
refrigerator, 49, 93
Relativity, Theories of, 116, 117, 118
reproductive system, 18–19
reptiles, 48, 56, 63
respiratory system, respiratory
    problems, 19, 132

rice, 42, 43, 47
Richter scale, 83
Ring of Fire, 71
robot(s), 77, 225
rock(s), 72–75, 81, 83, 131, 137, 218,
    220, 221, 225, 232
    see also magma
rockets, 222, 223, 224
ROM (read-only memory), 157, 159

safety, electric, 146
salmonella, 48
salt, 45, 48, 97, 122
samarium, 123
San Andreas Fault, 81
sand, sandstone, 72
satellite phone, 168
satellite radio, 172
satellite TV, 192, 193
satellites, 167, 168, 222, 223
Saturn, 217
savannas, 88
scabs, 22
scanners, 159, 161
Schmitt, Harrison, 223
science fair projects
    automobiles, 206
    barometric pressure, 113
    birds, 67
    brain, 39
    cars, 206
    cereal, 53
    computers, 169
    electricity, 153
    energy, 133
    food, 53
    fossils, 13
    gravity, 127
    music, 180
    photography, 191
    pollutants, 97
    rocks, 74
    shapes, building, 235
    Sun, 227
    weather, 113
science, nature of, 114–27
screw, 125
scrotum, 18
sea creatures, 57, 61, 64, 76, 81, 92,
    131, 225
    see also oceans
seasons, 215
seaweed, 51
Sedna, 225
seesaw, 125
Segway HT, 203
seismograph, 83
semen, seminal vesicles, 18
senses, five, 27–29
Sereno, Paul, 63
servers, computer, 164
Seven Wonders of the Ancient World,
    232–33
Shepard, Alan, 116
shock, electric, 142
shorthand, Internet, 163
silicon, 123
silver, 122, 149

skeletal system, 21
skin, 17, 21, 23, 29, 42
skyscrapers, 236–37, 238, 239
sleeping, sleepwalking, 26
slopes, 124
smallpox, 34, 35, 36
smell, 29
sneezing, 34
snot, 22
snow, 107
soda, 50
sodium, 49, 122, 123
software, 161
soil, 72, 89, 225
solar power, solar winds, 136, 214
solar system, 208–27
sonoluminescence, 138
sound, 28, 170–81, 186, 192, 193
sound cards, 158, 159
soup, chicken, 50
space, 205, 206, 208–27
space-time, 116, 118
speakers, 151, 174, 180, 193
species, 57, 60
sperm, 18, 19, 31, 33
spinal cord, 29
Splashpower™, 152
splicing, 46
stars, 138, 210, 211–13, 226
static electricity, 110, 142, 143, 144–45
steel, 236, 238, 242
stem cells, 8, 21
Stephenson, George, 204
steppes, 88
stereo, 179
stomach, 17, 18, 21, 22
stone. see rock(s)
streetcar, 205
submarines, 204, 205
subways, 203, 205
sugars, 51
sulfites, 49
sulfur, sulfur dioxide, 132, 218
Sullivan, Louis, 240
Sun, 90, 101, 136, 210, 211–12, 213,
    214–15, 216, 217, 218, 220, 221
sunspots, 215
supernova, 212, 213
superstructure, 236–37
surround sound, 179, 187
sweets, 42

T cells, 17, 34, 49
T-1 line, T-3 line, 164
talking pictures, 187
tapeworms, 48
taste, 29
taxonomy, 57
tears, 23
tectonic plates, 80, 81
    see also plate tectonics
teeth, 21

telephone, 164, 165, 166, 168
    see also cellphones
telescope, 118, 211, 212, 226
television. see TV (television)
telomeres, 9
temperature, air, 102
tendons, 21
tension, 230, 232, 236, 237, 243
terrorist attacks of September 11,
    2001, 238, 239
Tesla, Nikolai, 166
testes, testicles, testosterone, 17, 18,
    31
thermometer, mercury, 102
thunder, 109
thyroid, 45
tides, tidal power, tidal waves, 83,
    137, 219
tigers, 61, 62
time, 117, 118
tin, 123
tires, flat, 103
Titanic, 77
tongue, 29
tornadoes, 108–9
touch, 29
trackball, trackpad, 158
trains, 202, 204
transportation, 194–207
    airplanes, 198–99
    automobiles, 200–201
    engines, 196–97
    helicopters, 204
    hot-air balloons, 205
    new technology in, 206
    Segway, 203
    submarines, 205
    subways, 203
    timeline of, 204–5
    trains, 202
trees, 87, 91, 132
tsunamis, 83
tundra, 89
TV (television), 45, 151, 164, 172, 187,
    192–93
Twin Towers, 238
Twinkies, 49
twins, 32
Tyrannosaurus rex, 63

umbilical cord, 8
universe, origins of, 210
uranium, 123, 134, 135
Uranus, 217
urine, urinary system, 19
uterus, 19
Uup, Uut, 126

vaccines, 35, 47
vagina, 19
vegetables, 42, 47, 48
vehicles. see transportation
veins, 20
Venus, 216
video
    analog, 184, 186, 192–93
    cards, 159

digital, 185, 187, 188, 193
    games, 158, 190
viruses, 34, 35, 48
viruses, computer, 159, 161, 162
vitamins, 42, 43, 44, 45, 47, 49, 53
volcanoes, 71, 80–81
vomit, 23
Vomit Comet, 126

warming, global, 90–91, 96, 132
waste
    body, 18, 19, 23
    hazardous, 92
    nuclear, 135
water
    and oil, 50
    as energy source, 131, 137
    boiling and freezing points of, 102
    electricity and, 144, 146, 153
    for Hanging Gardens of Babylon,
        233
    from glacial melting, 96
    humidity and, 100–101
    on Mars, 225, 226
    pollution of, 48, 92
wax, ear, 23
Wearable Motherboard™, 38
weather, 98–113
wedge, 124
weight
    in humans, 45
    of objects, 230, 231, 235, 236, 237,
        238, 242, 243
wheel, 204
Wherify Wireless GPS watch, 167
white blood cells, 17, 21, 22, 50
whiteheads, 23
Wi-Fi (Wireless Fidelity), 168
wind, wind power, 101, 104–5, 131, 136,
    236, 238, 239
wings, 198, 199
woolly mammoth, 62, 75
work, 124, 130
World Trade Center, 238, 239
World Wide Web, 163, 164, 190
Wozniak, Steven, 162
Wright brothers, 199, 205
Wright, Frank Lloyd, 240
www.whitehouse.gov, 163

X-rays, 139

Yahoo, 163
Yamaha MusicCast, 180
Yamasaki, Minoru, 238
Yang, Jerry, 163
yellow fever, 36
yogurt, 42

zinc, 42, 43, 149
zits, 23

CREDITS

THANKS TO THE FOLLOWING EXPERT CONSULTANTS:

Ann M. Coulston, MS, RD, Nutrition Consultant, Mountain View, CA

Joel Evans, Chief Geek and Founder, Geek.com

Martha Wise Callan, Curriculum Director, National Energy Education Development (NEED) Project

Sander Goldman, Senior Construction Executive, Landair Project Resources Inc.

Dick Knapinski, Media/Public Relations, Experimental Aircraft Association

Frank J. Marsik, PhD, Dept. of Atmospheric, Oceanic and Space Sciences, University of Michigan, Ann Arbor

Patrick K. Sisterhen

Roger White, Transportation Specialist, Smithsonian Institution

THANKS TO THE FOLLOWING FOR THEIR THOROUGH EDITORIAL REVIEWS:

Laurie Goldman

JR Minkel

Adam Marcus

THANKS TO THE FOLLOWING FOR THEIR ADDITIONAL WRITING AND RESEARCH FOR BRAINPOP:

Sean Fitzgibbons

Jane Pickett

Josie Richstad

Alex Simon

Tamson Weston

Thanks to Morris Katz for his ideas for the book.

ILLUSTRATIONS AND PHOTOGRAPHY

Except where noted below, all illustrations by Mike Watanabe and Demian Johnson.

6: Institute of Human Origins. **7:** John B. Carnett/POPULAR SCIENCE MAGAZINE. **8:** A Peek in the Pod. **9:** Yale University Press/Brookhaven National Laboratory. **25:** Photodisc (cake); John B. Carnett/POPULAR SCIENCE MAGAZINE (diver, bike); Dean E. Biggins/U.S. Fish and Wildlife Service (bird). **26:** Library of Congress, Prints and Photographs Division, LC-USZ62-72266. **27:** National Eye Institute, National Institutes of Health. **29:** Scott Bauer, Agricultural Research Service, United States Department of Agriculture (USDA). **32:** Photodisc. **35:** National Library of Medicine, National Institutes of Health. **38:** Georgia Institute of Technology. **40-45:** DigitalStock. **46:** Agricultural Research Service, USDA (mango experiment); Scott Bauer, Agricultural Research Service, USDA (grapes). **47:** Jack Dykinga, Agricultural Research Service, USDA. **50-51:** DigitalStock. **57:** Robin Hunter, United States Fish and Wildlife Service (USFWS) (whale); Gary M. Stolz, USFWS (whale tail). **58:** LuRay Parker, USFWS (ferret); Bill Tarpenning, USDA (girl with pig, girls grooming dog); Lando Ettrick (dog); Laurie Newberry (cat). **59:** Bill Tarpenning, USDA. **60:** LuRay Parker, USFWS (grizzly); Doug Perrine, USFWS (manatee); Ryan Haggerty, USFWS (frog). **61:** Ryan Haggerty, USFWS (turtle); Gary M. Stolz, USFWS (panda, tiger). **63:** John B. Carnett/POPULAR SCIENCE MAGAZINE. **64:** Commander John Bortniak, NOAA, Department of Commerce (shark); Jackie Reid, NOAA, Department of Commerce (ray); Mr. Richard B. Mieremet, NOAA, Department of Commerce (dolphin). **65:** Gary M. Stolz, USFWS. **68-69:** Corbis. **76-77:** Corbis. **76:** Lisa Ebersole. **77:** Lisa Ebersole (fish); OAR/National Undersea Research Program (NURP)/Woods Hole Oceanographic Institute/NOAA (ALVIN). **79:** William McTigue, NOAA, NOAA, Department of Commerce. **80:** NASA. **81:** Robert E. Wallace, USGS. **82:** Library of Congress, Prints and Photographs Division, LC-USZ62-39698 (Japan); University of Colorado, US Department of Commerce, NOAA, National Environmental Satellite, Data and Information Service, National Geophysical Data Center (Peru); M. Mehrain, Dames, Moore, US Department of Commerce, NOAA, National Environmental Satellite, Data and Information Service, National Geophysical Data Center (Iran); Library of Congress, Prints and Photographs Division, LC-USZ62-70537 (Italy, women helping); Library of Congress, Prints and Photographs Division, LC-USZ62-73448 (Italy, makeshift house). **83:** NOAA Central Library, NOAA, Department of Commerce. **87:** Susan E. Meyer (macaw); National Park Service (Rocky Mountain National Park). **88:** Susan E. Meyer (camel); National Park Service (cactus, jackrabbit, bison). **89:** Marsha Melnick (Chile); National Park Service (caribou, Denali National Park).